GROUND WATER VULNERABILITY ASSESSMENT
Contamination Potential Under Conditions of Uncertainty

Committee on Techniques for Assessing Ground Water Vulnerability

Water Science and Technology Board

Commission on Geosciences, Environment, and Resources

National Research Council

NATIONAL ACADEMY PRESS
WASHINGTON, D.C. 1993

National Academy Press • **2101 Constitution Avenue, N.W.** • **Washington, D.C.** **20418**

Support for this project was provided by the U.S. Department of Agriculture Contract No. 59-0700-1-145, U.S. Environmental Protection Agency Grant No. CR-817614-01-1, and the U.S. Geological Survey Contract No. 14-08-001-AO834.

Library of Congress Cataloging-in-Publication Data

Ground water vulnerability assessment : predicting relative
  contamination potential under conditions of uncertainty / Committee
  on Techniques for Assessing Ground Water Vulnerability, Water
  Science and Technology Board, Commission on Geosciences,
  Environment, and Resources, National Research Council.
       p.   cm.
  Includes bibliograpical references and index.
  ISBN 0-309-04799-4
    1. Groundwater—Pollution. 2. Water—Pollution potential.
  I. National Research Council (U.S.). Committee on Techniques for
  Assessing Ground Water Vulnerability.
  TD426.G725   1993   93-32944
  628.1'68—dc20   CIP

iii

v

The National Academy of Sciences is a private, nonprofit, self-perpetuating society of distinguished scholars engaged in scientific and engineering research, dedicated to the furtherance of science and technology and to their use for the general welfare. Upon the authority of the charter granted to it by the Congress in 1863, the Academy has a mandate that requires it to advise the federal government on scientific and technical matters. Dr. Bruce M. Alberts is president of the National Academy of Sciences.

The National Academy of Engineering was established in 1964, under the charter of the National Academy of Sciences, as a parallel organization of outstanding engineers. It is autonomous in its administration and in the selection of its members, sharing with the National Academy of Sciences the responsibility for advising the federal government. The National Academy of Engineering also sponsors engineering programs aimed at meeting national needs, encourages education and research, and recognizes the superior achievements of engineers. Dr. Robert M. White is president of the National Academy of Engineering.

The Institute of Medicine was established in 1970 by the National Academy of Sciences to secure the services of eminent members of appropriate professions in the examination of policy matters pertaining to the health of the public. The Institute acts under the responsibility given to the National Academy of Sciences by its congressional charter to be an adviser to the federal government and, upon its own initiative, to identify issues of medical care, research, and education. Dr. Kenneth I. Shine is president of the Institute of Medicine.

The National Research Council was organized by the National Academy of Sciences in 1916 to associate the broad community of science and technology with the Academy's purposes of furthering knowledge and advising the federal government. Functioning in accordance with general policies determined by the Academy, the Council has become the principal operating agency of both the National Academy of Sciences and the National Academy of Engineering in providing services to the government, the public, and the scientific and engineering communities. The Council is administered jointly by both Academies and the Institute of Medicine. Dr. Bruce M. Alberts and Dr. Robert M. White are chairman and vice chairman, respectively, of the National Research Council.

Preface

The topic of assessing ground water vulnerability first came to the attention of the Water Science and Technology Board (WSTB) in December 1988. Concerned about the scientific basis for vulnerability assessments and the potential for their inappropriate application, the board organized and hosted a planning session in February 1990 to become better informed on the issues. The session was attended by experts from industry, academe, and federal, state, and local agencies interested in ground water protection issues; they concluded that the WSTB should undertake a study of techniques for assessing ground water vulnerability. The board then drew on the deliberations of the planning session to develop the terms of reference for this study.

With financial support from the U.S. Environmental Protection Agency, U.S. Geological Survey, and U.S. Department of Agriculture, the WSTB appointed the Committee on Techniques for Assessing Ground Water Vulnerability. The committee's study expands on two National Research Council reports: *Ground Water Models: Scientific and Regulatory Applications* (1990), and *Spatial Data Needs: The Future of the National Mapping Program* (1990). These reports served as points of departure for committee deliberations on broader, generic issues pertaining to regional assessments of ground water contamination.

Specifically, the committee's charge was to:

1. Identify the existing and proposed uses of vulnerability assessment

methods, identify extant methods, and review their scientific bases and effectiveness.

2. Review, in cooperation with other efforts, available spatially referenced databases to determine their applicability to regional assessments of ground water contamination potentials, and recommend parameters for inclusion in data collection and protocols for database development.

3. Develop generic guidelines and criteria for evaluating assessment methods in terms of (a) interpretation of their outputs and (b) their use in decision making.

4. Develop a research agenda for: (a) acquiring minimum databases required for making valid vulnerability assessments, and (b) developing more reliable assessment techniques.

Following an initial meeting in Washington, D.C., the committee met on four other occasions, in Barnstable, Massachusetts; Fresno, California; Orlando, Florida; and Oahu, Hawaii. At each site, the committee heard presentations from technical experts engaged in the development of vulnerability assessment methods and from managers actively involved in policy formulation and the application of these techniques in county, state, and national ground water protection programs. Firsthand discussions with leading practitioners of both the scientific and management aspects of ground water vulnerability assessment were extremely helpful to the committee's deliberations, which often took the form of lively debate, both during and following formal sessions. Each of these locations or states, along with Iowa, which was not visited, is the subject of a case study in Chapter 5 of this report.

The committee did not attempt to issue the last word on the problem it was given. Despite considerable progress over the last 20 years in research and understanding of contamination transport and fate processes, adequate understanding of these processes is still lacking in many areas. This gap in understanding precludes our ability to predict, with high certainty, the effects on ground water vulnerability of a change in management practices in a region. The members of this committee believe this report should be useful to managers who will rely on vulnerability assessments. The report includes guidance for making informed judgments on whether an assessment provides the necessary information to be useful in the decision making process and how the assessment might be lacking. For example, a key piece of information, which is rarely included in assessment results, is the uncertainty of the ground water vulnerability assessment.

The committee addressed fundamental questions regarding the definition of ground water vulnerability, a concept that is in turn subtle and obvious, and has stated its most general findings as the three Laws of Ground Water Vulnerability. The committee was not bound by preconceptions of validity or invalidity of existing vulnerability assessment techniques in its evaluation of the potential scope of the field and looked beyond the limitations of current techniques and databases. Our recommendations for further development of techniques and databases, and for directions of scientific research appear in Chapter 6.

Some readers may feel that this report provides an overly pessimistic view on the use of vulnerability assessments. It is true that the committee, in struggling with the manifold technical and practical difficulties affecting the performance of vulnerability assessments today, nearly concluded that their limitations are so great as to be no use in management decision making. Recognizing that managers will make decisions about ground water with or without vulnerability assessments, the committee instead asked whether it is better to have the information provided by a vulnerability assessment or not. With due regard to the danger of misapplication of vulnerability assessments by managers unfamiliar with the limitations of assessment methods, the committee felt that assessments provide an increment of useful information, albeit not enough to provide the sole support for any decision.

Early in its work, the committee decided to treat ground water vulnerability assessment foremost as a tool for management. Accordingly, this report is designed to be of direct use to managers as well as to those who develop techniques for assessing vulnerability and the science that supports these techniques. The report is consumer oriented in that it reflects current and future management needs and the ability or inability of existing or foreseeable assessment techniques to meet these needs.

On the immediate horizon, the most significant and potentially controversial use of vulnerability assessments is in differential management of ground water resources, as contemplated by federal programs that would have states perform assessments in support of management plans for areas based on their vulnerability to contamination. Differential management has as its goal efficient resource management and relies on an ability to discriminate between areas of higher and lower ground water vulnerability. Regulatory regimes developed under differential management could, for example, include differences in allowable uses and management practices for potential ground water contaminants, such as agricultural pesticides. Policy makers and regulators engaged in differential management should be cautioned by the sections of this report that describe the limits of existing assessment techniques in making discriminating predictions of the likelihood of ground water contamination. Reworded, the Third Law of Ground Water Vulnerability says extreme differences in vulnerability can be differentiated, but subtle ones cannot.

An important issue, which was not considered by this committee in an attempt to keep the scope of the report manageable, is the economics of vulnerability assessment. Risk-cost-benefit analyses are likely to play an integral role in determining whether vulnerability assessments are used in the future. Economics will be especially important in determining when it is cost-effective to collect additional data for newer or more complex approaches or whether existing data will suffice. This issue requires further consideration.

The committee comprised, by design, individuals representing diverse disciplines, expertise, interests, and geographies, and our report reflects this diversity. A problem with investigations of large-scale, multidisciplinary problems such as ground water vulnerability or contamination is that difficulties can arise in communicating ideas among scientific disciplines rooted in different philosophies and approaches to problems. In such cases, differences in concepts and terminology can become a problem. However, one of the strengths of the National Research Council study process is that it challenges members of the committee to reevaluate their own ideas in the context of the problem at hand. Members are required to convey what they see personally as truth and to communicate their ideas in terms that can be understood by people outside their individual disciplines. It should also be mentioned that, although this report reflects the consensus of the committee, it does not necessarily reflect each member's beliefs in their entirety.

It was a privilege for me to spend many hours struggling with these diverse and talented individuals over difficult and sometimes contentious questions, at times equipped only with metaphors to see us through to consensus. Many individuals from all parts of the country, acknowledged by name in Appendix C, gave generously of their time to share expertise and advise the committee on ground water science and management aspects of vulnerability assessment. The willingness of local hosts to provide access to both informed people and instructive field experiences was critically important to the project. The National Research Council and its Water Science and Technology Board unstintingly supported the committee's efforts during the course of this study. Senior Project Assistant Patricia Cicero proved indispensable as both logician and logistician. It is a pleasure to convey the entire committee's respect for Project Director Sarah Connick, without whose rare combination of insight, persistence, patience, and good humor this report truly would not have been possible. Last, on a personal note, I would like to acknowledge the support of Barnstable County and the Cape Cod Commission during this effort.

Armando J. Carbonell, *Chair*
Committee on Techniques for
Assessing Ground Water Vulnerability

Contents

EXECUTIVE SUMMARY   1
    Introduction, 1
    Management, 4
    Approaches to Vulnerability Assessment, 5
    Data and Databases, 9
    Case Studies, 9
    Research Recommendations, 10
    Reference, 11

1   INTRODUCTION   13
    Protecting Ground Water from Future Contamination, 14
    Assessing Ground Water Vulnerability, 19
    The Vulnerability Assessment Process, 26
    References, 29
    BOXES
    President's Water Quality Initiative, 15
    EPA's Pesticides and Ground Water Strategy, 16
    The Many Ways of Defining Ground Water Vulnerability, 17
    Scale, Size, and Maps, 23

2   CONSIDERATIONS IN THE SELECTION AND
   USE OF VULNERABILITY ASSESSMENTS   30
    Introduction, 30

Existing and Potential Uses for Vulnerability Assessments, 31
Factors Affecting Selection and Use of Vulnerability
   Assessments, 35
Summary, 40

3 APPROACHES TO VULNERABILITY ASSESSMENTS   42
Introduction, 42
Review of Current Approaches, 44
Uncertainty in Vulnerability Assessment Methods, 63
Testing and Evaluation of Vulnerability Assessments, 77
Computing Environments for Vulnerability Assessments, 86
Summary, 94
References, 97
BOXES
First-Order Uncertainty Analysis, 69
Uncertainty in Pesticide Leaching Assessments, 70
Field-Scale Model Testing and Validation, 78
Evaluation of Regional Vulnerability Assessment, 82
Geographic Information Systems, 88

4 DATA AND DATABASES   104
Introduction, 104
Topography, 109
Soils, 112
Hydrogeology, 121
Weather and Climate, 123
Land Use and Land Cover, 126
Management Factors, 129
Conclusion, 131
References, 132
BOXES
The Spatial Data Transfer Standard, 107
Soil Mapping, 113

5 CASE STUDIES   135
Introduction, 135
Iowa, 135
Cape Cod, 139
Florida, 144
The San Joaquin Valley, 151
Hawaii, 155
Application of a Vulnerability Index for Decision-Making
   at the National Level, 162

Summary, 165
References, 167

6   CONCLUSIONS AND RECOMMENDATIONS   170
    Management Implications, 171
    Approaches, 173
    Data and Databases, 174
    Research Agenda, 175

APPENDIXES

    A SOURCES FOR DIGITAL RESOURCE DATABASES   181

    B BIOGRAPHICAL SKETCHES OF COMMITTEE MEMBERS 185

    C CONTRIBUTORS TO THE COMMITTEE'S EFFORT   189

INDEX   193

GROUND WATER
VULNERABILITY ASSESSMENT

Executive Summary

INTRODUCTION

In recognition of the need for effective and efficient methods for protecting ground water resources from future contamination, scientists and resource managers have sought to develop techniques for predicting which areas are more likely than others to become contaminated as a result of activities at or near the land surface. Once identified, those areas could then be subjected to certain use restrictions or otherwise targeted for greater attention aimed at preventing contamination of the underlying ground water resources.

The concept that some areas are more likely than others to become contaminated has led to the use of the terminology "ground water *vulnerability* to contamination." This basic concept has taken on a range of definitions in the technical literature. For the purposes of this report, **ground water vulnerability to contamination** is defined as:

> *The tendency or likelihood for contaminants to reach a specified position in the ground water system after introduction at some location above the uppermost aquifer.*

As considered herein, ground water vulnerability refers to contamination resulting from nonpoint sources or areally distributed point sources of pollution and does not address individual point sources of pollution nor any situation where a pollutant is purposely placed into the ground water system. This definition of ground water vulnerability is flawed, as is any other, by a fundamental principle that is stated here as the **First Law of Ground Water Vulnerability:**

All ground water is vulnerable.

Vulnerability is not an absolute property, but a relative indication of where contamination is likely to occur; no ground water, with possible exceptions such as deep sedimentary basin brines, is invulnerable. Furthermore, it may be necessary to consider long term effects on ground water quality, perhaps over decades, in carrying out vulnerability assessments.

Ground water vulnerability is an amorphous concept, not a measurable property. It is a probability (i.e., "the tendency or likelihood") of contamination occurring in the future, and thus must be inferred from surrogate information that is measurable. In this sense, a ground water vulnerability assessment is a predictive statement much like a weather forecast, but for processes that take place underground and over much longer time scales.

The potential for contaminants to leach to ground water depends on many factors, including the composition of soils and geologic materials in the unsaturated zone, the depth to the water table, the recharge rate, and environmental factors influencing the potential for biodegradation. The composition of the unsaturated zone can greatly influence transformations and reactions. For example, high organic matter or clay content increases sorption and thus lessens the potential for contamination. The depth to the water table can be an important factor because short flow paths decrease the opportunity for sorption and biodegradation, thus increasing the potential for many contaminants to reach the ground water. Conversely, longer flow paths from land surface to the water table can lessen the potential for contamination for chemicals that sorb or degrade along the flow path. Recharge rates affect the extent and rate of transport of contaminants through the saturated zone. Finally, environmental factors, such as temperature and water content, can significantly influence the degradation of contaminants by microbial transformations.

An array of approaches for predicting ground water vulnerability has been developed from an understanding of the factors that affect the transport of contaminants introduced at or near the land surface. These methods fall into three major classes: (1) overlay and index methods that combine specific physical characteristics that affect vulnerability, often giving a numerical score, (2) process-based methods consisting of mathematical models that approximate the behavior of substances in the subsurface environment, and (3) statistical methods that draw associations with areas where contamination is known to have occurred.

Each of these methods requires that adequate data be available on factors that affect ground water vulnerability, such as soil properties, hydraulic properties, precipitation patterns, depth to ground water, land use and land cover, and other characteristics of the area to be assessed. Different types and amounts of data are necessary depending on the specific assessment method used. The product of most vulnerability assessments to date has been a map depicting areas of relative vulnerability. Some researchers have chosen instead to express results as probabilities with the associated uncertainties displayed in tabular form.

It is infeasible and perhaps impossible to formulate a universal technique for predicting vulnerability, one that considers all of the ways in which contamination occurs or that is appropriate for all situations. Key elements to consider in a vulnerability assessment for a particular application include the reference location, the degree of contaminant specificity, the contaminant pathways considered, and the time and spatial scales of the vulnerability assessment. The reference location is the position in the ground water system specified to be of interest. The ground water table is the reference location used in most existing techniques. However, managers may determine that another reference location is more useful for their purposes. Vulnerability assessments may or may not account for the different behavior of different contaminants in the environment. Thus, there are two general types of vulnerability assessments. The first addresses *specific vulnerability*, and is referenced to a specific contaminant, contaminant class, or human activity. The second addresses *intrinsic vulnerability* and is for vulnerability assessments that do not consider the attributes and behavior of specific contaminants. In practice, a clear distinction between intrinsic and specific vulnerability cannot always be made. Contaminants can enter aquifers by a variety of pathways. Most existing assessment techniques address only transport that occurs by simple percolation and ignore preferential flow paths such as biochannels, cracks, joints, and solution channels in the vadose zone. The omission of preferential flow paths is likely a significant limitation of vulnerability assessments in many environments. Some overlay and index methods have attempted to address contamination that might occur by wells and boreholes by mapping those features in combination with the results derived from other assessment methods. The overall utility of a vulnerability assessment is highly dependent on the scale at which it is conducted, the scale at which data are available, the scale used to display results, and the spatial resolution of mapping.

The combination of these elements makes up a vulnerability assessment method. Inherent in any such combination will be scientific uncertainties associated with errors in data, errors in method, and potential misapplication of an approach to a given area. The prediction of ground water vulnerability is an imprecise exercise, as stated in the **Second Law of Ground Water Vulnerability:**

Uncertainty is inherent in all vulnerability assessments.

The Vulnerability Assessment Process

Although a large degree of uncertainty is associated with the results of existing vulnerability assessment methods, much useful information can be gained by going through the process of assessing ground water vulnerability. Ground water vulnerability assessment is a potentially useful management concept for guiding decisions about ground water protection and thus requires the cooperative efforts of regulatory policy makers, natural resource managers, educators, and technical experts. The process of assessing vulnerability is dynamic and iterative. It requires determination of the purpose of the assessment, followed by selection of a method, identification of the type, availability, and quality of data needed, performance of the actual assessment, and, finally, use of the information gained from the assessment process to make decisions on ground water resource management. This process involves the gathering, organization, and, ideally, critical evaluation of as much information as possible relating to the potential for contamination to occur in the area being assessed. Through this process scientists and managers can develop a better understanding of ground water systems, which should help them make better decisions on how to protect ground water resources.

MANAGEMENT

The intended use of the vulnerability assessment process is the most obvious and important factor to consider in selecting a vulnerability assessment approach. Uses and needs for vulnerability assessments can be grouped into four broad categories. First, assessments can be used in the *policy analysis and development* process to identify potential for ground water contamination and the need for protection and to aid in examining the relative impacts of alternative ways to control contamination. Second, when scarce resources prevent uniform and high levels of spending, vulnerability assessments can be used in *program management* to guide allocation and targeting of resources to areas where the greatest levels of effort are warranted. Third, vulnerability assessments can be used in some instances to *inform land use decisions* such as alteration of land use activities to reflect the potential for ground water contamination, or voluntary changes in behaviors of land owners as they become more aware of the ground water impacts of their land-based activities. Finally, and perhaps most important, is the use of vulnerability assessments to *improve general education* and awareness of a region's hydrologic resources.

Often policy makers will not find in a vulnerability assessment the objective, scientific, and accurate product they need for making these decisions. Rather they will find that its usefulness may be severely constrained by scientific unknowns or lack of appropriate data. Thus, it is important that policy makers and resource managers become intelligent consumers of vulnerability assessments.

Important technical and institutional considerations should be taken into account in the process of developing a vulnerability assessment. Technical considerations include an evaluation of the type and form of the results or output, the appropriateness of the method for the physical characteristics of the geographic area being addressed, the adequacy of the data available or to be collected, and the analysis of uncertainty in the output and how it may affect the consequent decisions. Important institutional issues include the time frame in which the assessment is meant to apply, how the vulnerability assessment will be coordinated with other planning programs and needs, the cost of the assessment and the value of the information to be gained, the availability of personnel and physical resources to perform an assessment, and the plans and activities of other agencies and institutions that may have an interest in the assessment. These factors are not mutually exclusive.

APPROACHES TO VULNERABILITY ASSESSMENT

The three classes of methods for assessing ground water vulnerability range in complexity from a subjective evaluation of available map data to the application of complex transport models. Each class has characteristic strengths and weaknesses that affect its suitability for particular applications.

Overlay and index methods involve combining various physical attributes (e.g., geology, soils, depth to water table, well locations). In the simplest of these methods, all attributes are assigned equal weights with no judgment being made on their relative importance. Thus areas where specified attributes mutually occur (e.g., sandy soils and shallow ground water) are rated as more vulnerable. These methods were the earliest to be used in assessing ground water vulnerability and are still favored by many state and local regulatory and planning agencies. Overlay and index methods that attempt to be more quantitative assign different numerical scores and weights to the attributes in developing a range of vulnerability classes which are then displayed on a map.

Specific issues that need to be considered regarding the suitability of overlay and index methods for particular applications include the relative importance of the physical attributes in influencing vulnerability, the natural variability in the attributes used, and the availability and spatial resolution of data. The factors that affect ground water vulnerability vary from place to place, as does their relative importance. Therefore it is important that the attributes included in an assessment be appropriate for the specific situation and, if they are to be weighted, that their weights reflect the particular physical setting. No single set of factors or weights is suitable for all situations. Most methods use a single, average annual value for each attribute at each point location, but, attributes such as depth to ground water and recharge often vary in time, both seasonally and annually. Overlay and index methods are often preferred because the data they require are generally more available. In addition, these methods are relatively simple; while they include factors important in determining ground water vulnerability, they do not attempt to fully describe the processes that lead to contamination.

Approaches using process-based simulation models require analytical or numerical solutions to mathematical equations that represent coupled processes governing contaminant transport. Methods in this class range from indices based on simple transport models to analytical solutions for one-dimensional transport of contaminants through the unsaturated zone to coupled, unsaturated-saturated, multiple-phase, two- or three-dimensional models. These approaches are distinguished from others in that many of them attempt to predict contaminant transport in both space and time.

While process-based models attempt to incorporate a more complete description of the physical, chemical, and biological processes affecting ground water vulnerability, they may not necessarily provide more reliable results. The data these methods require often are not available and must be estimated by indirect means. In addition, these models do not account for flow and transport processes occurring at either smaller or larger spatial scales than those for which the models were developed, and they do not account for cases where preferential flow exists.

Statistical methods generally use a contaminant concentration or a probability of contamination as the dependent variable. These methods incorporate data on known areal contaminant distributions and provide characterizations of contamination potential for the specific geographic area from which the data were drawn. Statistical methods have been developed with the availability of data keenly in mind and are designed to deal with data of varying quality and types. They do not attempt to define processes or cause-effect relationships, and results are expressed as probabilities. These methods have been used in the definition and characterization of assessment areas and the assessment of vulnerability using probability models. Statistical approaches vary in complexity and generally include multiple independent variables.

The primary consideration in the use of statistical methods is that the area to which they are applied must be comparable to that in which they were developed. In addition, because statistical methods rely on information about where ground water has been contaminated, it is important that adequate monitoring and chemical use information be available.

Uncertainty in Vulnerability Assessment

Uncertainty is inherent in all methods of assessing ground water vulnerability. Uncertainties arise from errors in obtaining data, due to natural spatial and temporal variability, in computerization, processing, and storage of data, and in modeling and conceptualization. Results of vulnerability assessments are usually displayed on a map of a region depicting various subareas, called polygons or cells, having different levels of vulnerability. The distinction between each level is, however, arbitrary. Further, the estimates of vulnerability are associated with a level of uncertainty. Thus, confidence intervals associated with the numerical values assigned to neighboring cells or polygons may overlap to the point that subtle distinctions perceived in the vulnerabilities of adjacent cells are not defensible. The inability to distinguish differences between adjacent cells with differing vulnerability scores increases with increasing uncertainties in methods and data.

Few published vulnerability assessments account for uncertainties from either model or data errors, although an array of methods would be appropriate for this application. It is important that uncertainty analyses be included in vulnerability assessments so that users can develop an understanding of the level of knowledge about vulnerability and the hydrologic system in the area that is being studied. In addition, uncertainty analyses can help to identify which attributes require more accurate measurements in order to reduce overall uncertainty, identify attributes for which less precise information is required and thereby save in data collection efforts, and determine whether a simpler approach would suffice or if a more sophisticated approach is needed for better reliability (Heuvelink et al. 1989).

Testing and Evaluation of Vulnerability Assessments

Evaluation of a vulnerability assessment must address at least two questions: (1) Is the vulnerability rating assigned to a given subarea valid? and (2) Are the values assigned to neighboring subareas sufficiently different? To answer these questions, assessment results must be compared with observations in the environment.

It is not possible to test regional vulnerability assessments on even a field-scale in the same way that a site-specific simulation model can be tested, nor is it possible to make definitive statements about the predictive accuracy of one method compared to another. One difficulty is that a vulnerability assessment method may yield an index value or a probability, which, unlike a concentration, cannot be measured in the field. Also, to make meaningful comparisons of predicted levels of vulnerability and observed constituent concentrations, it is necessary either to know the history of contaminant loading to the subsurface or to assume that contaminant loading has been spatially and temporally uniform. Neither situation is likely to exist, except perhaps in a controlled field-plot study. Further, in that the goal of assessing ground water vulnerability is to assist in the protection of ground water resources, to allow contamination to occur on a regional scale as predicted would be counterproductive.

Despite these difficulties, the validity of a regional vulnerability assessment can be inferred through several lines of inquiry. Testing and evaluating vulnerability assessments may involve a hierarchal approach that evolves through several stages. The most sensible uses of vulnerability assessment techniques, in fact, may include plans to test, review, and refine the assessment over time, perhaps over many years.

Ground water vulnerability predictions are made in a relative, not an absolute, sense. Assessments only distinguish some areas in a region as being more or less vulnerable than other areas. Uncertainty is pervasive in both spatial databases and computational schemes; as a result, all vulnerability assessments are inherently uncertain. It may be fairly easy to identify areas where ground water contamination is highly probable, but may not be equally easy to delineate areas where it is highly improbable. For example, it is clear that ground water in a mature karst aquifer system or a shallow sand and gravel alluvial aquifer is highly vulnerable to contamination. However, it may be much more difficult to demonstrate that ground water underlying a clay-rich unsaturated zone indeed has low vulnerability to contamination because many difficult-to-quantify factors, such as preferential flow paths, can complicate the situation. Moreover, differentiating areas that are not highly vulnerable in terms of more subtle distinctions in vulnerability is very difficult. This concept can be summarized as the **Third Law of Ground Water Vulnerability:**

The obvious may be obscured and the subtle indistinguishable.

Computing Environments for Vulnerability Assessments

Regardless of method, much data on attributes and geography are required to conduct a ground water vulnerability assessment. In addition, suitable analytical tools are required to prepare, combine, study, and display the various components of the assessment. Numerous techniques have been used to perform these tasks, normally following advances in the allied fields of computer, graphic, and statistical sciences. The two computing environments used for vulnerability assessments are grid-cell based systems and geographic information systems (GIS). Grid-cell based systems were the first to evolve and are rapidly giving way to GIS, which in many ways is considered more flexible.

The oversimplification that can occur using any method that involves the display of results in the form of a map raises important concerns. Often these concerns can be mitigated by addressing critical questions about the intended use of the assessment and uncertainties associated with the results. GIS technology provides new opportunities to describe and display graphically uncertainty associated with each assessment, and exhaust the tabular data through the construction of many different maps.

DATA AND DATABASES

Most research has been concerned primarily with the processes that affect vulnerability; less attention has been paid to data collection, entry and management, and the computing environment. These issues, however, are critical to the ability to conduct a successful vulnerability assessment.

Federal, state, and local government agencies collect massive quantities of data each year. The Federal Geographic Data Committee has been established to provide oversight of federal agencies involved in collecting and using spatial data and their attributes, to coordinate data collection and sharing, and to establish federal standards for geographic data exchange, content, and quality. The quality and availability of geographic and attribute information at the state and local levels is highly variable.

Databases are available to varying extents for parameters relating to topography, soils, hydrogeology, weather and climate, land use and land cover, and management factors. Not all of these data are readily available in digital form or at the scale needed for different types of assessments. Accelerated efforts to improve and develop spatial and attribute databases will facilitate the improvement of ground water vulnerability assessment methods.

CASE STUDIES

An array of methods for assessing ground water vulnerability is being used around the country. Several examples illustrate the diversity in techniques and the factors that influenced their selection. In Iowa, a qualitative overlay method is used to assess intrinsic vulnerability; a single vulnerability map was prepared showing depth to ground water and the location of well holes. On Cape Cod, Massachusetts, where the geological setting is relatively homogeneous, deterministic models for ground water flow and solute transport in the aquifer were used to identify where contamination potentially could affect well fields. In Florida, overlay and index methods were used to assess ground water vulnerability to pesticide contamination. In the San Joaquin Valley of California an approach based on detection of contamination has been used to address potential for further pesticide contamination. The USDA has developed a hybrid approach using an index method coupled with a simulation model to assist decision making at the national level. Finally, on Oahu, Hawaii, process-based models were used to predict pesticide transport in the vadose zone.

RESEARCH RECOMMENDATIONS

Critical evaluation and understanding of uncertainty is vital to the use of any means of vulnerability assessment. The following recommendations constitute a research agenda aimed at reducing uncertainty in vulnerability assessments and improving opportunities to use them effectively.

• Develop a better understanding of all processes that affect the transport and fate of contaminants.

• Establish simple, practical, and reliable methods for measuring *in situ* hydraulic conductivities of the soil and the unsaturated and saturated zones. Develop methods for scaling measurements that sample different volumes of porous materials to provide equivalent measures. Develop simple, practical, and reliable methods for measuring *in situ* degradation rates (e.g., hydrolysis, methylation, biodegradation), and develop methods for characterizing changes in degradation rate as a function of other physical parameters (e.g., depth in soil).

• Develop improved approaches to obtaining information on the residence time of water along flow paths and identifying recharge and discharge areas.

• Develop unified ways to combine soils and geologic information in vulnerability assessments.

• Improve the chemical databases, currently the source of much uncertainty in vulnerability assessments.

• Determine the circumstances in which the properties of the intermediate vadose zone are critical to vulnerability assessments and develop methods for characterizing the zone for assessments.

• Establish in the soil mapping standards of USDA's Soil Conservation Service an efficient soil sampling scheme for acquiring accurate soil attribute data in soil mapping unit polygons and documenting the uncertainty in these data. A need exists to better characterize the inclusions of other soil types in soil mapping units, including fractional area of included soil and distribution of inclusions.

• Establish reliable transfer functions for estimating *in situ* hydraulic properties using available soil attribute data (e.g., bulk densities, particle-size distributions, etc.). Develop ways to determine the additional uncertainty arising from the use of transfer functions in ground water vulnerability assessments.

• Develop methods for merging data obtained at different spatial and temporal scales into a common scale for vulnerability assessment.

• Improve analytical tools in GIS software to facilitate integration of assessment methods with spatial attribute databases and the computing environment.

• Establish more meaningful categories of vulnerability for assessment methods.

Determine which processes are most important to incorporate into vulnerability assessments at different spatial scales.

• Obtain more information on the uncertainty associated with vulnerability assessments and develop ways to display this uncertainty. Methods are needed that can identify and differentiate among more sources of uncertainty.

• Develop methods for accounting for soil macropores and other preferential flow pathways that can affect vulnerability. These investigations should include evaluations of the uncertainty in methods and measurements as they affect the assessment.

• Develop method for incorporating process-based, statistical, and qualitative information into an integrated or hybrid assessment.

• Identify counterintuitive situations leading to greater true vulnerability than commonly perceived. For example, develop greater understanding of the circumstances in which low-permeability materials that overlay aquifers can transmit contaminants to ground water.

REFERENCE

Heuvelink, G.B.M., P.A. Burrough, and A. Stein. 1989. Propagation of errors in spatial modelling with GIS. Int. Jour. Geographical Information Systems 3(4):303-322.

1

Introduction

It is the mark of an instructed mind to rest satisfied with the degree of precision which the nature of the subject permits, and not to seek an exactness where only an approximation of the truth is possible.

— *Aristotle*

Ground water is an important natural resource throughout the world. In the United States, approximately 50 percent of the population and more than 90 percent of rural residents use ground water as their source of domestic drinking water (USGS 1990). Ground water is the source of about 34 percent of the irrigation waters in the United States. Other uses of ground water have grown dramatically; total use of ground water for 1985 was an estimated 73 billion gallons a day (USGS 1990), more than double the usage in 1950. In addition, ground water is the principal source of surface water during low flow periods. About 30 percent of river and stream flow comes from ground water, where it contributes to important ecological habitat as well as surface drinking water supplies (USEPA 1991a).

The importance of ground water has long been recognized, but the potential for ground water to become contaminated as a result of human activities at or near the land surface has only been recognized in recent years. Before about 1980 it was thought that soils served as filters, preventing harmful substances deposited at the surface from migrating downward into ground water. Today it is known that soils and other intervening layers have a finite capacity to filter and retard, and so protect ground water.

Over the past two decades, a large number of chemicals and wastes from human activities have been found in ground water throughout the United States. Ground water can be contaminated by localized releases from sources such as hazardous waste disposal sites, municipal landfills, surface impoundments, underground storage tanks, gas and oil pipelines, back-siphoning of agricultural chemicals into wells, and injection wells. Ground water can also become contaminated by substances released at or near the soil surface in a more dispersed manner including pesticides, fertilizers, septic tank leachate, and contamination from other nonpoint sources.

Nitrates from fertilizers and animal wastes are the most pervasive type of ground water contamination. An estimated 20.5 million tons of fertilizers were applied to crops during 1988-1989 (USDA 1989). Between 1960 and 1985, agricultural use of nitrogen quadrupled, to 12 million tons (USDA 1987). Nitrate levels in ground water have increased concurrently with these rises in fertilizer application.

Pesticides also contribute significantly to ground water pollution. Each year about 661 million pounds of active pesticide ingredients are used in agriculture (OTA 1990, USEPA 1987). The first reported instances of ground water contamination by pesticides occurred in 1979 when dibromochloropropane (DBCP) was detected in California and aldicarb in New York. Subsequently, DBCP was detected in ground water in four additional states. By 1983, ethylene dibromide (EDB) had been found in wells in 16 counties of California, Florida, Georgia, and Hawaii (USEPA 1987). These findings prompted the suspension of EDB use in the United States. By 1988, pesticides had been detected in the ground water of more than 26 states (USEPA 1988). The largest monitoring study conducted in the United States, EPA's National Pesticide Survey (USEPA 1990), concluded that about 10.4 percent of wells in community water systems and 4.2 percent of rural domestic well water had detectable residues of one or more pesticides; fewer than 1 percent of all wells, however, were estimated to contain at least one pesticide in excess of established levels of health concern.

Once contaminated, ground water is very expensive to clean up; in many cases, cleanup may not be possible within a reasonable time (Mackay and Cherry 1989, Haley et al. 1991). In addition, ground water is the only source of drinking water for many rural areas (USGS 1990). The cost of replacing contaminated sources with bottled water or other alternatives is high relative to that of existing ground water resources (Abdalla 1990).

PROTECTING GROUND WATER FROM FUTURE CONTAMINATION

The seriousness and intractability of the problem of contaminated ground water has led resource managers to pursue a policy of prevention. Boxes 1.1 and 1.2 provide background information on the ground water protection programs of two federal agencies—the U.S. Department of Agriculture (USDA) and U.S. Environmental Protection Agency (EPA).

The factors that affect the ability of contaminants introduced at the land surface to reach ground water vary from place to place. Many extreme

---

Box 1.1
President's Water Quality Initiative

The President's Water Quality Initiative was launched in 1989 in response to the widespread concern that agricultural activities contribute to the contamination of the Nation's ground waters. The goal of the initiative is to relate agricultural activities to ground water quality and to develop and implement farm management strategies that protect ground water. The USDA was directed to achieve this goal in a manner that maintains productivity and profitability, and minimizes regulation. Research, education, technical assistance, cost-sharing, and data collection programs have been implemented to achieve these objectives. The Initiative will extend through 1995; it is led by the USDA and involves eight principal USDA agencies, state agricultural experiment stations and cooperative extension services, the U.S. EPA, the U.S. Geological Survey, the National Oceanic and Atmospheric Administration, and state universities.

As part of the initiative, the USDA developed a ground water vulnerability index for use in setting priorities in program management and to provide insight on the impact of policy development. A description of the USDA Ground Water Vulnerability Index for Pesticides and its applications is presented in the national level case study in Chapter 5.

---

situations are relatively obvious. For example, ground water contamination is likely to occur in areas having shallow water tables and sandy soils with high recharge rates. Such relatively obvious situations, however, are found on land that comprises only a small fraction of the area of the United States. Efforts to protect against future contamination must focus on the much larger areas where relative vulnerability to contamination is more difficult to distinguish. Given this understanding, resource managers have sought to identify areas where contamination is more likely to occur than in other areas. Thus the concept of ground water vulnerability to contamination was developed.

Ground Water Vulnerability to Contamination

As illustrated in Box 1.3 the concept of ground water vulnerability to contamination has different meanings for different people. In its broadest context, ground water vulnerability refers to whether or not an underlying aquifer will become contaminated as a result of activities at the land surface. For the purposes of this report, **ground water vulnerability to contamination** is defined as:

Box 1.2
EPA's Pesticides and Ground Water Strategy

Protecting the Nation's Ground Water: EPA's Strategy for the 1990s (USEPA 1991a) articulates the overall goal of EPA's ground water policy as:

"[T]o prevent adverse effects to human health and the environment and to protect the environmental integrity of the nation's ground-water resources; in determining appropriate prevention and protection strategies, EPA will also consider the use, value, and vulnerability of the resource, as well as social and economic values."

The inclusion of vulnerability considerations in this policy objective recognizes that uniquely local hydrogeologic and land management practices are significant factors affecting the potential for contamination to occur and thus the need for different types of protection plans that are consistent with local needs and conditions.

Based on the policy goals and principles outlined in this strategy, EPA developed a ground water protection strategy specific to the use of agricultural chemicals. The centerpiece of the *Pesticides and Ground-Water Strategy* (USEPA 1991b) "is the development and implementation of State Management Plans (SMPs) for specific pesticides of concern." An SMP is supposed to describe a state's approach to ground water protection for a specific pesticide based on local differences in ground water use, value, vulnerability, and sensitivity. Thus, as a part of their ground water protection responsibilities, states are strongly encouraged to conduct vulnerability assessments.

EPA has taken a differential management approach to ground water protection. The major assumption underlying such an approach is that one can assess vulnerability well enough to reliably identify geographic areas that warrant separate treatment. This fundamental issue is addressed further in the following chapters.

The tendency or likelihood for contaminants to reach a specified position in the ground water system after introduction at some location above the uppermost aquifer.

Note that this definition of ground water vulnerability refers to contamination resulting from nonpoint sources or areally distributed point sources of pollution and does not address individual point sources of pollution nor any situation where a pollutant is purposely placed in the ground water system. Sources such as landfills and underground storage tanks are not considered because they represent point sources even though they may de-

Box 1.3
The Many Ways of Defining Ground Water Vulnerability

Vulnerability means different things to different people. Some view it as an intrinsic characteristic of soils and other parts of the natural environment. Others find that vulnerability depends on the properties of individual contaminants or contaminant groups, but is independent of specific land-use or management practices (e.g., the amount of pesticide applied). Still others associate vulnerability with a specific set of human activities at the land surface. Some authors have attempted to avoid the term vulnerability altogether and have substituted terms such as sensitivity. The following quotes illustrate the diversity in terminology.

Foster (1987)

Aquifer Pollution Vulnerability - "the intrinsic characteristics which determine the sensitivity of various parts of an aquifer to being adversely affected by an imposed contaminant load."
Ground Water Pollution Risk - "the interaction between (a) the natural vulnerability of the aquifer, and (b) the pollution loading that is, or will be, applied on the subsurface environment as a result of human activity."

U.S. General Accounting Office (1991)

Hydrogeologic Vulnerability - "a function of geologic factors such as soil texture and depth to groundwater."
Total Vulnerability - "a function of these hydrogeologic factors, as well as the pesticide use factors that influence the site's susceptibility."
Total Risk - "This last approach is even broader, for it incorporates the size of the population at risk from potential pesticide contamination—that is, the number of people who obtain their drinking water from ground water in the area."

Pettyjohn et al. (1991)

Aquifer Vulnerability - "The geology of the physical system determines vulnerability."
Aquifer Sensitivity - "Aquifer sensitivity is related to the potential for contamination. That is, aquifers that have a high degree of vulnerability and are in areas of high population density, are considered to be the most sensitive..."

continued

U.S. Environmental Protection Agency (1993)

Aquifer Sensitivity - "The relative ease with which a contaminant (in this case a pesticide) applied on or near the land surface can migrate to the aquifer of interest. Aquifer sensitivity is a function of the intrinsic characteristics of the geologic materials of interest, any overlying saturated materials, and the overlying unsaturated zone. Sensitivity is not dependent on agronomic practices or pesticide characteristics."

Ground Water Vulnerability - "The relative ease with which a contaminant (in this case a pesticide) applied on or near the land surface can migrate to the aquifer of interest under a given set of agronomic management practices, pesticide characteristics and hydrogeologic sensitivity conditions.

grade the quality of the ground water over a region. Contamination resulting from brine injection wells, enhanced oil recovery wells, artificial recharge wells, and subsurface nuclear detonations are not considered because they represent purposeful placement of contaminants in the ground water system; it is obvious that any ground water system is vulnerable to such activity. The mobilization of naturally occurring trace elements and salt water intrusion into coastal aquifers as a result of pumping are also excluded. While in many places these sources and pathways may be the dominant cause of contamination, the concept of ground water vulnerability addresses only contaminants introduced by humans above the water table at or near the land surface. Other potential contamination must be addressed on a case-by-case basis using other means.

In certain circumstances, a large number of certain types of point sources— such as septic tank systems—distributed over a region could be considered a regional nonpoint source problem and are included in this definition. Also, cracks and fractures on a regional scale would be considered. In all cases considered under this definition, the contaminant must move at least partially through surficial material. Any mechanism that causes a complete bypassing of this material, such as back siphoning during chemigation, is not directly addressed by the methods examined in this study.

This conception of ground water vulnerability is bounded, as are any others, by a fundamental principle which is stated here as the **First Law of Ground Water Vulnerability:**

All ground water is vulnerable.

Vulnerability is not an absolute or measurable property, but an indication of the relative likelihood with which contamination will occur; no ground water (with possible exceptions such as deep sedimentary basin brines) is invulnerable.

An important consequence of the First Law is that the time a potential contaminant would take to travel from the point of introduction to the specified position in the ground water system must be either an implicit or explicit part of any attempt to identify vulnerable areas. A long travel time by itself, however, does not guarantee that an aquifer has low vulnerability. Rather, a key issue is the extent to which processes such as dispersion, sorption, and biochemical transformations are likely to reduce concentrations of the contaminants of interest and/or transform the contaminants to benign products. Thus, it may be misleading to assign low vulnerability to a setting simply because the unsaturated zone is very thick. Dependent on the unsaturated zone materials, if the contaminants of interest are sufficiently persistent and mobile to reach ground water, then they will eventually reach the aquifer. For example, several investigators (e.g., Pratt et al. 1972) have shown that nitrates can take decades to reach ground water. By extension, pesticides that are persistent, but less mobile than nitrate due to sorption, could take even longer.

ASSESSING GROUND WATER VULNERABILITY

Ground water vulnerability is an amorphous concept, not a measurable property. It is a probability (i.e., "the tendency or likelihood") that contamination will occur, and thus must be inferred from surrogate information that is measurable. In this sense, a vulnerability assessment is a predictive statement much like a weather forecast, but for processes that take place underground and on much longer time scales.

An array of methods for predicting ground water vulnerability has been developed. Many of them are based on mathematical models using equations that approximate the behavior of substances in the subsurface environment. These methods are called process-based methods. Another set of methods combine physical characteristics that affect vulnerability in a weighted index or numerical score. A third approach uses statistical methods to draw associations with areas in which contamination is known to have occurred. Generally, the more complex and detailed methods require more complex and detailed knowledge of the system being assessed. Simpler methods incorporate more approximations and are less precise, but require less detailed information about the system being assessed. Although complex methods may describe transport mechanisms more precisely, the data required are often unavailable and must be approximated from limited existing information.

Uncertainty in the Assessment Process

Predicting ground water vulnerability is an imprecise exercise. Information about the subsurface is expensive to obtain, especially over large areas, and assessment methods can only approximate actual environmental processes or other associations. Thus one arrives at the **Second Law of Ground Water Vulnerability:**

Uncertainty is inherent in all vulnerability assessments.

All of these methods are based on abstractions of reality and are subject to uncertainty as a result of misspecification, misuse, and data errors. Uncertainty is inherent in vulnerability assessments because of limitations in knowledge of contaminant behavior in the subsurface, as well as significant limitations in the spatial databases used to make assessments. Most existing methods convey a misleading impression of the uncertainty of the vulnerability assessment. A consequence of the Second Law is that vulnerability should be expressed in probabilistic terms (i.e., likelihood) that provide information about the unreliability of the assessment.

Different approaches may give vulnerability ratings that do not agree with each other or with observations of ground water pollutants. The model evaluation problem for large areas, or even a field, is especially difficult because the results (i.e., vulnerability ratings) are not subject to experimental verification using normal scientific methods.

Elements of Vulnerability Assessment

It is impossible to formulate a universal technique for predicting vulnerability that considers all of the ways in which contamination occurs. Key elements to consider in a vulnerability assessment for a particular application include the reference location (e.g., the water table or a specified position within the ground water system), the degree of contaminant specificity, the contaminant pathways considered, and the time and spatial scales of the assessment.

Reference Location

Vulnerability may be assessed on the basis of the prediction of the arrival of a contaminant at the water table or at some location within the ground water system, such as a well or the interface between ground water and surface water. Although the water table is used as the reference location in many methods, the potential for contaminants to move elsewhere in an aquifer should also be considered. Important considerations include the locations of recharge zones (places where precipitation on the land surface may infiltrate downward toward the water table) and discharge zones (places where ground water moves upward toward a stream or other discharge point). For example, the vulnerability assessed using the water table as the reference location may be greater at discharge zones than at recharge zones because the water table is shallower in discharge zones, whereas the potential for contaminants to migrate farther in the ground water system once they arrive at the water table may be significantly greater at the recharge zones. In some situations, water recharging the ground water system may move essentially horizontally along the water table gradient from high to low elevation and discharge at a surface water body or land surface depression. In other situations, the recharge can move substantially downward in the aquifer below the water table. In the former case, the potential for contamination is greatest near the water table; in the latter case, contaminants can spread through a large portion of the aquifer.

Specific and Intrinsic Vulnerability

Vulnerability assessments may or may not account for the different behavior of different contaminants in assessing vulnerability. In general, two types of vulnerability assessment can be defined. The first, *specific vulnerability*, is used when vulnerability is referenced to a specific contaminant, contaminant class, or human activity. A second term, *intrinsic vulnerability*, refers to vulnerability determined without consideration of the attributes and behavior of particular contaminants. In practice, a clear distinction between intrinsic and specific vulnerability cannot always be made. Many vulnerability assessment methods do not refer to specific contaminants (and hence are intrinsic); however, many of the parameters used in assessment methods (e.g., organic carbon content) will have different influences on different contaminants.

Contaminant Pathways

Contaminants can enter aquifers by several different means as illustrated in Figure 1.1. In general, vulnerability assessments consider only those types of contamination that begin as downward percolation from a surface source or from sources in the shallow subsurface. Thus, for example, direct entry of contaminants into wells resulting from a spill or back-siphoning during chemigation is not a pathway considered in vulnerability assessment.

Most measures of ground water vulnerability to contamination assume simple percolation from the land surface and ignore preferential flow paths, such as biochannels (root holes and worm holes) and cracks, joints, and solution channels in the vadose zone. These pathways, however, may give

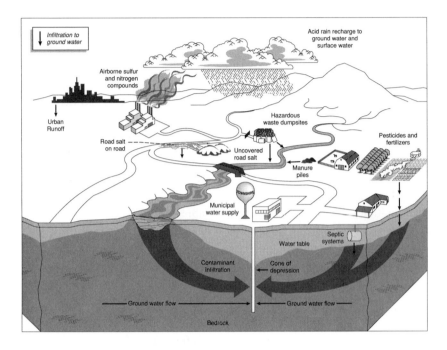

FIGURE 1.1   Pathways by which contaminants may reach ground water.

contaminants a more direct and rapid path to ground water than they would otherwise have.   In some cases, considerable potential exists for water to move from contaminated shallow aquifers to deeper aquifers via existing or improperly sealed abandoned wells.   Cross-contamination might take place in the wellbore or outside the well casing in an unsealed annulus.   It is difficult to incorporate these types of contaminant pathways into quantitative measures of ground water vulnerability, yet they may be the primary control on the vulnerability of deeper aquifers to contamination.   One approach is to overlay information on the potential for cross-contamination of deeper aquifers (e.g., sink holes or agricultural drainage areas) on traditional maps of shallow aquifer vulnerability as was done in Iowa (see case example in Chapter 5).

Vulnerability to contamination is commonly treated as a static property although ground water development can have a marked effect on vulnerability by changing the flow regime.   Pumpage-induced movement of contaminated shallow ground water into deeper aquifers may be a significant consideration in some situations.   Inclusion of these factors into a vulnerability assessment generally entails some level of computer simulation.

Spatial Scales

Often a key product of vulnerability assessment is a map delineating areas of different vulnerability. Overall, the utility of different methods of assessment is highly dependent on the scale at which data are available, the scale used to display the results, and the spatial resolution of the mapping. In general, vulnerability assessments are conducted at map scales that range from 1:12,000 to 1:250,000, although some multistate or larger area assessments might use map scales as small as 1:1,000,000 or 1:2,000,000. The spatial resolution of vulnerability maps depends on the resolution of the databases that are available for characterizing the region of interest. The situation is complicated because spatial databases tend to differ in their levels of detail and accuracy. Thus, it is difficult to make general statements about the resolution of vulnerability assessments. It is likely, however, that the resolution will be coarser than individual occurrences of contamination. Box 1.4 provides some additional information about maps and scales.

Box 1.4
Scale, Size, and Maps

Vulnerability assessments are performed over areas ranging from the national level, through state, county and hydrologic unit levels, to the field level, where a field is as small as 2 or 3 acres. The degree of resolution required for a vulnerability assessment will depend on the purpose for which it is intended. In addition, factors such as the size of the area being assessed, the level at which information is available, and the capacity to handle information will affect the scale at which an assessment can be done. Table 1.1 shows the ranges of map scales at which different levels of assessment are appropriate.

TABLE 1.1 Map Scales and the Corresponding Management Units

1:2,000,000	1:250,000	1:100,000	1:24,000	1:12,000
National Multistate				
	State Multicounty			
		County		
			Hydrologic Unit	Field

continued

The usage of the cartographer's term "scale" can be confusing. Maps that provide high resolution, such as 1:12,000 and 1:24,000, are considered "large-scale." Maps having a lower level of resolution, such as 1:250,000 and 1:2,000,000, are termed "small-scale." As a point of reference, Figures 1.2a, b, and c show a 3-acre field plot depicted on a 1:100,000, 1:24,000, and 1:12,000 maps, respectively.

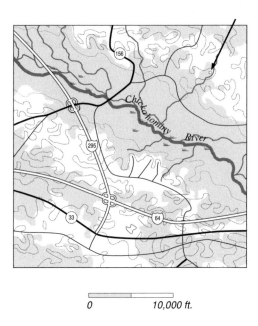

0   10,000 ft.

FIGURE 1.2a   A 3-acre field plot is shown on each of the maps in Figure 1.2a, b, and c.   The map in Figure 1.2a is drawn at 1:100,000; the 3-acre field plot appears in the upper right corner. Figure 1.2b is drawn at 1:24,000 and Figure 1.2c is drawn at 1:12,000. A comparison of these figures shows how resolution increases with map scale.

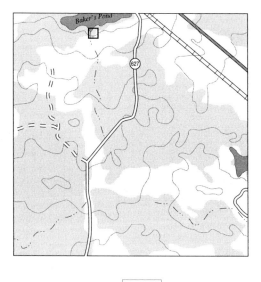

0   1,000 ft.

FIGURE 1.2b   See Figure 1.2a for description.

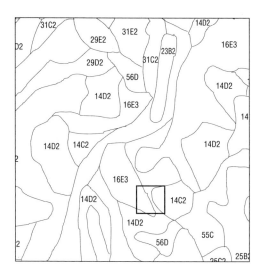

0   1,000 ft.

FIGURE 1.2c   See Figure 1.2 a for description.

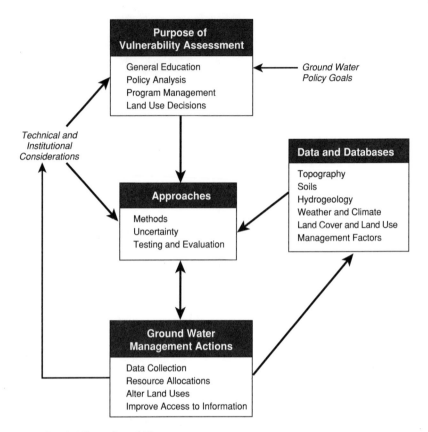

FIGURE 1.3 The vulnerability assessment process.

THE VULNERABILITY ASSESSMENT PROCESS

The flowchart in Figure 1.3 shows the major components of vulnerability assessment, which in general correspond to the chapters of this report. They include: determining the purpose of the assessment; selecting an assessment method, dealing with issues of uncertainty and evaluation; identifying the needs, availability, and quality of data; and eventually using the completed assessment in managing ground water resources.

As the flowchart shows, the approach used to assess ground water vulnerability is central to the process, but is also directly affected by inputs or considerations entailed by the purpose, data availability, and management use of the assessment. The selection and development of a method for vulnerability assessment is not simply a question of appropriate science, but also reflects concerns over the need for the assessment, the availability of suitable data, the level of uncertainty in the model or the data, and the impact of this uncertainty on the management actions resulting from the assessment.

Ground water vulnerability assessment is a dynamic and iterative process that requires the cooperative efforts of regulatory policy makers, natural resource managers, and technical experts. In performing vulnerability assessments these three groups are united by a common goal: the protection of ground water by the development and implementation of different management practices or policies, based on vulnerability to contamination, that minimize or prevent contamination of ground water resources.

The first step in the process of vulnerability assessment is to identify the purpose of the assessment. As indicated in the flowchart, an assessment's purpose is influenced by a variety of factors including the organization's ground water policy goal, technical considerations (such as the form of the output and the cost of the assessment), and institutional issues (such as the time frame for the assessment and resource availability). Purposes of vulnerability assessments range from improving information and education through analyzing the impact of alternative ground water policies, providing a tool for allocating resources, and guiding the decisions of land users or land use managers. These issues are described in Chapter 2.

The next stage in the process is to select a suitable approach for conducting the assessment. Various methods are available. This stage of the assessment process includes choosing a model or technique for the assessment, identifying the uncertainties inherent in the model and the data needed for the assessment, and testing the model and its assumptions. Each of these issues is discussed in Chapter 3.

Highly related to the performance of an assessment are considerations surrounding the availability and quality of the data required. These data questions influence both the choice of technique for the assessment and the confidence of policy makers and regulators in making decisions based on the results. Issues of data availability and quality are addressed in Chapter 4.

Once an assessment is complete, various management actions may be taken to protect ground water quality or minimize contamination. Management actions could range from altering land use practices, targeting resource allocations, or disseminating vulnerability information through an educational program to collecting additional data on factors relating to vulnerability or ground water quality. Actions based on a vulnerability assessment should be tempered by the uncertainty of the assessment and the confidence of the technical experts in the assessment they have produced. Therefore, the flowchart indicates another iteration via feedback to the boxes concerning the approaches, the data, and technical and institutional considerations. Findings and recommendations on the use and improvement of vulnerability assessments and related research needs appear in Chapter 6.

Case Studies

Chapter 5 of this report presents six case studies, covering a broad spectrum of uses, assessment methods, and spatial scales of analysis. In each study, the selection of assessment methods seems to have been influenced by the availability of spatial databases, ease of implementation, and the perceived credibility or validity of the selected method.

In Iowa, the vulnerability assessments were conducted to acquire improved information that would help develop ground water protection strategies based on voluntary action, but not to support regulatory activities. In contrast, vulnerability assessments are being used in Florida and on Cape Cod to delineate land areas that will be targeted for differential management in order to protect the quality of ground water resources. The assessment conducted by the USDA has a national perspective and is designed to be used as a decision aid in program management and policy development regarding the impacts of agricultural chemicals on ground water quality.

California's approach to ground water protection reflects one end of the spectrum in the types of methods used for vulnerability assessment. The state relies completely on ground water monitoring for regulatory purposes in identifying Pesticide Management Zones. None of the extant vulnerability assessment methods was considered adequate or practical because their associated uncertainties were judged to be too large for use in California. Regulatory action is taken only after a pesticide has been detected in ground water, and pesticide use restrictions are imposed only within the land section where the contaminated well is located. Many of the states (e.g., Florida and Iowa) have adopted overlay and index methods because the required databases were readily available and because these methods could be easily implemented given the resources available. In other cases, (e.g., Hawaii), the use of one-dimensional simulation models that predict pesticide leaching to ground water are being explored as a tool in regional vulnerability assessments. On the other hand, sophisticated three-dimensional ground water flow models are being used to delineate the zones of contribution to public wells on Cape Cod. The USDA assessment technique represents a hybrid approach in that it employs a numerical index based on outputs from a simulation model that are being used as adequate predictors of likely outcomes under diverse conditions. Ground water monitoring networks are being established in many states (e.g., Florida) to track the impacts of land-use activities on regional ground water quality.

The spatial scales at which the vulnerability assessments have been conducted range from the national scale (e.g., USDA), to statewide assessments (e.g., Florida, Iowa, Hawaii), to county-scale evaluations (e.g., Cape Cod). Some of the assessments are based on spatial aggregation of outputs from simulation models designed to represent field-scale processes (e.g., Hawaii, Cape Cod, USDA).

REFERENCES

Abdalla, C.W. 1990. Measuring economic losses from ground water contamination: An investigation of household avoidance costs. Water Resources Bulletin 26(3):451-463.

Foster, S.S.D. 1987. Fundamental concepts in aquifer vulnerability, pollution risk and protection strategy. Pp. 69-86 in Vulnerability of Soil and Groundwater Pollutants, W. van Duijvenbooden and H.G. van Waegeningh, eds. The Hague, The Netherlands: TNO Committee on Hydrological Research Proceedings and Information No. 38.

Haley, J.L., B. Hanson, C. Enfield, and J. Glass. 1991. Evaluating the effectiveness of ground water extraction systems. Ground Water Monitoring Record Winter:119-124.

Mackay, D.M., and J.A. Cherry. 1989. Groundwater contamination: Pump-and-treat remediation. Environmental Science and Technology 23(6):630-636.

Office of Technology Assessment (OTA). 1990. Beneath the Bottom Line: Agricultural Approaches to Reduce Agrichemical Contamination of Groundwater. Washington, D.C.: U.S. Government Printing Office.

Pettyjohn, W.A., M. Savoca, and D. Self. 1991. Regional Assessment of Aquifer Vulnerability and Sensitivity in the Coterminous United States. Washington, D.C.: U.S. Environmental Protection Agency.

Pratt, P.F., W.W. Jones, and V.E. Hunsaker. 1972. Nitrate in deep soil profiles in relation to fertilizer rates and leaching volume. Journal of Environmental Quality 1(1):97-102.

U.S. Department of Agriculture (USDA). 1987. The Magnitude and Cost of Groundwater Contamination from Agricultural Chemicals, A National Perspective. Staff Report AGES870318. Washington, D.C.: U.S. Department of Agriculture, Environmental Research Service. 54 pp.

U.S. Department of Agriculture (USDA). 1989. Agricultural Resources: Inputs, Situation and Outlook. Washington, D.C.: U.S. Department of Agriculture, Economic Research Service.

U.S. Environmental Protection Agency (USEPA). 1987. Agricultural Chemicals in Ground Water: Proposed Pesticide Strategy. Washington, D.C.: U.S. Environmental Protection Agency, Office of Pesticides and Toxic Substances.

U.S. Environmental Protection Agency (USEPA). 1988. Pesticides in Ground Water Data Base: Interim Report. Washington, D.C.: U.S. Environmental Protection Agency.

U.S. Environmental Protection Agency (USEPA). 1990. National Survey of Pesticides in Drinking Water Wells, Phase I Report. Washington, D.C.: U.S Environmental Protection Agency, Offices of Water and Pesticides and Toxic Substances. EPA 5709-90-0-5.

U.S. Environmental Protection Agency (USEPA). 1991a. Protecting the Nation's Ground Water: EPA's Strategy for the 1990s. Washington, D.C.: U.S. Environmental Protection Agency, Office of the Administrator.

U.S. Environmental Protection Agency (USEPA). 1991b. Pesticides and Ground-Water Strategy. Washington, D.C.: U.S. Environmental Protection Agency, Offices of Pesticides and Toxic Substances.

U.S. Environmental Protection Agency (USEPA). 1993. A Review of Methods for Assessing Aquifer Sensitivity and Ground Water Vulnerability to Pesticide Contamination. Draft. Washington, D.C.: U.S. Environmental Protection Agency.

U.S. General Accounting Office (GAO). 1991. Groundwater Protection: Measurement of Relative Vulnerability to Pesticide Contamination. Washington, D.C.: U.S. General Accounting Office. GAO/PEMD-92-8.

U.S. Geological Survey (USGS). 1990. National Water Summary 1987—Hydrologic Events and Water Supply and Use. U.S. Geological Survey Water-Supply Paper 2350. 553 pp.

2

Considerations in the Selection and Use of Vulnerability Assessments

INTRODUCTION

Numerous agencies and organizations have conducted or plan to conduct vulnerability assessments as part of their decision making, policy making, and/or planning functions. In most cases, these assessments are analytical tools that bridge the science that seeks to understand the relationship between land use activities and ground water contamination with the sociopolitical realities of making decisions and implementing programs to protect ground water quality.

Increasingly, policy makers and managers have demanded that vulnerability assessments provide objective, scientific, and accurate evidence they can use to make difficult choices and decisions. Similarly, scientists have struggled with providing simple, readily understandable products (often maps) containing the results of sophisticated models representing complex ground water processes and sometimes questionable data. An important corollary to the Second Law of Ground Water Vulnerability is that since all vulnerability assessments are uncertain, no management decisions based on them are ever clear-cut or certain. The tension between the need for and capability of vulnerability assessments to provide accurate and useful information forms the structure for this chapter.

The intended use of the vulnerability assessment process is the most obvious and important consideration in selecting an assessment approach. The uses of vulnerability assessments in policy making range from advising decision makers of the need for or consequences of their actions, to providing direction for allocating resources, to informing decisions about land use activities, to educating the general public about ground water contamination potential. Existing uses of and needs for vulnerability assessments can be grouped into four broad categories. First, assessments can be used in *policy analysis and development* to identify the potential for ground water contamination and the need for protection and to aid in examining of the relative effects of alternative ways to control contamination. Second, when scarce resources prevent uniform and costly expenditures, vulnerability assessments can be used in *program management* to allocate resources to areas where the greatest effort is warranted. Third, vulnerability assessments can be used in some instances to *inform land use decisions* such as site selection, alteration of land use activities to reflect the potential for ground water contamination, or voluntary changes in behaviors of land owners as they become more aware of the ground water impacts of their land-based activities. Finally, and perhaps most important, is the use of vulnerability assessments to *improve general education* and awareness of a region's hydrologic resources.

Often policy makers will not find the objective, scientific, and accurate product they need for the decisions identified above. Rather, they will find that the usefulness of a vulnerability assessment may be severely constrained by scientific unknowns or lack of suitable data. Hence, policy makers and managers need to become intelligent consumers of vulnerability assessments since the selection and use of assessments are significantly affected by several technical and institutional factors.

Several key factors will affect both the technical conduct of an assessment and its effectiveness in use. The more consideration given to these technical and institutional issues, the more likely are the needs for a vulnerability assessment to be matched with a useful, scientifically-based technique.

EXISTING AND POTENTIAL USES FOR
VULNERABILITY ASSESSMENTS

Policy Analysis and Development

Vulnerability assessments can be used to aid in the development and analysis of policies to respond to potential or actual ground water contamination. In this early stage of the policy making process, assessments can be used to predict, at least qualitatively, potential ground water quality outcomes of different policy scenarios. Vulnerability assessments can also be used as a tool in assessing the effectiveness of alternative responses to a problem.

In some cases, vulnerability assessments can be used to identify or predict the existence of potential for ground water contamination in a particular geographical or jurisdictional area. Therefore, these assessments often take the form of a map of existing levels of contamination or areas where contamination is known to have the potential to occur. In these cases, the assessment documents the problem needing to be resolved and provides the justification and rationale for further discussion, action, and/or policy development.

Another potential use of a vulnerability assessment in the policy development stage is to analyze proposed alternative policies that seek to respond to a particular ground water quality problem. A program manager faced, say, with a problem with the use of the herbicide atrazine in a particular region might need to examine several alternative policies—from education and technical assistance to regulation of usage rates to an outright ban on use. Various analytical tools could then be used by the policy analyst to determine the impacts of each of these options on a variety of factors including atrazine use, productivity, and ground water quality. For example, the predicted effectiveness of a policy that is implemented only in more vulnerable areas (versus all areas) can be estimated through the use of vulnerability assessments.

Program Management

Vulnerability assessments can also be used to guide various program-level management decisions. As stated above, assessments can document the level of severity and need to resolve a ground water contamination problem. Further, an assessment can highlight the need for financial or human resources to be directed toward the control of a particular ground water contaminant or contamination problem.

Vulnerability assessments also can give managers information they need to allocate resources to areas for particular purposes. These purposes could vary from providing the greatest benefit or protection with the least expenditure to preventing the worst possible contamination problem. For example, vulnerability assessments could be used to establish routine ground water monitoring programs, to establish databases, or to ensure compliance with standards or other protection requirements. More vulnerable areas would be monitored more closely than less vulnerable areas to identify incidences of contamination. Similarly, allocation of personnel to compliance programs could be based on vulnerability assessments. Assigning additional personnel to supervise land use regulations or mitigation plans in more vulnerable areas recognizes the need for closer control of activities in areas more susceptible to contamination.

In each of these instances, vulnerability assessments serve as a tool to improve the management of ground water resources. In one case, vulnerability assessments elevate the awareness of program managers to the problem of ground water contamination and provide a call for further action. In other instances, an assessment is used to direct the allocation of resources, financial or human, to particular types of problems or particular locations. Each of these uses of vulnerability assessments serves a critical management need.

Land Use Decisions

The vast majority of land use decisions in the United States are made by private land owners and owners operating within a framework of publicly adopted rules and regulations. Land use planning and control functions that establish and enforce these rules have typically been performed by local (municipal and county) government, although some states (Florida, Oregon, and Vermont are prominent among them) have exercised broad authority over land use. The federal role in land use management has generally been very limited, except for federally owned lands.

Land use decision making thus tends to be highly decentralized, and the application of ground water vulnerability assessments to such decisions presents special technical and institutional problems. Still, ground water vulnerability assessments may inform three principal categories of land use decision making: zoning and screening functions; permit conditioning, mitigation, and monitoring; and the voluntary behaviors of individual land users and owners.

Zoning and Screening

Zoning, one of the primary forms of managing land use, involves the assignment of a range of acceptable and/or unacceptable uses and activities to different areas of land. *Screening* is the search for suitable sites for specific activities or types of facilities. Often, suitable sites are found by eliminating unsuitable sites. The goal of both zoning and screening in protecting ground water is to preemptively direct facilities relatively likely to cause ground water contamination (such as landfills, wastewater discharges, and certain industrial uses) and activities of high contamination potential (such as the application of pesticides) away from areas of high vulnerability.

Zoning or screening aimed at preventing unacceptable impacts on ground water must address the most sensitive use or function of the ground water resource. For example, ground water can be used as a drinking water supply or play an important role in freshwater and marine ecosystems. Each of these uses or functions exhibits dramatically different tolerances for contamination that must be accounted for in identifying ground water impacts.

Zoning and screening functions ultimately involve decisions affecting individual sites. Regional vulnerability assessments do not provide site-specific resolution, but may appear to contain information relevant to site-level decisions. Limitations in the ability to predict the effect of land uses and activities on ground water include scale constraints, errors, and uncertainty. While it might be tempting to construct a hypothetical ground water zoning map based on a vulnerability map, such a zoning map could not of course, be more detailed or more certain than the underlying vulnerability assessment. Unfounded application of regional assessments at the site level could result in misinformed decisions with unfortunate and even tragic consequences for the land user, land regulator, and the ground water resource itself.

Conditioning, Mitigating, and Compliance Monitoring

In issuing permits for activities that may contaminate ground water, regulators often establish specific requirements that relate to the characteristics of the activity or site. Conditions or required mitigation may include treatment to acceptable levels of contaminant concentration, limits on discharge volumes, prohibition of discharge, and required containment to deal with accidental spills. Vulnerability assessments also can guide the establishment of sampling routines for compliance monitoring. Land uses in comparatively more vulnerable areas may, therefore, require more monitoring for compliance assurance than uses in less vulnerable areas.

As before, the utility of vulnerability assessments to the manager in setting conditions or establishing mitigation will vary with the specificity of the assessment. Vulnerability assessments conceivably could be used to establish more stringent requirements in areas of high vulnerability, including more frequent or intensive monitoring to demonstrate compliance with permit conditions.

Technical Assistance

The availability of a vulnerability assessment can give both land users (e.g., farmers) and managers (e.g., water supply superintendents) a proper sense of caution and some information on how to avoid excessively risky actions. A vulnerability assessment prepared by the Soil Conservation Service, for example, may be linked to a set of alternative land uses and conservation practices that would minimize contamination of the water system. Farmers would select from the acceptable alternatives based on resource protection factors as well as social and economic factors. Other responses may include voluntary restrictions of activity by the land user (such as self-imposed limits on pesticide use) to avoid contamination or the setting aside of land near wells of surface waters to prevent direct contamination. Again, the utility of the vulnerability assessment in technical assistance will depend on its specificity, level of detail, and degree of uncertainty.

General Education and Awareness

Although vulnerability assessments are rarely undertaken primarily to increase the awareness and knowledge of the public and decision makers on the potential for contamination of ground water resources, that may be their most valuable use. Because ground water resources are generally invisible, public knowledge of the ground water system, its use, and its susceptibility to contamination is often poor. A vulnerability assessment can improve such awareness by highlighting the surface or near-surface activities that lead to ground water contamination, by noting the movement of contaminants, and by indicating the factors leading to higher or lower levels of vulnerability. This increased knowledge often produces a greater willingness to take the necessary steps to protect against ground water contamination.

In some cases, this use of vulnerability assessments is explicitly intended. As illustrated in the Iowa case study in Chapter 5, learning more about the ground water system and its susceptibility to contamination was an essential part of that state's nonregulatory approach to ground water protection. In other situations, education can be an unstated or implicit goal of an assessment that provides the knowledge or awareness necessary to implement new policies, allocate resources, or affect land use decisions.

Such assessments also may help to create public support for protective measures. For example, the "sole source aquifer" designation under the Safe Drinking Water Act was successful in creating a widely shared image in places like Cape Cod of a fragile, interconnected, and irreplaceable resource requiring conscientious management and careful protection. More specific assessments also may contribute to greater sophistication and greater commitment to action on the part of the public, as was shown in the town meeting votes to acquire large holdings of land in wellhead protection areas on Cape Cod and elsewhere in the 1980s.

FACTORS AFFECTING SELECTION AND USE OF VULNERABILITY ASSESSMENTS

Varying levels of accuracy, certainty, resources, and data are required to meet each of the four uses identified above. Not all approaches or data can meet these needs. Decision makers must, therefore, reconcile their needs with the capability of the methods and data. Several technical and institutional factors affect this match between the selection and use of the vulnerability assessment and its eventual purpose. By addressing these issues, decision makers may be better able to request an assessment that meets their needs while still understanding its limitations and weaknesses. Further, those performing the assessments may be able to provide language that clarifies the proper use of the results.

Technical Considerations

Many technical issues affect the design and use of vulnerability assessments. They include the type and form of the results or output, the suitability of the technique for the physical characteristics of the area being assessed, the adequacy of the available data or data to be collected, and the analysis of uncertainty in the output and how it may affect the actions influenced by the assessment. These factors are not mutually exclusive.

Type and Form of Output

The first critical technical issue is the form of presentation of the results of the vulnerability assessment. What do users of the assessment wish to obtain from it? A variety of types and forms of output may be needed to meet various needs. For example, the USDA case (see Chapter 5) demonstrates the need for delineating regions with different vulnerabilities so that resource allocation decisions can be made. For this purpose, a map depicting numerous areas differently colored or shaded is desirable.

Alternatively, a vulnerability assessment could be used to determine areas where use of a particular pesticide should be restricted or specific management practices should be implemented. This use would require comparatively greater resolution among areas than the resource-allocation example, but may lead to a much simpler product, such as a map showing two types of regions: one where a pesticide is banned and another where use is permitted. Significant explanatory text would be essential to justify this map properly, to convey its assumptions and approach, and to illustrate its use.

In most cases, the product of a vulnerability assessment is a map of various areas—each area containing essentially similar vulnerability characteristics. Shading or coloring of these areas denotes different levels of vulnerability or characteristics affecting vulnerability. Such maps are very easily understood graphical means of conveying information for decision making. Maps, however, require aggregation of characteristics into defined areas. This aggregation can either mask important distinctions or emphasize minor differences. While a map is the output of choice in most existing vulnerability assessments, much care should go into preparing it, since the map, not the actual data, method, or process involved in preparing it, will be regarded as the true output of the assessment.

The map should be supported by a technical supplement describing the underlying assumptions of the assessment, the rationale for the selection of the method of analysis, an assessment of the adequacy of the data for the selected method, the uncertainties associated with the input data and analysis, and the sensitivity of the results to key assumptions and available data. This information makes possible an independent evaluation of the technical adequacy of the vulnerability assessment.

Size and Characteristics of Assessment Area

The analytical technique selected for a specific vulnerability assessment should be technically defensible with respect to the physical dimensions and characteristics of the area covered by the assessment. The area may be the entire nation, a subregion, a state, a single county or multicounty region, an entire watershed or part of a watershed, or a field. The characteristics may be quite uniform or highly variable within the region to be assessed. As a rule of thumb, the mathematical complexity of the vulnerability assessment technique is inversely related to the size of the area being assessed.

For smaller regions, on the level of a watershed or field, the vulnerability assessment technique may include numerical models of the physical processes of vadose-zone hydrologic flow and chemical transport and fate. Depending on the data available, the characteristics to be included in the assessment, and the technical skill of the people doing the assessment, these models could be very complex. At present, when the area being assessed is larger than a watershed, such as in a state, regional, or national assessment, these detailed physical models typically would be replaced by techniques that aggregate information across watershed boundaries.

Availability of Data

A major consideration in selecting an assessment technique is the type and amount of data required by the analysis and the level of certainty desired. For physical process models, the requirements are very specific: measurements of hydraulic and soil properties, such as conductivities, permeabilities, and bulk densities, should be available from one or more locations within the area being modeled. Without site- or area-specific data, the credibility of the modeling is diminished. Because these data are associated with physical measurements, specific requirements for the methods of collection can be stipulated to ensure comparability across different data collection activities.

The statistical and index techniques also require data, including flow-system characteristics, vadose zone transport times, population densities, and land use information, among others. Because these types of data are less tied to specific physical measurements, and because the geographic regions will vary from assessment to assessment, it is difficult to set standards for data collection and aggregation for these methods.

For any type of analysis, the quality of the data will affect the level of uncertainty associated with the assessment results. Thus, the desired level of certainty will also affect the selection of a technique.

Uncertainty of Results and Impact on Use

Any vulnerability assessment will be subject to uncertainty for many reasons. They include lack of available data, measurement errors in available data, incomplete understanding of the relevant environmental processes, uncertainty resulting from prediction of events, errors in aggregating information, and errors inherent in using statistical measures of association. Some of these errors or uncertainties can be measured, but others cannot. Uncertainties in data that describe field properties that can be directly measured are more easily quantified than the types of uncertainty that result from method used.

All forms of uncertainty are critical in the design and use of an assessment. Consideration should be given to the effects of uncertainty on how decisions will be made, what decisions are made, and how the results of the assessment are presented. In all cases, this discussion of uncertainty and errors should help elucidate which decisions are possible, the benefits of making correct decisions, and the consequences of making incorrect choices.

Simple methods may be appropriate for areas where more comprehensive data needed for detailed evaluations are not available. However, when data are available and more detailed methods can be performed, these results usually would be preferred to those from simpler methods. The eventual use of an assessment should, more or less, reflect the technical limitations of the method.

Therefore, the purpose of the vulnerability assessment, the level of uncertainty in the results that can be tolerated, and the limitations of the techniques and results will directly affect the design and use of the assessment. These and similar technical issues should be adequately considered by both the users of the assessment and the technical staff who prepare it.

Institutional Considerations

In addition to purely technical issues, several institutional factors are important to the design and eventual use of a vulnerability assessment. These issues include the time frame in which the assessment is meant to apply, how the proposed vulnerability assessment is coordinated with other planning programs and needs, the cost of the assessment and the value of the information to be gained, the availability of personnel and physical resources to perform the assessment, and the plans and activities of other agencies and institutions that may have an interest in the assessment. Again, these factors are not mutually exclusive, and they overlap with the technical issues discussed above.

Time Frame of a Vulnerability Assessment

Since a vulnerability assessment is done to predict the possibility of contamination of ground water or the potential worsening of existing conditions, the period to be covered by the proposed vulnerability assessment must be chosen carefully. As noted in Chapter 1, sufficiently persistent and mobile contaminants may eventually be observed in ground water at significant levels even though the travel times may be long. Thus, it may be necessary to consider effects on ground water quality over longer time spans and greater distances than is commonly done in vulnerability assessments.

Cost and Commitment of Personnel and Physical Resources

Any vulnerability assessment, no matter how simple, will incur programmatic costs, including the commitment of personnel and physical resources. Key questions to be considered include: How much funding is available for a vulnerability assessment? Are staff with the needed expertise available? If new staff must be hired, what are the long-term personnel and financial commitments? Are the physical resources, such as ground water sampling or testing equipment, or computer facilities for data management and analysis readily available?

Each of these questions considers a different feature of the human and financial costs of performing a vulnerability assessment. In general, the more resources available for the analysis, the more detailed and sophisticated it can be. In many cases, however, the intended use of the assessment may not require a detailed or sophisticated approach. Therefore, the resources invested in the analysis should be consistent with the value of the results.

Coordination with Other Planning Programs and Needs

Another important institutional issue in the design and use of a vulnerability assessment is its role in other ground water planning and protection efforts. Is the assessment an integral part of a well defined strategy for ground water protection, or is it designed to respond to a particular, rather specific, ground water question? If the vulnerability assessment is to be a one-time activity—for example, a survey of the status of a region's ground water—the approach would likely be to use existing data with a readily available assessment method to produce results in relatively short order.

On the other hand, a vulnerability assessment can be part of a long-term program to develop and monitor ground water protection strategies and intervention measures. In this case, the assessment would benefit from potentially significant investments in data collection, computer systems to manage the data, and personnel to produce an assessment tailored to the specific needs of the program. These longer-term assessments also may need to be flexible enough to adapt to programmatic changes and to incorporate advances in computer and data management technologies.

Coordination with Other Agencies and Institutions

A final consideration in planning and conducting a vulnerability assessment is the role of other organizations, agencies, or institutions in the performance or use of the assessment. Often, other agencies or institutions may need or have an interest in specific information to be produced by the assessment. In some cases, another group may be conducting or may have completed a similar vulnerability assessment. More commonly, however, several agencies may be undertaking assessments for somewhat different purposes. Coordination among these organizations and agencies may greatly decrease the cost of the assessment and increase its value and credibility.

SUMMARY

Vulnerability assessments can meet a variety of needs for ground water managers, land use regulators, resource conservationists, and the general public. Increasing awareness, informing land use decision making, allocating resources, and evaluating alternative policies are just a few of the uses noted in this chapter. Regardless of use, however, tension exists between managers' desire to obtain clear, incontrovertible vulnerability information and the ability of assessments to meet that need. At present, lack of knowledge, data, staff, and time prevent accurate assessments of ground water vulnerability.

To reduce this tension and make progress in developing and using vulnerability assessments, action is required from scientists and managers alike. Managers and policy makers should recognize the scientific limitations and expect less from current vulnerability assessments. To reduce uncertainty in assessments, managers will have to provide adequate support for the development and evaluation of improved approaches and data collection. Similarly, scientists should recognize manager's needs for assessments and focus their energies on responding to the uncertainties, high costs, and high levels of expertise needed. In addition, scientists should seek better methods for communicating underlying uncertainties to managers who may not have extensive technical training. Better communication among scientists and managers should surely improve the development of useful and valid vulnerability assessments and the soundness of policies informed by them.

3

Approaches to Vulnerability Assessments

INTRODUCTION

Numerous approaches have been used or proposed for assessing ground water vulnerability. They range from sophisticated models of the physical, chemical, and biological processes occurring in the vadose zone and ground water regime, to models that weight critical factors affecting vulnerability through either statistical methods or expert judgment. Each of these categories of techniques are reviewed in this chapter, with particular emphasis on their strengths and limitations.

A fundamental characteristic of all approaches to vulnerability assessment is uncertainty, either in the method itself or in the data it uses. These uncertainties are discussed, and ways to analyze and minimize them are presented. Possibilities for testing and evaluating models are discussed for both field-scale and regional-scale assessments. At the conclusion of this chapter, geographic information systems (GIS) are presented as a commonly used computing environment for executing some types of assessments and for displaying the results of virtually all types of assessments.

The potential for contaminants to leach to ground water depends on many factors, including the composition of the soils and geologic materials in the unsaturated zone, the depth to the water table, the recharge rate, and environmental influences on the potential for biodegradation. The composition of the unsaturated zone can greatly influence transformations and reactions. For example, high organic matter or clay content increases sorption and thus lessens the potential for contamination. The depth to the water table can be important because short flow paths decrease the opportunity for sorption and biodegradation and thus increase the potential for contamination. Conversely, longer flow paths from land surface to the water table can lessen the potential for contamination by chemicals that sorb or degrade along the flowpath. The recharge rate is important because it affects the extent and rate of transport of contaminants through the unsaturated zone. Finally, environmental factors, such as temperature and water content, can significantly influence the loss of contaminants by microbial transformations.

Some general geologic and hydrologic factors that influence an aquifer's vulnerability to contamination are shown in Table 3.1, along with examples of features that lead to low or high vulnerability. Although these factors may seem quite simple at first inspection, many of them interact in the

TABLE 3.1 Principal Geologic and Hydrologic Features that Influence an Aquifer's Vulnerability to Contamination (After Johnston 1988)

Feature Determining Aquifer Vulnerability to Contamination	Low Vulnerability	High Vulnerability
A. Hydrogeologic Framework		
Unsaturated Zone	Thick unsaturated zone, with high levels of clay and organic materials.	Thin unsaturated zone, with high levels of sand, gravel, limestone, or basalt of high permeability.
Confining Unit	Thick confining unit of clay or shale above aquifer.	No confining unit.
Aquifer Properties	Silty sandstone or shaly limestone of low permeability.	Cavernous limestone, sand and gravel, gravel, or basalt of high permeability.
B. Ground Water Flow System		
Recharge Rate	Negligible recharge rate, as in arid regions.	Large recharge rate, as in humid regions.
Location within flow system (proximity to recharge or discharge area)	Located in the deep, sluggish part of a regional flow system.	Located within a recharge area or within the cone of depression of a pumped well.

TABLE 3.2 A Listing of Some Key Parameters in Models of Pesticide Transport in Soils (Adapted from Wagenet and Rao 1990. Reprinted, by permission, from the Soil Science Society of America, 1990.)

Pesticide Parameters

Organic carbon-normalized sorption coefficient (K_{oc})
Distribution coefficient (K_d)
Aqueous solubility
Henry's constant
Saturated vapor density
Gas phase diffusion coefficient
Biological half-life
Hydrolysis half-life
Oxidation half-life
Foliar decay rate

Soil Parameters

Dispersion coefficient
Saturated water content
Field-capacity water content (θ_{FC})
Wilting-point water content
Hydraulic properties
Bulk density (ρ_b)
Organic carbon content (f_{oc})
pH
Cation exchange capacity
Heat flow parameters

Crop Parameters

Root density distribution
Maximum rooting depth
Pesticide uptake rates

Climatological Parameters

Rainfall or irrigation rates
Pan evaporation rates
Daily maximum and minimum temperature
Snow melt
Hours of sunlight

Management Parameters

Pesticide application rate and timing
Pesticide application method and formulation
Crop production-system variables
Soil-management variables

environment to create more complex and subtle distinctions in vulnerability than the extreme situations in Table 3.1. Furthermore, many of these factors affecting vulnerability are highly variable and difficult to characterize over any given area. One set of characterizations is shown in Table 3.2, which lists some of the key parameters often used in modeling one aspect of ground water contamination potential, pesticide transport and transformation in soils.

REVIEW OF CURRENT APPROACHES

Combinations of some or all of the factors noted above are included in the various approaches used to assess ground water vulnerability. These approaches range in complexity from a subjective evaluation of available map data to the application of complex contaminant transport models. The U.S. Environmental Protection Agency (EPA 1992a) evaluated the methods currently available for assessing aquifer sensitivity or ground water vulnerability to pesticide contamination. Their categorization includes three broad classes of approaches depending on the factors included in the assessment method. Each class is broken down further into specific types of approaches, such as aquifer sensitivity assessment methods which consider only hydrogeologic factors; hybrid methods, which consider hydrogeologic and pesticide factors; and ground water vulnerability assessment methods, which consider hydrogeologic, pesticide, and agronomic factors. Statistical tools are also noted for their usefulness in validating methods or providing hydrogeologic setting information.

Our alternative classification scheme places assessment methods in three general categories: (1) overlay and index methods, (2) methods employing process-based simulation models, and (3) statistical methods.

Assessment methods in the first category, overlay and index methods, are based on combining maps of various physiographic attributes (e.g., geology, soils, depth to water table) of the region by assigning a numerical index or score to each attribute. In the simplest of these methods, all attributes are assigned equal weights, with no judgment being made on their relative importance. Thus, areas where simple confluence of the specified attributes occurs (e.g., sandy soils and shallow ground water) are deemed vulnerable. Such methods were the earliest to be used and are still favored by many state and local regulatory and planning agencies. Overlay and index methods that attempt to be more quantitative assign different numerical scores and weights to the attributes in developing a range of vulnerability classes, which are then displayed on a map. Popularization of GIS technology has made it increasingly easy to adopt map overlay and index methods.

The assessment methods in the second category, methods employing process-based simulation models, require analytical or numerical solutions to mathematical equations that represent coupled processes governing contaminant transport. Methods in this category range from indices based on simple transport models to analytical solutions for one-dimensional transport of contaminants through the unsaturated zone to coupled, unsaturated-saturated, multiple phase, two- or three-dimensional models.

Statistical methods having a contaminant concentration or a probability of contamination as the dependent variable form the basis for the third category. These methods incorporate data on known areal contaminant distributions and provide characterizations of contamination potential for the specific geographic area from which data were drawn. Statistical methods are sometimes used by regulatory agencies that have the regional databases on ground water contamination needed to develop models.

Some characteristics of selected vulnerability assessment methods used in the United States are listed in Table 3.3. Comparative details on these

TABLE 3.3 Selected Methods Used in the United States to Evaluate Ground Water Vulnerability to Contamination

Method	Reference	Map Scale[1]	Reference Location	Intrinsic and/or Specific
Overlay and Index Methods				
Kansas Leachability Index	Kissel et al. 1982	Small	Soil	Intrinsic
DRASTIC	Aller et al. 1985, 1987	Variable	Ground Water	Intrinsic
California Hotspots	Cohen et al. 1986	Large	Water Table	Intrinsic and Specific
Washington Map Overlay Vulnerability	Sacha et al. 1987	Small	Ground Water	Intrinsic and Specific
SEEPPAGE	Moore 1988	Variable	Ground Water	Intrinsic
Iowa Ground Water Vulnerability	Hoyer and Hallberg 1991	Small	Ground Water	Intrinsic
EPA/UIC	Pettyjohn et al. 1991	Small	Ground Water	Intrinsic

Process-Based Simulation Models

PESTANS	Enfield et al. 1982	Large	Soil	Specific
BAM	Jury et al. 1983	Large	Soil	Specific
MOUSE	Steenhuis et al. 1987	Large	Ground Water	Specific
PRZM	Carsel et al. 1984	Large	Soil	Specific
RF/AF	Rao et al. 1985	Variable	Soil	Specific
GLEAMS	Leonard et al. 1987	Large	Soil	Specific
CMLS	Nofziger and Hornsby 1986	Large	Soil	Specific
RITZ/VIP	McLean et al. 1988	Large	Soil	Specific
LEACHM	Wagenet and Hutson 1987	Large	Soil	Specific
RUSTIC	Dean et al. 1989	Large	Ground Water	Specific and Intrinsic

Statistical Methods

Discriminant Analysis	Teso et al. 1988	Small	Ground Water	Specific
Regression Analysis	Chen and Druliner 1988	Small	Ground Water	Specific

[1]"Large scale" means that the method is typically applied at a level of detail of at least a 1:24,000 scale map to a small spatial area; "small scale" means that the method is typically applied at a level of detail less than that of a 1:50,000 scale map to a larger spatial area.

and other methods were published recently by EPA (1992a). Inspection of Table 3.3 reveals some general similarities within the broad classes of methods. Overlay and index methods tend to be applied at small map scales (large study areas), typically greater than 1:50,000, whereas most current process-based models apply to problems at much larger map scales (smaller study areas). Most overlay and index methods and most statistical methods refer to the saturated zone (the ground water resource) or water table as the reference location. In contrast, most process-based models have a floating reference location depending on the extent to which contamination is investigated through the vadose zone (for example, the reference location may be the bottom of the crop root zone for agricultural scenarios). Most overlay and index methods are designed to evaluate intrinsic vulnerability or have mixed specific and intrinsic utility. In contrast, most process-based models and statistical methods are designed for specific classes of contaminants such as pesticides or nitrate.

Overlay and Index Methods

Overlay and index methods rely primarily on qualitative or semiquantitative compilations and interpretations of mapped data. Selected overlay and index methods are listed in Table 3.4 together with the parameters used in their application. Additional methods are summarized by the U.S. Environmental Protection Agency (1992a). Variables used in the overlay and index methods typically include approximate depth to the water table, ground water recharge rate, and soil and aquifer material properties.

Depth to Ground Water

The shorter the distance to ground water, the less soil and underlying unsaturated zone material is there to act as a filter or adsorbent. Depth to ground water also affects the transit time available for various abiotic and biotic processes to degrade the chemical. Depth to ground water corresponds to the depth to water table in unconfined aquifers or to the depth to the bottom of a confining geologic unit when the uppermost aquifer is confined. Varying degrees of confinement over an area are common. Overlay and index methods use a single depth to ground water at each location. However, large seasonal fluctuations in water levels in unconfined aquifers can complicate the estimate of single representative values. Seasonally high water table depths may be used to provide conservative estimates. Information on the depth to ground water is available from many sources, including well logs, federal and state agency computer files, and water-level maps published by federal and state agencies, universities, and consulting firms.

TABLE 3.4 Parameters Used in Selected Overlay and Index Methods for Vulnerability Assessments

Method	Author(s)	Parameters Related to			
		Depth to Ground Water	Recharge	Unsaturated Zone and Aquifer Material	Other
DRASTIC	Aller et al. 1985 Aller et al. 1987	Depth to water table	Net recharge	Soil media Vadose zone media Aquifer media Hydraulic conductivity	Slope
Wisconsin Ground Water Contamination Susceptibility	Wisconsin Department of Natural Resources, Wisconsin Geological and Natural History Survey 1987	Depth to water table	—	Soil characteristics (4 classes based on texture) surficial deposits Depth to bedrock Bedrock type	—
Potential for Contamination of Shallow Aquifers in Illinois by Agricultural Chemicals	Berg and Kempton 1988 McKenna and Keefer 1991	—	—	Soils and geologic materials differentiated by thickness, texture, permeability, and stratigraphic position	—
Ground Water Vulnerability Regions of Iowa	Hoyer and Hallberg 1991	Depth to private well water sources	—	Aquifer type (alluvial, bedrock, glacial drift) and thickness of confinement by low permeability drift or shale	Locations of sinkholes and agricultural drainage wells
State-by-State Assessment of Aquifer Vulnerability and Sensitivity for the Conterminous U.S.	Pettyjohn et al. 1991	—	—	Geologically based classification of surficial and relatively shallow aquifers	—

Recharge

Estimates of ground water recharge used in vulnerability assessments should account for all inputs (e.g., rainfall, irrigation, artificial recharge, and wastewater applications) and losses (e.g., runoff, evapotranspiration) of water. Typically, average annual values of recharge are used, and recharge is assumed to be uniform over large areas. In reality, recharge is commonly quite variable in time, both seasonally and annually, and it can be highly variable over a region.

The identification of recharge and discharge zones may be particularly useful in assessing the potential for contaminants introduced at the water table to move deeper into the ground water system. Evaluating recharge and discharge zones can be difficult in hydrogeologic systems where ground water flow systems occur at different scales. For instance, a given area may have local flow systems with discharge zones within hundreds of meters of the recharge zones, intermediate-scale systems of one or a few kilometers that encompass two or more local flow systems, and regional-scale flow systems many kilometers long that begin at the major ground water system divide and traverse the entire regional system to the major drain. The extent to which flow systems of different spatial scales can be defined as parts of regional assessments of ground water vulnerability is subject to significant limitations. Nonetheless, the identification of recharge and discharge zones may be one of the more important elements of a vulnerability assessment.

Properties of the Unsaturated Zone and Aquifer Material

Many different properties of the unsaturated zone and aquifer material may be incorporated into overlay and index methods. Ideally, one might consider properties of the unsaturated zone to indicate the potential for vertical transport of contaminants to ground water, while properties of the aquifer indicate the potential for lateral transport. Because the aquifer material commonly is also part of the unsaturated zone, such a clear distinction does not always exist in application of overlay and index methods. In fact, for many overlay and index methods, it is not always obvious whether the reference location is the water table or some unspecified location within the ground water flow system.

Properties of the unsaturated zone and aquifer material listed in Table 3.4 illustrate considerable diversity among vulnerability assessment methods. Many of the methods consider geology, but neglect soils, others focus on soils, but ignore geology. Some indexing methods, like DRASTIC, attempt to be universally applicable and incorporate parameters that should be available to some degree virtually everywhere; other methods are adjusted to the setting and data bases available in a particular area. An advantage of the latter approach is that geologic and geographic features unique to a particular area can be taken into account. For example, the Illinois method (Berg and Kempton 1988, McKenna and Keefer 1991) involved an intensive examination of stratigraphy and the identification of low and high permeability units in a three-dimensional context throughout the state.

Finally, in addition to the foregoing factors related to hydrology, geology, and soils, some overlay and index methods have combined use of these factors with surrogate data on contaminant loading. For example, Moreau and Danielson (1990) used DRASTIC scores in combination with estimated pesticide use rates to produce vulnerability maps for selected pesticides for the state of North Carolina.

Major sources of data used in overlay and index methods include: 1) soil maps generated by the Soil Conservation Service (SCS) in conjunction with state and local agencies, 2) topographic maps produced by the U.S. Geological Survey (USGS), 3) geologic maps published by the USGS, state geological surveys, and other sources, and 4) regional and local land-use planning maps.

Discussion

A simple overlay-type vulnerability map is prepared by superposing a series of maps showing the areal distributions of attributes considered important in characterizing the potential for ground water contamination (e.g., soil types, depth to ground water, recharge rate). Each attribute is given equal weight, and areas with different vulnerability ratings are defined by the patterns or ranges of attribute values that overlap in the area. Typically, the product is a single map depicting areas of differing vulnerability, designated by a score, pattern, or color. In some instances, overlay methods identify areas with different expected ground water vulnerabilities, but no attempt is made to rank the areas from most to least vulnerable.

Perhaps the simplest overlay method is that used by Pettyjohn et al. (1991) for evaluating the potential for ground water contamination in the contiguous United States on a state-by-state basis. They developed their method specifically for the U.S. EPA's Underground Injection Control Program, but indicated that "the products are equally valuable to assess the potential for ground water contamination from other surface or near surface sources." Their vulnerability assessment is based solely on a geologic classification of surficial and relatively shallow aquifers. Pettyjohn et al. (1991) also evaluated aquifer sensitivity in which they included population density as an additional factor.

Overlay methods are commonly used for vulnerability assessments at the state level. For example, Illinois (Berg and Kempton 1988, McKenna and Keefer 1991) and Iowa (Hoyer and Hallberg 1991) have developed GIS-based maps using overlay methods with an emphasis on geology as the key attribute for assessing vulnerability. An overlay map for the state of Wisconsin considers depth to water, geology, and soils information (Wisconsin Department of Natural Resources and Wisconsin Geological and Natural History Survey 1987).

In contrast to simple overlay methods, index methods assign a numerical value to each attribute based on its magnitude or qualitative ranking. Each attribute, in turn, is assigned a relative importance or weight compared to the other attributes. A consensus of experts may be solicited (the Delphi approach) to determine the relative weights assigned to different attributes and the numerical values assigned to different levels of each attribute. The weighted-attribute ratings are summed to obtain an overall numerical score for ground water vulnerability. These numerical scores are used to group similar areas into classes or categories of vulnerability (e.g., low, medium, and high) that are then displayed on a map. Some methods multiply the numerical scores or values assigned to the attributes together rather than adding them (c.f., Back et al. 1984).

Several types of indices have been developed for ground water vulnerability assessments. The DRASTIC index (Aller et al. 1987) is perhaps the best known of these methods. Some state regulatory agencies have developed index assessment methods similar to DRASTIC (cf., Rupert et al. 1991). Using information about pesticide leaching abilities, Kellogg et al. (1992) developed the GWVIP and GWVIN indices to generate national-scale vulnerability maps for pesticides and nitrates, respectively (see Chapter 5).

Overlay and index methods have often been developed with the availability of information keenly in mind. These methods are driven largely by data availability and expert judgment, with less emphasis on processes controlling ground water contamination. One can argue whether the factors included in the methods are the relevant ones for vulnerability assessment and whether the factor ratings are appropriate. For example, Banton and Villeneuve (1989) questioned the basis for the numerical weighting scheme used by Agricultural DRASTIC after comparing its results with those from a process-based modeling approach (PRZM). Further, Holden et al. (1992) concluded that "the complex weighting and coding procedures used in the DRASTIC scoring are self defeating," and that in the short-term, "simpler classification schemes, focusing on only a few major vulnerability factors, look to be more useful than DRASTIC." There are no quantitative criteria for evaluating the scientific basis of these methods.

Many overlay and index methods address intrinsic vulnerability, although some of them address what might be called pseudospecific vulnerability. The latter methods (e.g., Agricultural DRASTIC) were developed with a particular type of contamination in mind, but generally lack any real specificity among the contaminants considered. For example, a method that lumps all agricultural contaminants clearly lacks specificity, given the wide range of properties among pesticides and other agricultural chemicals.

Process-Based Simulation Models

"Everything must be made as simple as possible, but not simpler."
—Albert Einstein

Process-based simulation models are distinguished from all other methods because many of them attempt to predict contaminant transport in both space and time. For example, simulations of one-dimensional transport in the unsaturated soil zone may predict contaminant concentrations with depth at discrete time intervals during and after the time the contaminant is applied to the land surface. Similarly, the computer algorithms available for contaminant transport in the saturated and unsaturated zones (NRC 1990) predict the vertical and areal extent of contamination with time and mathematically incorporate many of the physical, chemical, and microbial processes in the unsaturated and saturated zones.

Process-based models can be used in both regional and site-specific studies and have been developed and applied primarily by research scientists rather than by regulators. The complex simulation models for solving coupled and/or multiphase contaminant transport in two or three dimensions have been used almost exclusively to evaluate physical, biological, and chemical controls in hypothetical settings or well-evaluated local incidences of contamination (NRC 1990). Such complex models have not been used to evaluate ground water vulnerability on a regional scale; therefore, this discussion will focus on simpler process-based models of one-dimensional transport through the vadose zone.

Table 3.5 indicates the various process representations used in several simulation models that have been used to predict pesticide behavior in the unsaturated zone. Outputs from three of these models are detailed in Table 3.6. These tables are included for illustrative purposes; more recent versions of these models include enhancements in areas of process representation, input parameter estimation, and output capabilities. The models listed in these tables differ in complexity. LEACHM is the most complex in terms of the number of processes included and the most sophisticated in terms of process description. Models such as LEACHM have large data requirements, but they offer the flexibility of being applicable to more diverse scenarios and provide detailed outputs (see Table 3.6). Models such as GLEAMS and PRZM are designed to assist in management decisions;

TABLE 3.5 A Comparison of Process Conceptualization in Five Models
Used to Predict Pesticide Behavior in the Vadose Zone (Adapted from
Pennell et al. 1990. Copyright by the American Geophysical Union.)

Process	Simulation Model	
	CMLS (Ver. 4.0, 1987)[1]	**GLEAMS (Ver. 1.8, 54, 1989)**[2]
Water Flow	Piston displacement of water. Instantaneous redistribution between field capacity and wilting point.	Predicts water flow between soil layers based on a storage similar to the "tipping bucket" method.
Runoff	Runoff not considered.	Runoff based on SCS curve-number method. Erosion calculated using overland, channel, and impoundment elements, and soil particle characteristics.
Solute Transport	Piston displacement of solute.	Convection transport of solute using water flow between soil layers. Solute can move upward by capillary flow.
Solute Dispersion	Tracks a nondispersive solute point.	Numerical dispersion, from convective transport equation, used to simulate actual solute dispersion.
Sorption	Input solute K_{oc}. Input organic carbon by soil horizon or enter K_d by soil horizon.	Input K_{oc}s for up to ten solutes and metabolites. Input organic matter by soil horizon.
Degradation	Input solute half-life by soil horizon.	Input half-life for each solute or metabolite by horizon. Input one coefficient of transformation for each component.
Evapotranspiration	Input daily PET. Water removed from wettest soil horizons in the root zone first.	Potential evaporation calculated from solar radiation and air temperature. Actual ET is then calculated using leaf area index and soil-water content.
Roots	Input maximum rooting depth. Root biomass constant.	Input maximum rooting depth. Water use is a function of depth based on an exponentially decreasing function.

[1]Nofziger and Hornsby 1986, [2]Knisel et al. 1989, [3]Wagenet and Hutson 1987, [4]Carsel et al. 1984

LEACHM (Ver. 1.0, 1987)[3]	**PRZM (Release 1, 1985)[4]**
Solves Richards' equation. Requires moisture release curve data which must be fit to a modified Campbell's function.	Water flow based on "tipping bucket" method. Operates between field capacity and wilting point. Instantaneous or time dependent water redistribution.
Runoff not considered.	Runoff based on SCS curve-number method. Erosion based on the Universal Soil Loss Equation.
Solves the convective-dispersive transport equation.	Convective transport of solute based on water flow between soil increments.
Calculated hydrodynamic dispersion.	Numerical dispersion, from convective transport equation, used to simulate actual dispersion.
Input K_{oc} for solute and two metabolites. Input organic carbon by soil increment.	Input solute K_d by soil horizon.
Input five degradation rate coefficients for three components by soil increment.	Input solute degradation rate coefficients by soil horizon.
Input weekly PET total. Water removal based on root distribution, root resistance, and soil-water potential.	Input daily ET and crop ET coefficient. Water removal based on root distribution and soil-water content.
Root biomass can be constant or increasing. For constant root biomass, input relative root fraction by soil increment.	Root biomass can be constant or increasing. Root distribution decrease linearly to maximum rooting depth.

TABLE 3.6 Major Outputs of Four Types of Pesticide Simulation Models (Adapted from Wagenet and Rao 1990. Reprinted, by permission, from the Soil Science Society of America, 1990.)

Output[1]	Type of Model			
	LEACHM (Ver. 1.0, 1987)	**GLEAMS** (Ver. 1.8, 54, 1989)	**PRZM** (Release 1, 1985)	**CMLS** (ver. 4.0, 1987)
Pore-water solute concentration	+	+	+	−
Depth of maximum solute concentration	+	+	+	+
Maximum depth of solute penetration	+	+	+	−
Soil-water flux	+	+	−	−
Soil-water content	+	+	+	−
Phase partitioning of solute mass	+	+	+	−
Temperature	*	*	−	−
Water uptake	+	+	+	−
Pesticide uptake	*	+	*	−
Volatile losses	+	−	−	−
Runoff	−	+	+	−

[1]A plus sign indicates that the output parameter values are provided, and a minus sign indicates that the parameter values are not provided. An asterisk indicates that the parameter can be considered, but usually is not because of insufficient data.

they are constructed to include most of the major processes, but some or many of the processes are represented in a less sophisticated manner. A loss of scientific rigor and conceptual detail is usually accompanied by a reduction in computational time and greater ease of use. Management and screening models usually require less data, but also provide commensurately less detailed prediction of system behavior. Finally, models designed primarily for instructional purposes (e.g., CMLS) are based on simplified representations of fewer processes and so require the least data. The models listed in Tables 3.5 and 3.6, and others like them, are similar in that they are deterministic, with model parameters assumed to have no variability. Thus, given a specific set of parameters (usually the mean or modal values), these models generate a set of unique outputs (not necessarily the mean values). Stochastic models, in contrast, are formulated with the premise that all input parameters, or even the processes included in the model, are inherently variable; they provide outputs in terms of means (expected values), the associated variances, and in some cases probability distributions. In practice, the lack of realistic probabilistic information from deterministic models can be overcome by employing Monte Carlo simulation techniques, which require assumptions about the probability density functions representing the spatial or temporal variability of the input parameters in the simulation models. Model outputs from multiple runs of a deterministic model, each run using a randomly chosen set of input parameters, are then represented as probability density functions of the prediction of certain likely outcomes (e.g., concentration in excess of a certain value). Such stochastic extensions of otherwise deterministic models have been presented by Jones et al. (1983), Villeneuve et al. (1987), Carsel et al. (1988a, b), and Laskowski et al. (1990) (see Box 3.2).

Discussion

It must be recognized that sophisticated models may not necessarily provide more reliable outputs, especially for regional-scale, and even for field-scale applications. Since data for many of the required input parameters for sophisticated models are not always available, their values have to be estimated by indirect means using surrogate parameters or extrapolated from data collected at other locations. Errors and uncertainties associated with such estimates or extrapolations can be large and may negate the advantages gained from a more rigorous process description in the simulation model.

After comparing measured data on pesticide leaching in a 1.6 hectare citrus grove with outputs from simulation models listed in Table 3.5, Pennell et al. (1990) concluded that deterministic pesticide simulation models should not be expected to predict observed solute concentration distributions accurately because the measured concentration distributions themselves are subject to considerable error. If the observed concentrations have a large measurement error then one would want the model to predict the most likely distribution rather than the observed distribution. One major source of error in measured pesticide concentrations cited is variability introduced by the method used to apply pesticide at the ground surface. Such variability is neither characterized in most field studies nor accounted for in any of the current models. Pennell et al. (1990) also concluded that the pesticide simulation models they evaluated were able to predict the location of the solute center of mass and the solute mass remaining in the soil profile within plus or minus 50 percent of the actual values. Measured values for these two parameters were found to be much less variable than the measured concentration profiles. Thus, the parameters that a more sophisticated model (LEACHM) is designed to predict cannot be measured with certainty, while the outputs of the simpler models (CMLS) appear to be subject to less variability. These findings suggest that models based on simplified process representation may be more useful for certain types of vulnerability assessments. The convective-dispersive solute transport approach employed in LEACHM and other models predicts the asymptotic behavior and is least likely to be valid when used for shallow depths. This problem can be circumvented by calibrating the model parameters using experimental data from the zone of interest (i.e., near soil surface), but extrapolation to much greater depths in the vadose zone can lead to significant errors.

All of the simulation models discussed here suffer from another major limitation, arising from the spatial scales over which the process conceptualization is valid. None of the models included in Tables 3.5 and 3.6 has the ability to simulate water flow and solute transport in cases where preferential flow exists. An increasing number of scientists argue convincingly that such bypass flow may be the rule rather than the exception for field situations (Bowman and Rice 1986, Germann 1988, Butters et al. 1989, Jury and Ghodrati 1989, Beven 1991, Jury and Flüher 1992).

Preferential flow can be the dominant transport phenomenon under certain circumstances, even in soils that exhibit no identifiable macrostructure (Ghodrati and Jury 1990, Roth et al. 1991). Even the most sophisticated model, LEACHM, cannot handle the complexities in flow and transport at finer spatial scales than those for which the model was formulated. Nicholls et al. (1982a, b) compared measured leaching and transformations of pesticides in field plots with predictions of two simulation models, one similar to LEACHM, and the other an empirical model, CALF, that considers preferential flow and transport in structured soils. They concluded that both models provided adequate predictions, and preferred the use of the simpler model CALF for management purposes since herbicide leaching was described as accurately by the CALF model as the more complex model and the CALF model required much less input data. Complex models that explicitly account for certain types of preferential flow in structured soil are available, but the required information on spatial distribution of preferential flow paths is practically impossible to determine using existing soils databases (Beven 1991) and models remain virtually untested in any practical sense. Conceptual qualitative explanations have been presented describing transport in soils with no macrostructural features. Models may be calibrated to produce agreement between predictions and field observations, however, the fitted parameter values have no physical basis and their values cannot be estimated based on measured soil properties (Roth et al. 1991). Most process models are based on the assumption of local sorption equilibrium, which likely is not achieved under natural conditions. However, transport nonequilibrium arising from preferential flow likely is more significant than sorption nonequilibrium.

In applying these models at various spatial scales, it has been assumed that the area of interest can be represented as a patchwork of homogeneous polygons, and that the model adequately represents the processes within each of these subareas. Thus, regional-scale behavior is assumed to be predicted by the composite representation of local-scale behavior simulated in each polygon. Such an approach does not consider the possibility that other processes or factors might be significant at the regional scale, necessitating formulation of new models appropriate for larger areas. For example, surface and subsurface water flow focused toward the bottom of a hill slope can lead to greater solute leaching compared to that at the top of the hill. The importance of such regional-scale features often is not represented by simply aggregating outputs of models designed to represent processes at local spatial scales.

An analogous situation exists in watershed modeling, where field-scale models are used to calculate runoff and contaminant loadings, which are then used in stream or river models to calculate flow and water quality for the entire watershed. Typically, field-scale models are calibrated on one or more small sites within the watershed, and these results are aggregated to the watershed scale through a network of channel sections simulated by the river model. These procedures have been shown to be realistic as long as the field-scale models and sites include all the processes that are important over larger areas (Donigian et al. 1983, Imhoff et al. 1983). For example, the field-scale model will need to represent both surface and subsurface flow components (and contaminant loadings), since both components are important at the watershed scale. If the model represents only field-size areas (e.g., 5 to 20 hectares) where only surface contributions are modeled, the regional watershed cannot be adequately modeled through aggregation of the individual field areas since subsurface contributions are not included. The problem is significantly greater for ground water, partly because of the difficulties in defining multidimensional subsurface flow and transport processes.

The foregoing discussion suggests that a principal limitation of simulation models currently used to make vulnerability assessments may be their failure to account for flow and transport processes at spatial scales either smaller or larger than those for which the models were developed. Although this situation can be remedied by use of other simulation models, the data needed to estimate many of the needed model parameters are not available currently, and the effort and cost of gathering such information for regional-scale assessments may be prohibitively large.

Statistical Techniques for Vulnerability Assessment

While statistical approaches for assessing ground water vulnerability have not received as much attention as overlay, index, and simulation modeling techniques, they have interesting potential applications to vulnerability assessment. Statistical methods can be used to evaluate, determine, and quantify the association between measures of vulnerability and various types of information that are thought to be related to vulnerability. Statistical methods are based on the concept of uncertainty which is described in terms of probability distributions for the variables of interest.

Since ground water vulnerability is a probabilistic notion, statistical methods should have more application in vulnerability assessments than they have had to date. Statistical methods can more easily deal with differences in scale than other methods that are based on the description of physical relationships. Also, the variety of statistical techniques available for treating assorted types of data makes statistical approaches inherently flexible. They include methods designed to deal with qualitative, quantitative, or mixed data sets, as well as truncated or censored data (e.g., data exhibiting detection or reporting limit effects). Examples of statistical methods include simple and multiple regression for single and multivariate variables, analysis of variance, discriminant and cluster analyses, geostatistical analyses (including kriging), and time series. The uncertainty methods applied to process models that are described in the previous section are based on statistical and probabilistic methods.

Typical of many statistical applications to ground water vulnerability is the goal of describing in mathematical terms (function or model) a relationship between water quality and natural and/or human-generated features in a discrete area or region through the use of surrogate or independent variables. In general, no a priori decisions are made about the subset of candidate variables to be included in the model, nor do the results purport to identify or define cause-effect relationships. Parameters from simple process-based indices (e.g., travel time, retardation factor) can be used as variables in a statistical analysis. To our knowledge such a hybrid approach has not yet been attempted for assessing ground water vulnerability.

Two possible applications of statistical techniques in vulnerability assessments described here are: (1) regionalization, and (2) assessment of vulnerability with probability models.

Regionalization

Delineation and description of an assessment area is of interest to managers and scientists alike. Agencies involved in land use planning and management have demonstrated needs for employing regionalization concepts. Regions delineated by natural drainage basins are convenient management tools. However, the applicability of regionalization schemes based on drainage systems to ground water management has been questioned, since aquifer boundaries do not necessarily coincide with drainage boundaries and are not themselves readily distinguished and measured.

Regionalization based on statistical analyses of hydrologic, geologic, and human activity data have been useful in differentiating ground water regions. Several examples appear in the literature, and a few are examined below. Seyhan et al. (1985) found that hydrochemical data from a dolomitic reef aquifer subjected to multivariate cluster analysis supported earlier conclusions that hydrogeological partitioning existed within the aquifer. The original partitioning study that was confirmed by Seyhan et al. used more traditional hydrogeological techniques to define aquifer compartments. Pedroli (1990) identified 16 classes of shallow ground water within a 20 km^2 area using cluster and discriminant analyses of hydrochemical data. Pedroli associated the variations in water quality with ecohydrological patterns, including landscape features, infiltrating and discharging water components and fertilizer pollutants resulting from farming practices. A study with immediate impacts on the hydrologic study unit (HSU) concept was conducted by Riley et al. (1990) in the vicinity of the Hanford Reservation in Washington. In an application of exploratory and confirmatory statistical analysis of existing hydrochemical data, Riley et al. (1990) quantitatively determined by multivariate cluster analysis (later confirmed through a combination of MANOVA, canonical, and discriminant analyses) that ground waters taken from opposing sides of the Columbia River were distinctly different. Such cases bring into question the logic of using surface water drainage basins as regions for conducting vulnerability assessments. The statistically-based regionalization schemes considered here do not depend on pollutant databases, but require adequate and largely routine water quality data.

Vulnerability Assessment

The integrity of and confidence in vulnerability assessment can be bolstered by statistical analyses. Statistical methods such as principal components analysis, discriminant analysis, cluster analysis, time series and regression analyses and an assortment of other parametric and nonparametric techniques are used in ground water studies to estimate the likelihood that a pollutant will contaminate an experimental unit or subset of a region. Riley et al. (1990) and many others have observed that "water quality is a multivariate concept. . . [that is] not defined by any single constituent." Thus multivariate statistical techniques may be well suited to analysis of water quality data and other regional data, which can include soils and geologic information, vegetal coverage and land management practices. Vulnerability assessments that use overlay/indexing techniques are an eyeballed form of multivariate discriminant analyses that lack probability estimates.

Interpretations of statistical applications vary in difficulty, and depend on the method used, the researcher(s') experience, and the amount and quality of the data investigated. Simple linear regression models using single independent and dependent variables ($Y = a + b_1X_1$) are not commonly applied to complex issues of ground water quality. More complex models, like multiple regression, can accommodate additional independent variables ($Y = a + b_1X_1 + b_2X_2 + . . .$). For example, Chen and Druliner (1988) used multiple regression to describe the relationship of nine variables to observations of triazine concentrations in ground water in Nebraska. The variables included data that can be practically collected (well characteristics, nitrate concentrations) or that have some demonstrated effect on pollutant transport (hydraulic gradient and conductivity). The best-fit model suggested a strong relationship ($R^2 = 84$ percent) between specific discharge (well characteristic), the surrogate nitrate pollutant concentrations, and the dependent triazine concentrations.

Statistical procedures such as discriminant analysis are more complex. Discriminant analysis is a tool for assigning observations described by multiple independent variables ($X_1, X_2, . . .$) to multiple discrete classes. Teso et al. (1988) used discriminant analysis to describe relationships between soil mapping unit data from 1 square mile areas (sections) and areas vulnerable to DBCP contamination in California. The discriminant model developed proved to be useful in delineating the DBCP contamination status of sections in a different county whose center of contamination was 100 kilometers from the model development region.

In addition to the methods discussed above, nonparametric statistical techniques are also used in vulnerability assessment. Berryman et al. (1988) has reviewed these techniques for their application to the detection of trends in water quality time series. A more general discussion of nonparametric approaches to environmental impact assessment is offered by Hipel (1988).

Geostatistical methods describe the spatial distribution of process parameters that affect vulnerability. Spatial statistical simulation methods then can be used to link nearby polygons through the continuity of the underlying processes. Such simulations do not show the discontinuities in the results between individual polygons. As with other techniques, one must pay attention to the uncertainty associated with the apparent gradations in vulnerability.

All statistical techniques require data. Some place more stringent requirements on data quality than others. As with most other forms of vulnerability assessment there is no replacement for high quality data. Since ground water data are used in developing statistical models, these methods are best applied to areas having adequate monitoring programs and/or a good hydrogeologic database coverage. In some cases, statistical models can be applied to regions outside the region of model development. The extent to which this is possible is limited to areas where available or obtainable data are similar to those used in model development. Application should also be guided by review of the assumptions and presuppositions made in data collection and model development. In general, the more complex approaches require greater expertise for interpretation and are best used in a team effort, where the team is composed of a statistician and other experts familiar with available data and their sources.

UNCERTAINTY IN VULNERABILITY ASSESSMENT METHODS

"To be absolutely certain about something, one must know everything or nothing about it."
—*Olin Miller*

Uncertainties inherent in all approaches to ground water vulnerability assessments may be derived from: (1) model related errors, which include uncertainty resulting from inadequate or incomplete representation of the system processes, and (2) data related errors, which include uncertainty resulting from errors in input data, even if the model used is correct (Loague and Green 1991). Thus, uncertainties are likely even when the model(s) or data are perfect. Imperfect model(s) and data are the norm rather than the exception.

Sources of Errors

Numerous reviews of errors and sampling methodology appear in the literature. Several reviews pertinent to ground water vulnerability assessment include those by Burrough (1986), who describes many important sources of error that result from inappropriate use of GIS systems, and by Kempthorne and Allmaras (1986), who review sampling errors as they relate to soil sampling. Statistical procedures for identifying extreme values that are indicative of error are described by Dixon (1986).

In Table 3.7, sources of error are grouped into six classes, which, in

TABLE 3.7 Sources of Errors in Ground Water Vulnerability Assessment (Adapted from Burrough 1986. Principles of Geographical Information Systems for Land Resource Assessment. Reprinted by permission of Oxford University Press.)

I. Errors in Obtaining Data
   1. Accuracy in locating sites
   2. Sample collection and handling
   3. Laboratory preparation and analysis
   4. Interpretation
II. Errors Due to Natural Spatial and Temporal Variability
   1. Random sampling error
   2. Bias
   3. Regionalization, extrapolation, interpolation
   4. Scale effects, changes in variance due to averaging
   5. Interpretation
III. Errors in Computerization (Digitizing) and Storage of Data
   1. Data entry
   2. Data age
   3. Changes in storage format
   4. Errors in programs to access data
   5. Use of surrogate data and procedures
   6. Adjustments in scale
   7. Determining boundaries
   8. Changes in representation of data
   9. Interpretation
IV. Data Processing Errors
   1. Numerical, truncation, and round-off errors
   2. Discretization errors
   3. Problems in solution convergence
   4. Interpretation
V. Modeling and Conceptual Errors
   1. Process representation and coupling
   2. Parameter identification
   3. Scale effects
   4. Interpretation
VI. Output and Visualization Errors
   1. Determination of boundaries
   2. Classification into vulnerability categories
   3. Interpretation

effect, represent the various stages involved in developing a vulnerability assessment. Although a list of possible errors is very long, the following discussion will be directed toward these six general classes. The first three classes are related to data errors and the final three to model errors. Because each step in a vulnerability assessment requires some degree of interpretation, Table 3.7 lists interpretation as one source of error in each class.

Errors in Obtaining Data

A large number of errors can be made in obtaining data. These include errors in the methods used to collect, transport, handle, and analyze field data, and errors introduced by laboratory or other methods used to determine the property of interest.

Errors Due to Natural Spatial and Temporal Variability

Many, if not most, of the data used in vulnerability assessments display significant spatial and temporal variability. Thus, large sampling errors can occur because different estimates of attributes or model parameters will be obtained from different samples at different locations or time periods. Bias may also be present because the sites selected for data collection may not truly represent the area or volume they are intended to characterize, or the timing of data collection may not account for seasonal effects on measured values. In fact, the concept of a representative value for processes that vary continuously in time or space is difficult to justify in theory. For practical purposes, however, it is necessary to assume representative values, particularly when data are limited.

Consequently, at any given spatial and temporal scale of interest, the model parameters should represent effective values at the appropriate scale. Any method to obtain averages will not eliminate uncertainty due to variability occurring at smaller scales. Large scale average values have reduced variance compared to values obtained over the same spatial and temporal domain but at a smaller scale, thus increasing the uncertainty of localized behavior. Appropriate averaging schemes and the magnitude of the associated uncertainty are model and problem specific and depend on the spatial and temporal structure of the variability. For example, areas of missing information in the mapped region should be found and data obtained as needed to create as complete a database as possible. Where empirical data are not available, estimates can be made by conditional simulations, interpolation, or extrapolation. One simple method is to assign the nearest data series available to a nearby map cell and assume that the value is constant over each cell. Alternatively, collected data can be used to develop estimates for the data at locations where data are missing. This process may involve a geostatistical technique such as kriging in which a model of the spatial correlation is developed from existing data and used to estimate an unknown value and the estimation variance. Statistical time series methods may be used for data exhibiting temporal variability. In any event, these or any other methods of interpolation or extrapolation will introduce additional sources of error and/or uncertainty.

Errors in Computerization (Digitizing) and Storage of Data

Computerization and storage errors are associated with preparing, entering, and processing data into a computer storage medium, such as GIS. Many such errors can be minimized by suitable quality control procedures. The uncertainty associated with many of the factors in Table 3.7, including surrogate data, density of observations, and the determination of boundaries, may be difficult, if not impossible, to determine quantitatively.

Data Processing Errors

Data processing errors include inaccuracies in the computational scheme used to obtain numerical values from a model or other quantitative measures of ground water vulnerability. These errors can include numerical dispersion errors, discretization errors, round-off errors, precision errors, possible solution convergence, and uniqueness errors. If the computational algorithm used is appropriate for the application, these errors will be a relatively minor part of the overall error.

Models and Conceptualizations

Modeling and conceptual errors result from lack of understanding of the spatial and temporal nature of transport processes, especially at a regional scale. No model currently available provides a completely accurate simulation of the flow of water and transport processes at the field scale, let alone at the regional scale. This shortcoming introduces some model error into every simulation. Model error is very difficult to measure quantitatively. The task would require a perfectly known system, which is never possible.

Conceptual errors are due to our view of a given part of the transport process. For example, if the transport of a chemical is subject to degradation, this process must be conceptualized before developing a model of the degradation process. The model developer chooses whether to describe the process using a first-order decay equation or some other formulation. The formulation the modeler uses, however, may only approximate the true process. Conceptual errors can also be caused by using a model that is not appropriate for the system considered. These errors may include errors in the approach used to describe the governing process, initial and/or boundary conditions, processes included in the models, and how these processes are coupled.

Output and Visualization Errors

The completed ground water vulnerability assessment results in a map or some other output. Errors at this stage include determination of the boundaries between areas, the classification of vulnerability levels into categories, and the misinterpretation of displays caused by indistinguishable colors or patterns.

The output reflects the ideas, conditions, and biases of its creator. However, the user may not clearly understand the assumptions, limitations, and restrictions that were built into the output (i.e., map). These errors may be obvious to the mapmaker, but not to the user. Errors associated with presentation using GIS are discussed later in the section on Geographic Information Systems.

Uncertainty Analyses

"In these matters, the only certainty is that there is nothing certain."
—Pliny the Elder

Vulnerability assessments using a specific method usually generate a map of the region depicting various polygons or cells; the distinctions between levels of vulnerability, however, are arbitrary. The vulnerability assigned to a particular point or polygon is uncertain because of model and data errors and is subject to spatial variability. Therefore, confidence intervals associated with the numerical values assigned to neighboring cells or polygons may overlap to the point that subtle distinctions made between vulnerability classes in adjacent cells are not defensible; hence, the boundaries delineating vulnerability classes are indeterminate because of both model and data errors. This inability to distinguish differences between adjacent cells with differing vulnerability scores increases with increasing magnitude of the relevant model and data uncertainties.

Few published vulnerability assessments account for uncertainties from either model or data errors. More is usually implied about the apparent certainty in vulnerability assessments than is stated about the underlying uncertainties. Little attention has been paid to the problem of errors in GIS databases and propagation of such errors where these databases are used for generating thematic maps (Mead 1982, Chrisman 1984, Burrough 1986, Goodchild and Dubuc 1987, Goodchild and Min-hua 1988).

Uncertainty analyses are used to evaluate the spatial and temporal variability and the propagation of errors in model calculations (i.e., variance in model outputs and the sufficiency of existing spatial databases) (Eisenberg et al. 1989). Such techniques have been used extensively in development of criteria for site selection and for designing radioactive waste-disposal facilities (Buxton 1989), but not for vulnerability assessments. Methods for evaluating uncertainty associated with data errors can be grouped into the following five categories (Brandstetter and Buxton 1989):

1. Classical statistical variance component analysis, which can be used to partition the total observed variance in the output to contributing factors.

2. First-order uncertainty analysis (FOUA) based on Taylor series expansion of the function (model) to evaluate variance of the output as a function of the variance in input parameters.

3. Statistical sampling methods that utilize a range of likely values for input parameters to assess the probable range of output parameters. Examples are Monte Carlo simulation, Latin hypercube sampling, discrete-event simulation, and boot-strapping methods.

4. Stochastic modeling approaches that directly incorporate the parameter or process uncertainties into the model itself and provide direct uncertainty estimates of model outputs.

5. Bayesian methods when uncertainties in input parameters can be specified by either expert judgment, or estimated from existing databases from which input parameter values have been determined.

Of these techniques, only FOUAs statistical sampling methods, and stochastic modeling techniques have been applied to vulnerability assessments. A description of the FOUA technique is presented in Box 3.1 and an example of the use of Monte Carlo methods in Box 3.2. Recent examples of first-order uncertainty analysis applied to a process-based index of vulnerability are reviewed below. Small and Mular (1987) and Jury and Gruber (1989) present examples of the applications of stochastic modeling approaches to evaluate uncertainty associated with climatic and soil variability in assessments of ground water vulnerability.

Applications of FOUA to Vulnerability Assessment

The earliest attempt to utilize spatial modeling techniques for regional-scale assessment of pesticide leaching potential was reported by Khan et al. (1986) and Khan and Liang (1989). They used two simple indices—the Retardation Factor (RF) and the Attenuation Factor (AF) developed by Rao et al. (1985)—as measures of leaching potential, and a GIS database—the Hawaii Natural Resource Information System (HNRIS) developed by Liang and Khan (1986)—in conducting an assessment for the Hawaiian island of Oahu. An example of the vulnerability maps generated by Khan and Liang (1989) is shown in Figure 3.3. The RF index is a measure of the relative time needed for a pesticide pulse to leach past some specified depth when compared to a nonsorbed tracer, whereas the AF index is the fraction of the

Box 3.1
First-Order Uncertainty Analysis

First-order uncertainty analysis (FOUA) is a well-known method for evaluating error propagation when mathematical operations are performed to calculate values of some parameter of interest, referred to as the dependent or derived variable, given the values for a set of other variables, referred to as the independent variables. The objective is to estimate the uncertainty, such as variance, in the derived parameter given the error in the independent variables. Here, we will briefly examine the basis for FOUA approximation method and its application in estimating the uncertainty in numerical measures of ground water vulnerability calculated by simple methods.

Consider some dependent variable, U, which is calculated as some function, $f(X_1, X_2,...,X_k)$, of independent variables, $X_1, X_2, ... ,X_k$. Given that $\overline{X}_j$ and $S^2_{x_j}$ represent mean and variance of the independent variables, respectively, and assuming that the $\overline{X}_j$ are uncorrelated, the mean (expected value), $\overline{U}$, and the variance, S^2_u, of the dependent variable is given by

$$\overline{U} \approx f(\overline{X}_1, \overline{X}_2, \cdots \overline{X}_k) \tag{1}$$

$$S^2_u \approx \sum_{i=1}^{k} \left(\frac{\partial U}{\partial X_i} \Big|_{x_i = \overline{x}_i} \right)^2 S^2_{xi} \tag{2}$$

In case $\overline{X}_1$ and $\overline{X}_2$ are correlated and r_{ij} is the correlation coefficient, the variance of U is given by,

$$S^2_u \approx \sum_{i=1}^{k} \left(\frac{\partial U}{\partial X_i} \Big|_{x_i = \overline{x}_i} \right)^2 S^2_{xi}$$

$$+ \sum_{i=1}^{k} \sum_{\substack{j=1 \\ i \neq j}}^{k} \left(\frac{\partial U}{\partial X_i} \Big|_{x_i = \overline{x}_i} \right) \left(\frac{\partial U}{\partial X_j} \Big|_{x_j = \overline{x}_j} \right) S_{xi} \, S_{xj} \, r_{ij} \tag{3}$$

Usually in practice, if any of the independent variables is not distributed normally, some sort of transformation (usually, taking logarithms) will be necessary such that the transformed variable (say, log X) follows a normal frequency distribution. The FOUA technique is recommended when U can be specified by a differentiable and well-behaved function of the independent variables.

Burrough (1986) and Heuvelink et al. (1989) presented examples of the application of the FOUA technique to a GIS-based spatial analysis. Loague et al. (1989, 1990) presented the first examples of the application of FOUA in regional assessments of ground water vulnerability.

Box 3.2
Uncertainty in Pesticide Leaching Assessments

The movement of pesticides to ground water is the end result of complex interactions involving physical, chemical, and biological processes which are further impacted by meteorologic conditions, soil and chemical characteristics, and agricultural practices. Movement within ground water (i.e., the saturated zone) is further affected by hydrogeological characteristics and conditions, in addition to the chemical characteristics of the pesticide. Most scientists recognize the uncertainty in attempting to quantify this complex system, yet attempts to quantify the uncertainty itself have been rare. The simulation models discussed in this chapter are primarily deterministic models that attempt to simulate the soil system without considering the inherent uncertainty in both the soil processes and system characteristics.

Several attempts have been made to integrate the application of Monte Carlo techniques with simulation models for predicting pesticide leaching and migration processes within a framework that allows consideration of uncertainty in both process and soil and ground water system characterization.

Carsel et al. (1988a) describe use of the Pesticide Root Zone Model (PRZM) (Carsel et al. 1984) in conjunction with probability distributions of soil characteristics in a simple screening procedure to assess pesticide leaching potential. National statistical distributions of selected soil parameters required by the model were generated from information on almost 3000 soil series in 40 states obtained from the U.S. Soil Conservation Service. Monte Carlo techniques were then used to generate randomized parameter sets, including SCS soil hydrologic group, weather data, pesticide degradation rate, and correlated values for field capacity, wilting point, and organic matter for each soil layer. The results of the 2,000 runs, for aldicarb application to corn in Ohio, were analyzed in a variety of ways, including cumulative distribution of aldicarb leached below selected depths in the soil as shown in Figure 3.1. This type of information indicates that, for the simulated conditions, in 97 percent of the simulations the model predicted that aldicarb residues of less than 0.1 kg/ha would leach below 1.5 m, and 99 percent of the simulations showed movement of less than 0.1 kg/ha below 3.0 m.

Laskowski et al. (1990) described a procedure they called probability modeling for assessing the regional variations expected in pesticide-use impacts on ground water quality. Their scheme is similar to that used by Carsel et al. (1988a) and involves the use of a simulation model (PRZM) for predicting pesticide behavior in the soil. The regional variations in rainfall and temperature distribution patterns are represented by the outputs of a weather generator model, and the SCS soil survey database is used to generate soil property distribu-

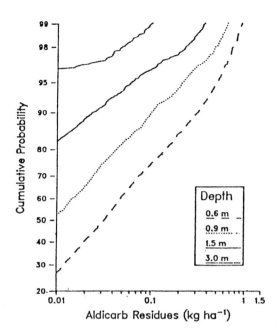

FIGURE 3.1 Cumulative probability distribution for annual pesticide movement below selected depths for 2,000 selected multivariate combinations of
PRZM runs for aldicarb in Ohio. (Carsel et al. 1988a. Reprinted, by permission, from Elsevier Science Publishers B.V., 1988.)

tions. As in Carsel et al. (1988a), Monte Carlo simulations are performed to produce frequency distributions for model inputs and the
corresponding model outputs. The Monte Carlo simulations are pre-
ceded by a Fourier Amplitude Sensitivity Test (FAST) that identifies
model input parameters that have the greatest impact on the model
outputs. Thus, the Monte Carlo simulation analysis is more efficient.
The output frequency distributions are then used as a basis for evaluating the probability that the maximum pesticide leaching depth is
sufficient to result in ground water contamination.

An extension of the Monte Carlo techniques to include PRZM
linkage to a simple ground water solute transport model is described
further by Carsel et al. (1988b). In this study, PRZM was again used
with Monte Carlo techniques applied to both the PRZM parameters
and the ground water model parameters using soils information appropriate for peanut production in North Carolina. Since the models
predicted pesticide residues in both soil and ground water, the results

continued

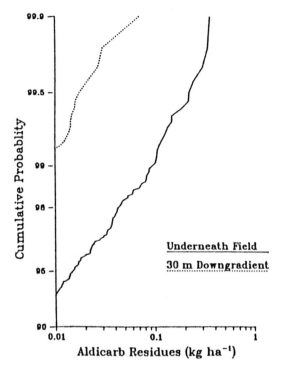

FIGURE 3.2 Cumulative probability distribution for aldicarb loadings under-
neath source area and 30 m downgradient for peanut production in North
Carolina. (Carsel et al. 1988b. Reprinted, by permission, from Elsevier Science Publishers B.V., 1988.)

were analyzed to compare residue remaining both beneath the field
site and 30 m downgradient in the shallow surface aquifer, as shown
in Figure 3.2. These results show that the residues 30 m downgradient
were generally an order of magnitude less than they were beneath the
field, and the downgradient values exceeded 0.01 kg/ha in less than 1
percent of the simulations.

The output probability distributions produced by the integration
of simulation modeling and Monte Carlo techniques allow consideration of uncertainties in soils properties, pesticide characteristics,
meteorology, and hydrogeologic conditions of pesticide migration to
and within ground water systems. This type of information will help
managers make the types of decisions needed to protect vulnerable
ground water regions with scarce resources.

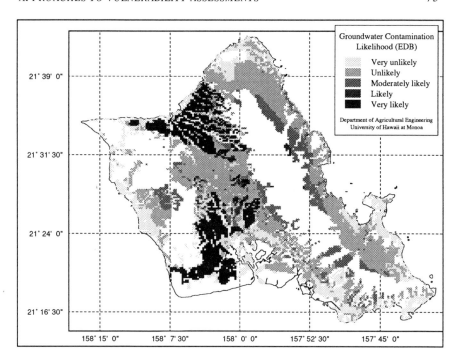

FIGURE 3.3   Map for Island of Oahu, Hawaii depicting relative vulnerability to ground water contamination with the pesticide ethylenedibromide (EDB). Vulnerability ratings are based on the values of retardation factor (RF), which is used as an index of pesticide leaching through soils. (Khan and Liang 1989. Reprinted, by permission, from Springer-Verlag, 1989.)

applied pesticide mass that is likely to leach past the depth of interest. Equations used for calculating RF and AF are shown in Table 3.8. The scales used to group contaminants on the basis of RF and AF indices in Figure 3.3 are entirely arbitrary.

Two principal assumptions made in deriving RF and AF indices must be noted: (1) water is assumed to move through the soil under steady, unsaturated conditions, with net ground water recharge rate (q) representing the steady flux, and (2) the soil profile is assumed to be homogeneous, where the soil property values used are depth-weighted averages. Computational schemes to eliminate both restrictions can be waived, as discussed by Rao et al. (1985).   Model errors resulting from the use of these simple indices may be partially evaluated by comparing the ranking of the leaching potentials of several pesticides as determined from RF and AF with rankings from more rigorous model simulations.   Of particular interest are evaluation of: (1) errors introduced by using annual recharge rate neglecting temporal

TABLE 3.8 Equations used to calculate the Retardation Factor (RF) and the Attenuation Factor (AF)

The AF index is given as:

$$AF = \exp\left[-\frac{(0.693\,d\,RF\,\theta_{FC})}{(q\,t_{1/2})}\right]$$ (1)

$0 \leq AF \leq 1$

where,
  d = distance to reference depth from ground surface (L)
  q = net annual ground water recharge (LT^{-1})
  $t_{1/2}$ = pesticide half-life (T) ($t_{1/2}$ = 0.693/k)
  k = first-order degradation rate coefficient (T^{-1})
  RF = retardation factor (dimensionless)

The RF index is given as:

$$RF = 1 + \frac{\rho_b f_{oc} K_{oc}}{\theta_{FC}}$$ (2)

$1 \leq RF \leq \infty$

where,
  ρ_b = soil bulk density (ML^{-3})
  f_{oc} = soil organic carbon content (mass fraction)
  K_{oc} = pesticide sorption coefficient (L^{3}M^{-1})
  θ_{FC} = soil-water content at field capacity (volume fraction)

---

variations in soil water and solute fluxes resulting from episodes of rainfall and irrigation, and (2) errors arising from use of depth-averaged soil properties in place of depth-varying values. Rao et al. (1985) and Kleveno et al. (1992) performed such evaluations and reached similar conclusions on the utility of the AF index for vulnerability assessments. Their results suggest that the relative order in which the pesticides were ranked in terms of their leaching potentials was not significantly different, whether the AF index or a more rigorous simulation model (e.g., CMLS, PRZM) was used. Thus, indices, such as AF, derived from simplified models may be adequate for vulnerability assessments because model errors are likely to be acceptable, in this case for relative rankings of contamination potentials.

Data errors, and their effects on uncertainty in vulnerability assessments, have been examined in some detail for the AF and RF indices. In particular, Loague and coworkers (Loague et al. 1989, 1990, Loague 1991, Kleveno et al. 1992) have used first-order uncertainty analysis (FOUA) to

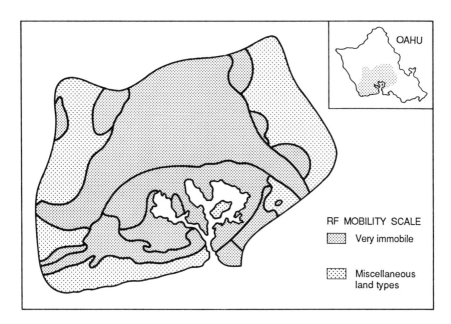

FIGURE 3.4a   Map depicting the potential for ground water contamination with diuron herbicide at the Pearl Harbor basin. The relative vulnerability ratings are based on RF values, which is used as an index for pesticide mobility in soils. (Loague et al. 1990. Reprinted, by permission, from Elsevier Science Publishers B.V., 1990.)

illustrate the need for recognizing the uncertainties associated with delineating areas of different levels of vulnerability using these indices. An example of such uncertainty is shown by comparing Figures 3.4.a and 3.4.b. Figure 3.4a shows vulnerability ratings, developed using the RF index, for the herbicide diuron in the Pearl Harbor Basin of Hawaii. Figure 3.4.b is a rating map with one standard deviation subtracted from the RF. Estimates of uncertainty were determined by first-order uncertainty analysis of the pesticide parameter K_{oc} and soil parameters (e.g., ρ_b, f_{oc}, and θ_{FC}). Note the large change in the RF map rating classes, largely resulting from uncertainty in f_{oc} and K_{oc}.

The large change in vulnerability ratings shown in Figure 3.4b, caused simply by accounting for a single standard deviation due to data errors, suggests the need for considerable caution in making regulatory decisions that distinguish between vulnerabilities in adjacent cells. Such uncertainties, and the likely changes in vulnerability classification of a subregion, clearly have considerable impacts on regulatory policy or land use management. Deterministically derived pesticide rating maps can be attractive to

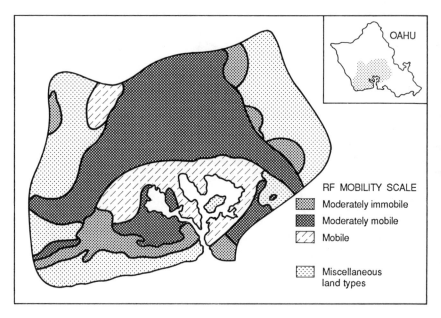

FIGURE 3.4b   Uncertainty in vulnerability maps shown in Figure 3.4a is represent-
ed by the rating maps produced with one standard deviation subtracted from average
RF values. (Loague et al. 1990. Reprinted, by permission, from Elsevier Science
Publishers B.V., 1990.)

decision makers because they provide sharp boundaries that lead to definitive interpretations of relative vulnerability. However, pesticide rating maps
that incorporate existing knowledge of data uncertainty are preferable to
those that do not because they give decision makers additional information.

The practical significance of uncertainty analyses in providing reliable
and cost-effective vulnerability assessments for resource managers and regulatory
officials can be summarized as follows (Heuvelink et al. 1989):

•   Identification of spatial attributes that need to be measured more
accurately to reduce uncertainty of the outputs to a specified level.

•   Identification of spatial attributes that are known too precisely (i.e.,
model outputs are insensitive to this input), so that fewer measurements
need be made in future data collection efforts. Cost savings can be redi-
rected to measurement of more sensitive attributes.

•   Determination of whether a simpler or a more sophisticated model
is needed for reliable vulnerability assessment. Data requirements for complex models may be such that the variability in required input parameters is

large, or available data are unreliable, or the error propagation through the model greatly magnifies errors in the input data.

Uncertainty of Uncertainty Analyses

Uncertainty analyses require information on the statistical properties of the attributes used in vulnerability assessments. For example, to use FOUA it is necessary to know the mean values for the input parameters, their variances, and the correlations among them. Information on statistical frequency distributions of the input parameters is needed to implement Monte Carlo simulation techniques to assess uncertainties in model outputs. Other, more sophisticated stochastic techniques may require knowledge of the spatial structure of parameter variance and covariance.

In most practical situations, two types of problems are encountered in attempts to perform uncertainty analyses: (1) no information is available on uncertainty of the spatial attributes or model coefficients, and (2) uncertainty information extrapolated from other sources is often of questionable quality. Thus, in many cases uncertainty analyses cannot be performed or themselves contain uncertainty. Despite these limitations, uncertainty analyses should be done to the extent practicable when conducting vulnerability assessments and can be useful in determining the impact of different levels of uncertainty on the results of the vulnerability assessment. Uncertainty information should be presented as a part of the results.

TESTING AND EVALUATION OF VULNERABILITY ASSESSMENTS

Evaluation of a vulnerability assessment must address at least two questions:

1. Is the vulnerability rating assigned to a given subarea (a polygon or a cell) valid?
2. Are the values assigned to neighboring subareas sufficiently different?

Issues of data quality and the scientific basis for the method play dominant roles in answering these questions. The vulnerability index assigned to a polygon or a cell may be incorrect because the model is inappropriate or because the input data used are unreliable. Even if a model is valid locally, it is not necessarily reliable for regional-scale simulations. As noted earlier, since the confidence intervals associated with the vulnerability index assigned to a cell or a polygon can often be large (because of data and model errors), we may not be able to distinguish differences in vulnerabilities of neighboring subareas.

General considerations in model testing and evaluation at the field scale are discussed in Box 3.3. Note that the term model, as used throughout this section, corresponds most directly to process-based assessment methods, but some of the concepts are also relevant to index or overlay methods.

One must be careful in extrapolating the experiences and results from field-scale testing of models to inferences of their applicability to regional-scale assessments. One limitation is that the sites where a model has been tested may not be representative of the conditions throughout a region. Second, it is likely that the available data will be much more detailed at the field scale than at the regional scale. For comprehensive evaluation of a regional vulnerability assessment model, the application at the field-plot scale should be based on the same type and detail of data as exists at the regional scale to the greatest extent possible.

Model validation and testing is more a process than an absolute yes or no result. According to Hern et al. (1986), ". . . model development and subsequent validation is an evolutionary process by its very nature." It involves multiple assessments of the model's abilities to represent observed data under a range of conditions. Each time new data are observed to agree with the predictions of a model, confidence in that model is increased.

Box 3.3
Field-Scale Model Testing and Validation

Models of contaminant transport through the vadose zone have received limited testing in real-world situations even at the field scale. Model testing and evaluation at the field scale is considered in greater detail by U.S. EPA (1982, 1989), Smith et al. (1988), and Donigian and Rao (1990).

The field testing of models can be viewed as a systematic analysis of errors, including most of the uncertainties discussed earlier. In any model testing effort, the user is continually faced with the need to analyze and explain differences between observations and model predictions. This requires assessments of the accuracy and validity of observed model input data, parameter values, system representation, and observed output data.

Model testing and evaluation against field data ideally should include three steps: calibration, validation, and postaudit. We say ideally because in many applications existing data will not support performance of all steps. In chemical-fate modeling, measured data for validation are often lacking and postaudit analyses are rare for any type of modeling exercise. Confusion surrounds model testing because of the different meanings that have been attached to the terms calibration, validation, etc. Here, we adopt the standardized concepts developed by the American Society for Testing and Materials (ASTM 1984).

Calibration is probably the most misunderstood of all the model testing components. Calibration is the process of adjusting selected model parameters within an expected range until the differences between model predictions and field observations are within selected criteria for performance. For all operational deterministic models (or portions thereof), calibration is usually needed and highly recommended.

Validation is the complement of calibration; model predictions are compared to field observations that were not used in model development or calibration. This is usually the second half of split-sample testing procedures, where the universe of data is divided (either in space or time), with a portion of the data used for calibration and the remainder used for validation. In essence, validation is an independent test of how well the model (with its calibrated parameters) is representing the important processes occurring in the natural system. Split-sample testing is common for surface-water models, but independent data sets may be difficult or impossible to obtain for ground water systems owing to the slowness of response times (NRC 1990, Konikow and Bredehoeft 1992). Verification and validation have been used interchangeably by many investigators, but the ASTM definition of verification is restricted to verifying the operation of the numerical procedures in the code.

Postaudit Analyses are the ultimate tests of a model's predictive capabilities. Model predictions for a proposed alternative are compared to field observations following implementation of the alternative. The degree to which agreement is obtained, given the acceptance criteria, reflects both the model capabilities and the assumptions made by the user to represent the proposed alternative. However, postaudit analyses have been performed in only a few situations (Alley and Emery 1986, Konikow and Bredehoeft 1992).

The recent U.S. EPA resolution (through its Science Advisory Board) on the use of models recognizes and advocates this view of model performance testing, as indicated in their quotation below:

"The stepwise procedure of checking the numerical consistency (i.e., code verification) *of a model, followed by field calibration, validation, and a posteriori* (postaudit) *evaluation should*

be an established protocol for environmental quality models in all media, recognizing that the particular implementation of this may differ for surface water, air and ground water quality models" (EPA 1989) (Note: Parenthetical text added by authors).

However, many investigators (e.g., Popper 1959) consider that a scientific hypothesis, such as a model, cannot be validated, but only invalidated. They argue that a good match between observations and model predictions does not prove the validity of the model. The match may be fortuitous owing to compensating errors in the model or erroneous observations. Conversely, a poor match does not necessarily mean the model is wrong or invalid. In reality, uncertainties and variabilities in measurements of the natural environment also limit the extent to which a model can be adequately tested to assess its validity, especially in the ground water arena.

The term validation itself may be part of the problem; inherently it implies a positive result—the model is valid for the conditions simulated. However, results showing lack of agreement between model and observed data are just as valuable, if not more valuable, because they help to demonstrate the bounds of applicability, or limitations, of the model. Ultimately, the purposes of model testing and evaluation are to identify the level of confidence in the form and structure of the model and to provide statements on the appropriate use of the model and its outputs.

Regional-Scale Testing and Evaluation

Ideally, regional vulnerability assessments could be tested against field observations of vulnerability to lead to improved methods and a better understanding of the factors affecting aquifer vulnerability to contamination. However, it is not possible to test regional vulnerability assessments in the same way that a field-scale simulation model can be tested, nor is it possible to make definitive statements about the predictive accuracy of one method compared to another at the regional scale. One difficulty is that a vulnerability assessment method may yield an index value or a probability, rather than a concentration. Thus, vulnerability, as treated in many methods, is not a property that can be directly measured in the field. A second difficulty is that to compare predicted values of vulnerability with observed constituent concentrations meaningfully one must either know the history of contaminant loading to the subsurface or assume that the contaminant loading has been spatially and temporally uniform. Neither situation is likely, except perhaps with a very small, well controlled field-plot study.

Despite these difficulties, and others noted below, inferences about the validity of a regional vulnerability assessment can be made through several lines of inquiry. Testing and evaluating vulnerability assessments may involve a hierarchical approach that evolves through several stages. In fact, the most sensible applications of vulnerability assessments may include explicit plans to test, review, and refine the assessment over time, perhaps over many years.

One approach to evaluating an assessment method is to compare the concentrations or the percent detections of one or more contaminants among different vulnerability classes predicted by the method. An example is provided by Meeks and Dean (1990), who compared the frequency of detections of DBCP to a vulnerability index applied to part of the San Joaquin Valley in California (see Box 3.4).

The use of ground water quality data to examine differences among vulnerability classes should be done with considerable caution for a number of reasons. Some of these are:

• The production zone of the well may be quite different from the reference location of the vulnerability method.

• Differences in ground water quality observed among vulnerability classes may be an artifact of spatial and temporal variations in chemical loadings.

• Short-circuiting of natural flow paths by movement down wells or their annuli can cause misleading results.

• Contaminants introduced at or near the land surface may have had sufficient time to reach the water table but may do so at a future date if they are sufficiently persistent and mobile.

• Information on well construction features, condition of the well, and location of the sampling point relative to water distribution, storage, or treatment are needed to evaluate the suitability of the well for sampling the constituents of concern. This information is incomplete for many wells. Information on the location of open interval(s) and the hydrogeologic unit(s) to which the well is open also may be lacking for many wells.

• Temporal variations in water quality may be a complicating factor, particularly for wells in shallow aquifers or with significant variations in pumping.

• Limitations in the protocols used for water quality monitoring may cause considerable uncertainty in the measured concentrations of constituents that are to be compared to model predictions.

As an example, some comparisons of ground water quality data with DRASTIC scores have been made using data from two national monitoring programs—the National Pesticide Survey (EPA 1992b) and the National Alachlor Well Water Survey (Holden et al. 1992). In both studies, little association between contamination by agricultural chemicals and DRASTIC scores was found, indicating that individual DRASTIC parameters were poorly correlated with contamination. The lack of association between contamination and the DRASTIC scores (or individual parameters) in these studies may reflect significant limitations in DRASTIC as a vulnerability assessment method. Conversely, the lack of association may be related to the problems listed above in relating ground water quality to vulnerability

Box 3.4
Evaluation of Regional Vulnerability Assessment

Meeks and Dean (1990) have proposed an index, the Leaching Potential Index (LPI), defined as follows: $LPI = [(10^3 \ v \ / \ (R \ \lambda \ z)]$ where v is the average pore water velocity in the vadose zone; R is the solute retardation factor; λ is the first-order degradation rate coefficient; and z is the depth from land surface to some reference plane within the vadose zone. This index is closely related to the AF index discussed earlier. After setting $v = (q/\theta_{FC})$, $R = RF$, $\lambda = (0.693/t_{1/2})$, and $z = d$, we note that LPI is, in fact, the reciprocal of the exponent term in the equation for defining AF (see Table 3.8); the additional factor of 10^3 was introduced by Meeks and Dean (1990) "in order to convert the index to a practical range." Note that larger values of LPI indicate a greater potential for contamination of ground water.

The utility of the LPI index for making regional-scale vulnerability assessments was evaluated by Meeks and Dean (1990) for a 381 square mile (975 km^2) study area in Stockton East Water District in the San Joaquin Valley of central California. The study area was discretized into 381 township and range sections, and for each sec-

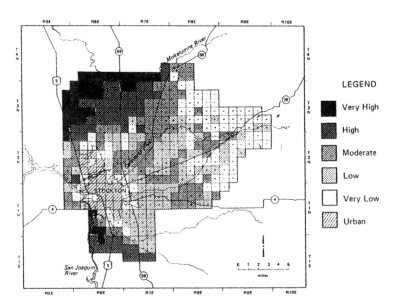

FIGURE 3.5   Geographic distribution of LPI ranks. (Meeks and Dean. 1990. Evaluating ground-water vulnerability to pesticides. Journal of Water Resources Planning and Management. Reprinted, by permission, from American Society of Civil Engineers, 1990.)

tion the LPI value was calculated. The calculated LPI values ranged from 2 to 133 (a mean LPI value of 19.3), with a strongly skewed frequency distribution. This finding suggests that a vast majority of the sections have a small leaching potential, with only a few sections having high vulnerability rating. The sections were then ranked by the LPI index and grouped into areas of similar leaching potential. A map showing the geographic distribution of the vulnerability classes is shown in Figure 3.5. Note that sections rated very high and high are clustered in a three-mile wide (4.84 km wide) band corresponding to an area of sandy soils, high recharge rates, and shallow water tables.

The next step in the Meeks and Dean (1990) assessment involved comparison of ground water quality monitoring data with the vulnerability ratings based on LPI values. The results from analyses of DBCP pesticide in ground water samples from wells throughout the study area were compiled; of the total 272 analyses, 202 were nondetects, while 70 were positive detections. The distribution of the negative and positive detects for the wells within each of the five areas grouped by vulnerability (plus urban areas, which were not rated) is shown in Table 3.9. The greatest percentage of positive detects was in areas rated as having very high or high vulnerability (45 and 50 percent, respectively), with progressively smaller percentage of positive detects for wells in areas with lower vulnerability.

Despite this evidence of the validity of the vulnerability assessment, the areas identified as very high and high are perhaps the trivial cases, and in the absence of uncertainty information, further subdivision of the study area may not be defensible.

TABLE 3.9 Percentage of Wells Tested with Detectable DBCP Categorized by Leaching Potential Index (Adapted from Meeks and Dean 1990. Evaluating ground-water vulnerability to pesticides. Journal of Water Resources Planning and Management. Reprinted, by permission, from American Society of Civil Engineers, 1990.)

Leaching Potential Category	Number of Wells in which DBCP was Detected	Number of Wells Tested	Percentage of Tested Wells in which DBCP was Detected
Very High	17	38	45
High	38	71	54
Moderate	11	56	20
Low	2	46	4
Very Low	2	47	4
Urban	0	16	0
Total	70	272	26

indices. For example, the screened intervals for the wells in the studies are at a wide range of depths from the water table, and many of the wells, particularly the community water system wells in the National Pesticide Survey, are from deeper, confined aquifers. Note, however, that in the National Alachlor Well Water Survey, a simple measure of vulnerability (based on the most likely aquifer tapped) is associated with pesticide contamination despite a less than clear relationship between the well-specific DRASTIC score and pesticide occurrence.

In addition to evidence from ground water observations of chemicals introduced by humans, various types of geochemical data may be useful in evaluating a vulnerability assessment, particularly the intrinsic vulnerability of an aquifer system. The types of ions in solution and their concentrations result from chemical processes responding to the lithology and hydrologic flow pattern of a particular hydrologic system (Freeze and Cherry 1979). Thus, the ionic composition of water in different locations may be an important indicator of flow paths of water through the subsurface and, in some instances, of the sources of water. For example, in a study of part of the coastal plain in Maryland and Delaware, Hamilton and Denver (1990) found that areas affected by agricultural chemicals could be identified by a distinct chemical signature of major inorganic constituents. Furthermore, measurements of isotopic data may be useful in the evaluation process. For example, elevated levels of tritium (a hydrogen isotope associated with the atmospheric testing of nuclear weapons) indicate that at least part of the ground water withdrawn from a well originally recharged the system after the early 1950s and hence helps distinguish young water from older water. The use of environmental isotopes and selected other chemicals as indicators of young ground water is reviewed in Plummer et al. (1993).

Limitations of Ground Water Quality Sampling

Vulnerability approaches are calibrated and validated using measured concentrations of contaminants in samples of ground water. In addition to analytical errors, the accuracy of the water quality data is constrained by how ground water samples are taken (Nelson and Dowdy 1990). The methods for obtaining representative ground water samples are relatively controversial, and errors can occur when: (1) samples are inappropriately handled, preserved, or stored, (2) ground water chemistry is stratified with depth below the water table, (3) and different pumping and purging methods are used. In addition, errors related to inappropriate sample processing occur when air is accidently introduced to the sample (changing the redox status, which affects solubility of dissolved metals) and when samples are not preserved for later analysis (bioactivity may affect nutrients, organic compounds, and dissolved metals). Three further examples of limitations in obtaining representative ground water samples are briefly noted below.

Difficulties in Characterizing the Mobile Fraction of Contaminants

Many ground water samples have excess turbidity caused by clay and silt entrained in the water column during sampling. The suspended solids are difficult to remove without filtering the sample, and digestion of the suspended solids routinely results in anomalously high concentrations of metals and other solutes that may not be transported naturally in the flow field. Nevertheless, some federal and state environmental regulations stipulate that samples must not be prefiltered before analysis of the "mobile fraction (particularly metals)" because of the possibility of removing contaminants sorbed onto colloid-sized particles that otherwise might be ingested (e.g., Puls and Barcelona 1989a, b). To remove clays and other solids entrained during sampling, it is recommended that wells be screened with narrower slits and that finer grained material be packed around the exterior of the screened interval (Puls and Barcelona 1989a, b). In this case, samples are still filtered, but *in situ*, at the well screen rather than during or after sampling.

A balance must be reached between the ideal sampling protocol and the realities of monitoring numerous locations in heterogeneous soils. For example, Ryan and Gschwend (1990) recently used the combination of field light scattering methods, sampling and storage under anoxic conditions, and pumping rates lower than 100 ml/minute to evaluate the amount of trace metal transport associated with colloids in a sand aquifer. Research reported by Kearl et al. (1992) and Puls and Powell (1992) similarly suggests that ambient water without artifactual turbidity can be obtained when low pumping rates are used to sample monitoring wells. However, until such methods are more widely used, analyses for total concentrations of many substances of interest may be suspect.

Sampling Near the Water Table

The elevation of the water table rises and falls on a seasonal basis in many areas. To ensure that some water always enters water table monitoring wells, well screens are usually positioned partly above and partly below the water table. Thus when water levels are low, only a small water column will be in the screened portion of the monitoring well. When water levels are high, the water table will still be in the screen, although there will be a larger column of water in the well (Driscoll 1986). In many contamination cases, however, solute concentrations below the water table are not uniform, but rather decrease or increase quick with depth below the water table. Therefore, measured contaminant concentrations will be affected by dilution, depending on how much of the water column below the water table is sampled and how the sample is obtained. Sampling error caused by screen placement relative to the water table has been evaluated by Robbins (1989), Robbins et. al. (1989), and Robbins and Martin-Hayden (1991). Robbins and colleagues conclude that concentrations of contaminants in water sampled from partially submerged well screens may be in error by orders of magnitude. To avoid these sampling problems, piezometers near the water table must be closer spaced vertically and have smaller screened intervals (e.g., Cherry 1983).

Purging and Pumping

Compounding the sampling problem is the process by which three to five casing volumes of water are purged from monitoring wells before a representative sample of ground water is collected. Empirical studies show that different pumping methods during purging produce different concentrations of contaminants (e.g., Gibb et. al. 1981, Robin and Gillham 1987). Robbins and Martin-Hayden (1991) have used mass continuity models of monitoring well purging to show that the number of casing volumes cannot be set *a priori* without information on the degree of contaminant stratification in the aquifer. Given all the uncertainties of sampling, standard monitoring wells may in fact provide only relative qualitative information on the concentrations of many contaminants.

COMPUTING ENVIRONMENTS FOR
VULNERABILITY ASSESSMENTS

Regardless of the approach chosen, a large quantity of data (attribute and geographic) are required to conduct a ground water vulnerability assessment. In addition, suitable analytical tools are needed to prepare, combine, study, and display the various components of the assessment. Numerous techniques have been used to perform these tasks, normally following advances in the allied fields of computer, graphic, and statistical sciences.

The earliest assessments were produced manually by compiling known information into an overall impression of the vulnerability of a certain area. Contaminated areas were studied and their site-specific environmental characteristics analyzed. Other areas with similar characteristics were then depicted as potential problem areas. Weighting of the various factors and regional differences were not generally included in these assessments.

More sophisticated assessments became possible with the advent of the computer. More factors could be simultaneously compared to determine relative risk. Environmental conditions could be codified into models of vulnerability. Many of the original forms of this type of assessment used grid-cell based models partly to standardize data collection and partly owing to the technical requirements of the computer in the days of punch-card data entry. This form of assessment, still used by many researchers, offers a more systematic approach and is relatively easy to create. However, these grid-cell models are inflexible to data of varying resolutions and accuracies, cannot be applied to various scales, and generally oversimplify complex, real world situations.

Recently, a computer model has been developed that uses geography to relate data layers, thereby allowing simultaneous use of data of varying scales, accuracies, and extents. A geographic information system (GIS) combines spatial information (geographic coordinates) with attributes to more accurately depict natural or man-made phenomena. GIS may also provide a wide array of functions to access, manage, manipulate, and display data. Further description of GIS systems is provided in Box 3.5.

Use of GIS has been growing in recent years. Specifically, GIS have been useful in ground water analysis and other spatial applications by federal, state, and local governments and private organizations. Generally, GIS have been used to create digital geographic databases, to manipulate and prepare data as input for various model parameters, and to graphically display model output. Primarily these functions have supported overlay or index approaches, but new GIS functions that are available or under development could further support the analytical requirements of process-based approaches.

Building and Making Databases Available for Assessment Approaches

Ground water vulnerability assessments require the input of data into an assessment approach where they are manipulated or analyzed to produce a measure of vulnerability. The large volumes of data often needed have led to a growing demand for computerized data sets and the development of computerized databases.

Most GISs have significant geographic database building capabilities. Map digitizing, map scanning, database editing, and data importing and exporting are standard GIS database development features. GISs can apply spatial estimation and smoothing techniques to convert line area data (vector polygons) to cell data (rasters). For example, point data, such as weather station data, can be converted into area surface data through surface generation algorithms and then accessed as cell input parameters.

Box 3.5
Geographic Information Systems

GIS is an integrating information technology that includes aspects of geography, surveying, mapping, cartography, photogrammetry, remote sensing, landscape architecture, and computer science. GIS technology links the characteristics of a place, a resource, or a feature with its spatial location. This linkage between the cartographic aspects of spatial information with characteristics or attributes of a resource or place creates an expanded database management system that could lead to new uses of emerging insights into the interrelationship between the environment and human activities.

Geographic information systems are commonly described by the functions they perform; they collect, manage, analyze, and display spatially-referenced data and their associated attributes. These functions and their relationships in a GIS are illustrated in Figure 3.6. While each function is important to the operation of a system, the figure does not adequately capture their interaction in the technology. More useful may be a definition of the system—GIS is the computer hardware, specialized spatial database software, database management system, spatial and attribute databases, and applications software that is interfaced or integrated with the GIS software, the data, and the people necessary to operate the system. This definition is illustrated in Figure 3.7. GIS provides a computing environment for scientific investigation and for information management and utilization that is particularly conducive to data display and spatial data stratification.

A wide selection of GIS software is available for either personal computers (PCs) or mainframes; the current computer preference is a workstation running some form of UNIX operating system. Software prices can range from $1,000 to $100,000, with a concomitant range

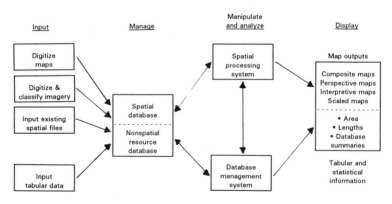

FIGURE 3.6 GIS functions and their relationships.

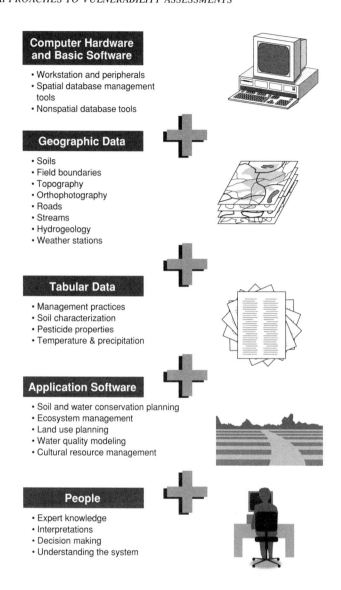

Computer Hardware and Basic Software

- Workstation and peripherals
- Spatial database management tools
- Nonspatial database tools

Geographic Data

- Soils
- Field boundaries
- Topography
- Orthophotography
- Roads
- Streams
- Hydrogeology
- Weather stations

Tabular Data

- Management practices
- Soil characterization
- Pesticide properties
- Temperature & precipitation

Application Software

- Soil and water conservation planning
- Ecosystem management
- Land use planning
- Water quality modeling
- Cultural resource management

People

- Expert knowledge
- Interpretations
- Decision making
- Understanding the system

FIGURE 3.7   Geographic information system components with examples of data and applications software.

in capabilities. Automated systems closely related to GIS include computer cartography and mapping systems, computer aided design (CAD) systems, and image processing systems; however, GIS is distinctive in its ability to manage and analyze topologically structured and geographically referenced data.

Since GISs also manage nonspatial attribute databases that are linked to the spatial data, information such as soil characteristics can be made available to each spatial location (each cell) or other desired spatial model input parameter. Thus, numerous data sets on a variety of characteristics can be combined into a coordinated, georeferenced database. GISs can be used to derive additional data layers from original source materials. Functions are available that can combine two or more data files, either spatially or by recomputing attributes.

This concept of derived data simply reflects the fact that required parameters often have not been measured for a specific site or region, are not at the scale of the assessment, or are not identified as specific data parameters. These parameters must be estimated from derived database(s), or other measurements or interpolated and/or extrapolated from data points. Most process-based approaches include some parameters that are difficult or impossible to measure directly and so must be calculated or estimated by other means. Among the reasons:

• It may be physically impossible to measure the parameter (e.g., diffusion coefficient).
• Limited resources may preclude obtaining the number of measurements needed for the scale and/or time period of interest.
• Point measurements may not have sufficient coverage for regional assessments, considering issues of spatial variability.

A number of automated procedures are available for estimating specific model parameters from existing databases. The most commonly used procedures estimate soil parameters from existing soil databases; examples are DBAPE, SOILPROP, and GRASS Waterworks. Data Base Analyzer and Parameter Estimator (DBAPE) (Imhoff et al. 1990), an U.S. Environmental Protection Agency product, is an interactive system designed to allow users to estimate soil parameters and develop meteorologic input for the EPA PRZM (Carsel et al. 1984) and RUSTIC (Dean et al. 1989) models using soils and meteorological databases. The soils database is a selected subset of the SCS national archival data system, NSSAD/SIRS (USDA 1985), that focuses only on agricultural soils. County soils information is included for almost 8,000 soil series with information on soil layering, soil texture class, percent sand, percent clay, bulk density, percent organic matter, available water, hydrologic soil group, and potential crops. From these basic data extracted from NSSAD/SIRS, DBAPE provides procedures for calculating model parameters for wilting point, water content at field capacity (0.1 and 0.33 bar tension), residual water content, saturated hydraulic conductivity, and soil water retention parameters from correlations developed by van Genuchten (1978), Rawls and Brakensiek (1985), and others.

The meteorologic data in DBAPE include a 25-year record of daily precipitation, air temperature, and wind speed for more than 200 NOAA weather stations across the country. Procedures are provided to calculate pan evaporation and solar radiation from these data for use by process-based simulation models.

SOILPROP is a proprietary program distributed by Scientific Software Group of Washington, D.C., that provides an interactive capability to estimate saturated hydraulic conductivity, soil water retention parameters, and associated uncertainty from particle size distribution information. The estimation procedures are similar to those used by DBAPE, but in addition covariances of parameter values are estimated using first-order error analysis. Input data must be supplied by the user since no database is associated with SOILPROP.

GRASS Waterworks (Vieux and Kang 1990) is GIS application software that performs analyses of spatial input parameters for hydrologic and water quality models. The program encompasses a generic set of analyses for hydrologic models, using spatial data sets and the GRASS GIS developed by the U.S. Army Corps of Engineers (U.S. Army Corps of Engineers 1988). GRASS Waterworks currently allows users to generate slope and aspect maps, delineate watershed boundaries and outlets, calculate land surface parameters (flow path length, average channel slope, watershed slope) from digital elevation data and do hydrologic modeling with the SCS TR-55 watershed model (USDA 1986). Although it is currently limited to surface parameters, linkages to other models and estimation of soil and vegetation parameters are planned in ongoing development efforts.

These three procedures—DBAPE, SOILPROP, and GRASS Waterworks—are examples of efforts to offset the lack of data for vulnerability assessments by using computerized databases and GIS technology to derive needed parameter values. These parameter derivation procedures are limited by the scale, accuracy, and validity of the basic data in the databases from which the parameters are calculated. More importantly, since the calculated values are simply estimates based on available information, they may introduce additional data errors into the vulnerability assessment. As discussed in the section on Uncertainty in Vulnerability Assessment Methods, such errors may substantially increase the uncertainty of the vulnerability assessment.

Geographical Display of Assessment Results

In most ground water vulnerability assessments, the results are portrayed on a map of the study area, typically in the form of polygons shaded or colored to depict the levels of vulnerability for all locations on the map. Too often, these maps oversimplify the results of the assessment or include too much information and so confuse or mislead the viewer. Ineffective maps are due to a combination of poor definition of the purpose of the map, poor assessment of the viewers' knowledge, and poor cartographic skills. Attention to each of these factors and tests of alternative methods can lead to maps that more effectively portray the results of the assessment. GIS technology is a useful tool for creating vulnerability maps and for quick and simple testing of methods of display.

Vulnerability assessment maps typically have not conveyed the uncertainty arising from errors in data and assessment methods. With GIS, for example, a very poor assessment (in terms of errors) can be mapped in a manner that, though very sophisticated, misrepresents the quality of the assessment. Thus, ways should be developed to assist in displaying uncertainty as well as results.

GIS technology presently offers excellent capabilities for displaying vulnerability assessment results on maps. With improvements in assessment methods and uncertainty analyses, GIS may also prove useful for depicting associated uncertainties on these same maps. These improvements will require the collection of better information on data quality, development of techniques for visualizing component and net uncertainty of individual data layers, development of models of the propagation of error through the assessment process, and production of maps depicting these factors.

One way of depicting uncertainty is the case of a two-color vulnerability map showing areas of comparatively high and low vulnerabilities in red and green, respectively. Uncertainty could be indicated by variations in the intensity of the basic colors. A pale green could indicate high uncertainty for a low vulnerability area; intense green could indicate high confidence. As each of the two basic colors becomes paler, they could bleed into a white area representing high uncertainty. These white areas are expected in the zone separating a vulnerable region from a less vulnerable one. The uncertainty associated with the color intensities should be included on the map legend.

Analytical Functions

GIS technology can support ground water vulnerability assessments in the analysis and modeling of spatial and physical relationships of critical environmental elements. Functions such as map overlay, reclassification, and query assist in analyzing these conditions. Many simple models for surface water applications have been developed by federal, state, and local water authorities using only basic GIS tools.

One example is the use of GIS to compute soil loss using SCS's Universal Soil Loss Equation (USLE). USLE estimates average annual soil loss in tons per acre as a product of factors representing climate (R), soil erodibility (K), topography (LS), vegetative cover (C), and supporting conservation practices (P). Actual soil loss (A) can be computed by the equation:

$$A = R \times K \times LS \times C \times P$$

For each of these factors, an intermediate map layer is generated using GIS. Some of these maps are created by simply regrouping the classes on another map (e.g., soil mapping units on a soils map are regrouped into classes of erodibility to create an erodibility factor map). Maps for other factors are created by applying mathematical formulae between map layers. For example, the topography factor (LS) is computed from the steepness of slope (S) and the length of the slope (L), with the formula:

$$LS = (\lambda/72.6)^m (65.4 \sin^2\theta + 45.6 \sin\theta + 0.065)$$

where, λ = slope length in feet; θ = angle of slope; and m = 0.5 if the percent slope is 5 or more, 0.4 on slopes of 3.5 to 4.5 percent, 0.3 on slopes of 1 to 3 percent, and 0.2 on uniform gradients of less than 1 percent.

Such equations can be solved with generic GIS tools, using the map layers to supply the variables. Likewise, to create a map of soil loss using GIS, the intermediate maps representing the five USLE factors are simply multiplied together, resulting in a map of estimated soil loss as well as the associated statistical data.

In these examples, the computations are applied across the map, with the equations applied independently for each point on the map. Although the concept of adding two maps or multiplying several maps may seem unusual, this is a routine capability of GIS technology and is duplicated in most non-GIS based approaches that attempt to deal with the spatial distribution of simple models like USLE.

New GIS functions and developments in related technologies have resulted in the ability to model environmental factors in a more sophisticated manner. Examples of these functions are:

• Diffusion functions can be used to depict the migration of entities across surfaces based on attributes of those surfaces.

• N-dimensional queries allow the user to interrogate the database for attribute information from multiple data layers at the same time, which is very useful in data visualization and model validation.

• Neighborhood analysis develops information on the adjacency, size, and geometry of physical features to further model them and their relationship to other features.

• Direct linkages between databases and software facilitate transfer of up-to-date information among applications, which promotes collaboration rather than duplication of efforts among supporting technologies.

• Software programs can transform an arduous set of commands into a simple procedure, thus providing sophisticated analyses to GIS novices.

Many GIS environments, however, still lack some of the basic analytical capabilities needed by modelers. For example, GIS analytical functions use static information and are run on demand. The dynamic nature of environmental phenomena is lost by these static models. Additionally, most GIS techniques today work only in two dimensions, which makes it difficult to visualize the relationships among surface and subsurface features. Some of these problems may be solved by software developments and should be reevaluated over time.

GIS technology can be used beneficially in ground water vulnerability assessments by supplying tools for encoding and producing geographic and attribute data, by computing spatial and attribute relationships, and by graphically portraying these relationships and model output. The technology can also be particularly useful to overlay and index methods by allowing various data layers to be integrated and/or weighted. Since GIS technology is designed to be adaptable to different technical and procedural requirements of vulnerability assessments, developments in the field can be expected to strengthen the support GIS can offer other assessment approaches.

SUMMARY

The methods used to assess ground water vulnerability range from simple overlay and index methods to more complicated process-based simulation models. Each method has advantages and limitations, and none is best for all situations.

Process-based models at the appropriate scale would be ideal in a perfect world, since they attempt to capture the true physical, chemical, and biological reactions that occur from the surface through the ground water regime. Process-based models, however, have not been demonstrated to be more effective than other techniques. The limitations of process-based models derive from model structure (i.e., lack of knowledge of how to formulate processes mathematically) and, more significantly, from limitations in data availability and quality. Furthermore, limited field experimentation with pesticide simulation models suggests that models based on simplified process representation may be more useful for many vulnerability assessments than more complicated models.

Most approaches for ground water vulnerability assessment assume undisturbed surficial deposits with spatially uniform percolation. Preferential flow paths, such as roots and worm holes, cracks, joints, and solution channels, are ignored. Yet these may well be the fundamental pathways affecting vulnerability, providing more direct and rapid paths for contaminants to reach ground water than they would otherwise have. Recent literature suggests that under certain circumstances preferential flow can be a dominant phenomenon (cf., Roth et al. 1991), that it can occur in soils with no apparent structure (cf., Ghodrati and Jury 1990), and that it can channel virtually all of the water and chemical flux through a small portion of the matrix in highly permeable soils that have subsurface lenses in them (cf., Kung 1990a, b).

Statistical methods incorporate uncertainty and attempt to explicitly minimize error, but require observations of surrogates for vulnerability (e.g., ground water samples from shallow wells). Using these surrogates, the methods directly derive parameter coefficients instead of assigning weights to attributes based on expert judgment as is done in overlay and index methods. Parameters from simple process-based indices (e.g., travel times) could be used in statistical methods, making for a sort of hybrid approach. However, the results of these methods can only be applied to the geographic areas in which the data were collected to regions where similar factors are associated with the likelihood of ground water contamination.

Overlay and index methods have been developed because of limitations in process-based models and because of a lack of monitoring data required for statistical methods. Overlay and index methods are based on assumptions that a few major factors largely control ground water vulnerability and that these factors are known and can be weighted (explicitly in index methods or implicitly in overlay methods). These assumptions have not been demonstrated, particularly with respect to assigning weights to different factors.

In reviewing vulnerability assessment methods, it is useful to distinguish between (1) the ability to explain the factors and processes leading to potential contamination of ground water, and (2) the ability to predict likely contamination of ground water at the desired spatial scale. Research over the past two to three decades has contributed significantly to our knowledge and enables us to offer explanations of contamination of ground water. However, our ability to translate this understanding into reliable predictive models is not as sound. Although we can identify many of the factors leading to ground water contamination and construct process-based models that incorporate these parameters, our ability to apply these models in real-world situations is significantly limited.

The foregoing remarks suggest that predictions of ground water vulnerability are probabilistic—that is, we may be able to forecast the probability of ground water contamination over a given area, but the level of confidence in such forecasts for any particular location is quite low. Furthermore, it is difficult, if not impossible, to test the validity of these predictions.

The challenge of vulnerability assessments resembles the problem of weather forecasting. For example, a forecast of a 70 percent chance of thunder showers in a specific location might be equated to identification of areas with high vulnerability. According to the National Weather Service, such a forecast does not predict rain at any given location or over the entire region, but only a 70 percent probability of rain somewhere (locations unspecified) in the region.

It can be argued that vulnerability assessments predict ground water contamination in a relative, not an absolute sense. That is, an assessment only identifies some areas in the region as more or less vulnerable than other areas. Uncertainty is pervasive in both spatial databases and computational schemes; as a result, all vulnerability assessments are inherently uncertain. It may be fairly easy to identify areas where ground water contamination is highly probable but not areas where it is highly improbable. For example, it is relatively easy to determine that ground water in a mature karst aquifer system or in a shallow sand and gravel alluvial aquifer is highly vulnerable to contamination. However, it may be much more difficult to demonstrate that ground water underlying a clay-rich unsaturated zone indeed has low vulnerability to contamination, because many factors difficult to quantify, such as preferential flow paths, may complicate the situation. Moreover, differentiation of areas that are not highly vulnerable to ground water contamination into more subtle distinctions in vulnerability is very difficult. This conclusion may be summarized as the **Third Law of Ground Water Vulnerability**:

The obvious may be obscured and the subtle indistinguishable.

Uncertainty in vulnerability assessments needs to be better recognized and revealed in the outputs. Assessment methods coupled with GIS and other sophisticated presentations can suggest greater knowledge than truly exists. Ways in which uncertainty could be better integrated into presentations include identifying the data sites used, developing companion uncertainty maps based on uncertainty analysis of data errors (these maps could be further broken down to show uncertainty associated with different parameters), and presentation of vulnerability maps generated by different methods. Maps produced by different methods, however, should be interpreted with caution as indicators of error because different methods use many of the same data and hence are not independent tests.

Vulnerability assessment is an interactive process that should be continually modified and improved using new information. Although assessment methods cannot be validated in the traditional sense, efforts to develop multiple lines of evidence for evaluating these assessments are encouraged.

Ground water quality data, however, should be used with considerable caution to examine differences among vulnerability classes, for a number of reasons. These include uncertainty in the reference location of the production zone of the well used to obtain the sample, uncertainty about the spatial and temporal variations in chemical loadings at the land surface, possible short-circuiting of natural flow paths by wells, and limitations in obtaining representative ground water samples from wells.

Several approaches for vulnerability assessments are available, and each has its own strengths, and limitations. All approaches combine uncertainty and should explicitly capture or reflect that uncertainty. Testing and evaluating these approaches is critical to producing a more justifiable, useful, and reasonable assessment.

REFERENCES

Aller, L., T. Bennett, J.H. Lehr, and R.J. Petty. 1985. DRASTIC: A Standardized System for Evaluating Ground Water Pollution Potential Using Hydrogeologic Settings. Ada, Oklahoma: U.S. Environmental Protection Agency.

Aller, L., T. Bennett, J.H. Lehr, R.J. Petty, and G. Hackett. 1987. DRASTIC: A Standardized System for Evaluating Ground Water Pollution Potential Using Hydrogeologic Settings. EPA-600/2-87-035. Ada, Oklahoma: U.S. Environmental Protection Agency.

Alley, W.M., and P.A. Emery. 1986. Groundwater model of the Blue River basin, Nebraska—Twenty years Later. Journal of Hydrology 85:225-249.

American Society for Testing and Materials (ASTM). 1984. Standard Practice for Evaluating Environmental Fate Models of Chemicals, 1978-84. Philadelphia, Pennsylvania: American Society for Testing and Materials.

Back, R.C., R.R. Romine, and J.L. Hansen. 1984. Rating system for predicting the appearance of temik aldicarb residues in potable water. Environmental Toxicology and Chemistry 3:589-597.

Banton, O., and J.P. Villeneuve. 1989. Evaluation of ground water vulnerability to pesticides: A comparison between the quantities. Journal of Contaminant Hydrology 4:285-296.

Berg, R.C., and J.P. Kempton. 1988. Stack-Unit Mapping of Geologic Materials in Illinois to a Depth of 15 Meters. Champaign: Illinois State Geological Survey Circular 542.

Berryman, D., B. Bobée, D. Cluis, and J. Haemmerli. 1988. Nonparametric approaches for trend detection in water quality time series. Water Resources Bulletin 24(3):545-556.

Beven, K. 1991. Modeling preferential Flow: An uncertain future? In Preferential Flow, T.J. Gish and A. Shirmohammadi, eds. Proceedings National Symposium, December 16-17, 1991. St. Joseph, Michigan: American Society of Agricultural Engineers.

Bowman, R.S., and R.C. Rice. 1986. Accelerated herbicide leaching resulting from preferential flow phenomenon and its implications for ground water contamination. In Proceedings of the Conference on Southwestern Ground Water Issues, Pheonix, Arizona, October 20-22, 1986. Dublin, Ohio: National Water-Well Association.

Brandstetter, A., and B.E. Buxton. 1989. The role of geostatistical, sensitivity and uncertainty analysis in performance assessment. Pp. 89-220 in Geostatistical, Sensitivity, and Uncertainty Methods for Ground-Water Flow and Radionuclide Transport Modeling, B.E. Buxton, ed. Conf-870971, Columbus, Ohio: Battelle Press.

Burrough, P.A. 1986. Principles of Geographical Information Systems for Land Resource Assessment. Monographs on Soil and Resources Survey No. 12. Oxford, U.K.: Oxford Science Publications, Clarendon Press.

Butters, G.L., W.A. Jury, and F.F. Ernst. 1989. Fieldscale transport of bromide in an unsaturated soil: I. Experimental methodology and results. Water Resources Research 25:1575-1582.

Buxton, B.E., ed. 1989. Geostatistical, Sensitivity, and Uncertainty Methods for Ground-Water Flow and Radionuclide Transport Modeling. Conf-870971. Columbus, Ohio: Battelle Press.

Carsel, R.F., C.N. Smith, L.A. Mulkey, J.D. Dean, and P. Jowise. 1984. User's Manual for the Pesticide Root Zone Model (PRZM): Release 1. Athens, Georgia: U.S. Environmental Protection Agency, Environmental Research Laboratory.

Carsel, R.F., R.S. Parrish, R.L. Jones, J.L. Hansen, and R.L. Lamb. 1988a. Characterizing the uncertainty of pesticide leaching in agricultural soils. Journal of Contaminant Hydrology 2:111-124.

Carsel, R.F., R.L. Jones, J.L. Hansen, R.L. Lamb, and M.P. Anderson. 1988b. A simulation procedure for groundwater quality assessments of pesticides. Journal of Contaminant Hydrology 2(2):125-138.

Chen, H., and A.D. Druliner. 1988. Agricultural Chemical Contamination of Ground Water in Six Areas of the High Plains Aquifer, Nebraska. National Water Summary 1986—Hydrologic Events and Ground-Water Quality. Water-Supply Paper 2325. Reston, Virginia: U.S. Geological Survey.

Cherry, J.A. 1983. Piezometers and other permanently installed devices for groundwater quality monitoring. Pp. IV-1 to IV-39 in Proc.: Petroleum Association for Conservation of the Canadian Environment, Seminar on Groundwater and Petroleum Hydrocarbons Protection, Detection, Restoration. Ottawa.

Chrisman, N.R. 1984. The role of quality information in long-term functioning of geographical information systems. Cartographica 21:79-87.

Cohen, D.B., C. Fisher, and M.L. Reid. 1986. Ground-water contamination by toxic substances: A California assessment. Pp. 499-529 in Evaluation of Pesticides in Ground Water, W.Y. Garner, R.C. Honeycutt, and H.N. Nigg, eds. ACS Symp. Series 315, Washington, D.C.: American Chemical Society.

Dean, J.D., P.S. Huyakorn, A.S. Donigian, Jr., K.A. Voos, R.W. Schanz, Y.J. Meeks, and R.F. Carsel. 1989. Risk of Unsaturated/Saturated Transport and Transformation of Chemical Concentrations (RUSTIC). Volumes I and II. EPA/600/3-89/048a. Athens, Georgia: U.S. Environmental Protection Agency.

Dixon, W.J. 1986. Extraneous values. Pp. 83-90 in Methods of Soil Analysis, Part I, Physical and Mineralogical Properties, Second Edition, A. Klute, ed. Agronomy Servies No. 9. Madison, Wisconsin: American Society of Agronomy.

Donigian, A.S., Jr., and P.S.C. Rao. 1990. Selection, application, and validation of environmental models. Pp. 577-600 in Proceedings of the International Symposium on Water Quality Modeling of Agricultural Nonpoint Sources, Part 2. ARS-81. Washington, D.C.: USDA Agricultural Research Service.

Donigian, A.S., Jr., J.C. Imhoff, and B.R. Bicknell. 1983. Modeling Water Quality and the Effects of Agricultural Best Management Practices in Four Mile Creek, Iowa. Athens, Georgia: U.S. Environmental Protection Agency.

Driscoll, F.G. 1986. Groundwater and Wells. St. Paul, Minnesota: Johnson Division, UOP.

Eisenberg, N.A., L.D. Richerstein, and C. Voss. 1989. Performance assessment, site characterization, and sensitivity and uncertainty methods: Their necessary association for licensing. Pp. 9-38 in Proceedings of the Conference on Geostatistical, Sensitivity, and Uncertainty Methods for Ground-Water Flow and Radionuclide Transport Modeling, B.E. Buxton, ed. Conf-870971. Columbus, Ohio: Battelle Press.

Enfield, C.G., R.F. Carsel, S.Z. Cohen, T. Phan, and D.M. Walters. 1982. Approximating pollutant transport to ground water. Ground Water 20(6):711-722.

Freeze, R.A., and J.A. Cherry. 1979. Groundwater. Englewood Cliffs, New Jersey: Prentice-Hall.

Germann, P.F., ed. 1988. Rapid and far-reaching hydrologic processes in the vadose zone. Journal of Contaminant Hydrology 3:115-380.

Ghodrati, M., and W.A. Jury. 1990. A field study using dyes to characterize preferential flow of water. Soil Science Society of America Journal 54:1558-1563.

Gibb, J.P., R.M. Schuller, and R.A. Griffin. 1981. Procedures for the Collection of Representative Water Quality Data from Monitoring Wells, Cooperative Ground Water Report 7. Champaign: Illinois State Water Survey.

Goodchild, M.F., and O. Dubuc. 1987. A model of error for choroplett maps, with applications to geographic information systems. Pp. 165-172 in Proc. Auto-Carto 8. Falls Church, Virginia: Amer. Congress of Surveying and Mapping.

Goodchild, M.F., and W. Min-hua. 1988. Modelling error in raster-based spatial data. Pp. 97-106 in Proc. Third Internl. Symp. Spatial Data Handling. Sydney, Australia.

Hamilton, P.A., and J.M. Denver. 1990. Effects of land use and ground-water flow on shallow ground-water quality, Delmarva Peninsula, Delaware, Maryland, and Virginia. Ground Water 28(5):789.

Hern, S.C., S.M. Melancon, and J.E. Pollard. 1986. Generic steps on the field validation of vadose zone fate and transport models. In Vadose Zone Modeling of Organic Pollutants, S.C. Hern and S.M. Melancon, eds. Chelsea, Michigan: Lewis Publishers, Inc.

Heuvelink, G.B.M., P.A. Burrough, and A. Stein. 1989. Propagation of errors in spatial modelling with GIS. Int. Jour. Geographical Information Systems 3(4):303-322.

Hipel, K.W. 1988. Nonparametric approaches to environmental impact assessment. Water Resources Bulletin 24(3):487-492.

Holden, L.R., J.A. Graham, R.W. Whitmore, W.J. Alexander, R.W. Pratt, S.F. Liddle, L.L. Piper. 1992. Results of the national alachlor well water survey. Environmental Science and Technology 26(5):935-43.

Hoyer, B.E., and G.R. Hallberg. 1991. Groundwater Vulnerability Regions of Iowa, Special Map 11. Iowa City: Iowa Department of Natural Resources.

Imhoff, J.C., B.R. Bicknell, and A.S. Donigian, Jr. 1983. Preliminary Application of HSPF to the Iowa River Basin to Model Water Quality and the Effects of Agricultural Best Management Practices. EPA Contract No. 68-03-2895. Athens, Georgia: U.S. Environmental Protection Agency.

Imhoff, J.C., R.F. Carsel, J.L. Kittle, Jr., and P.R. Hummel. 1990. Data Base Analyzer and Parameter Estimator, DBAPE (User's Manual). EPA/600-3-89-083. Athens, Georgia: Environmental Research Laboratory, U.S. Environmental Protection Agency.

Johnston, R.H. 1988. Factors Affecting Ground-Water Quality. National Water Summary 1986: Hydrologic Events and Ground-Water Quality. Water-Supply Paper 2325. Reston, Virginia: U.S. Geological Survey.

Jones, R.L., P.S.C. Rao, and A.G. Hornsby. 1983. Fate of aldicarb in florida citrus soils: 2. Model evaluation. Pp. 959-978 in Proceedings of a Conference of Characterization and Monitoring in the Vadose (Unsaturated) Zone, D.M. Nielson, and M. Curl, eds. Dublin, Ohio: National Water Well Association.

Jury, W.A., and H. Flüher. 1992. Transport of chemicals through soil: Mechanisms, models, and field applications. Advances in Agronomy 47:141-201.

Jury, W.A., and M. Ghodrati. 1989. Overview of organic chemical environmental fate and transport modelling approaches. Pp. 271-304 in Reactions and Movement of Organic Chemicals in Soils, B.L. Sawhney, and K. Brown, eds. Special Publication No. 22. Madison, Wisconsin: Soil Science Society of America.

Jury, W.A., and J. Gruber. 1989. A stochastic analysis of the influence of soil and climatic variability on the estimate of pesticide groundwater pollution potential. Water Resources Research 25(12):2465-2474.

Jury, W.A., W.F. Spencer, and W.J. Farmer. 1983. Behavior assessment model for trace organics in soil: I. Description of model. Journal of Environmental Quality 12:558-564.

Kearl, P.M., N.E. Korte, and T.A. Cronk. 1992. Suggested modifications to ground water sampling procedures based on observations from the colloidal baroscope. Ground Water Monitor Review 12:155-161.

Kellogg, R.L., M.S. Maizel, and D.W. Goss. 1992. Agricultural Chemical Use and Ground Water Quality: Where Are the Potential Problems? Washington, D.C.: U.S. Department of Agriculture, Soil Conservation Service.

Kempthorne, O., and R.R. Allmaras. 1986. Errors and variability of observations. Pp. 1-32 in Methods of Soil Analysis, Part 1. Physical and Mineralogical Methods, Agron. Monograph, No. 9 (2nd edition). Madison, Wisconsin: American Society of Agronomy.

Khan, M.A., and T. Liang. 1989. Mapping pesticide contamination potential. Environmental Management 13(2):233-242.

Khan, M.A., T. Liang, P.S.C. Rao, R.E. Green. 1986. Use of an interactive computer graphics and mapping system to assess the potential for ground water contamination with pesticides. EOS 67(16):278.

Kissel, D.E., O.W. Bidwell, and J.F. Kientz. 1982. Leaching Classes in Kansas Soils. Bulletin No. 641. Manhatten, Kansas: Kansas State University.

Kleveno, J.J., K. Loague, and R.E. Green. 1992. Evaluation of a pesticide mobility index: Impact of recharge variation and soil profile heterogeneity. Journal of Contaminant Hydrology 11(1-2):83-99.

Knisel, W.G., R.A. Leonard, and F.M. Davis. 1989. GLEAMS User Manual. Tifton, Georgia: Southeast Watershed Research Laboratory.

Konikow, L.F., and J.D. Bredehoeft. 1992. Ground-water models cannot be validated. Advances in Water Resources 15:75-83.

Kung, K.S. 1990a. Preferential flow in a sandy vadose zone: 1. Field observations. Geoderma 46:51-58.

Kung, K.S. 1990b. Preferential flow in a sandy vadose zone: 2. Mechanism and implications. Geoderma 46:59-71.

Laskowski, D.A., P.M. Tillotson, D.D. Fontaine, and E.J. Martin. 1990. Probability Modelling. London: Phil. Trans. Royal Society B329:383-389.

Leonard, R.A., W.G. Knisel, and D.A. Still. 1987. GLEAMS: Ground water loading effects of agricultural management systems. Trans. Amer. Soc. Agric. Eng. 30:1403-1418.

Liang, T., and M.A. Khan. 1986. A natural resource information system for agriculture. Agricultural Systems 21:81-105.

Loague, K. 1991. The impact of land use on estimates of pesticide leaching potential: Assessments and uncertainties. Journal of Contaminant Hydrology 8:157-175.

Loague, K., and R.E. Green. 1991. Statistical and graphical methods for evaluating solute transport models: Overview and application. Journal of Contaminant Hydrology 7:51-73.

Loague, K.M., R.S. Yost, R.E. Green, and T.C. Liang. 1989. Uncertainty in a pesticide leaching assessment for Hawaii. Journal of Contaminant Hydrology 4:139-161.

Loague, K., R.E. Green, T.W. Giambelluca, T.C. Liang, and R.S. Yost. 1990. Impact of uncertainty in soil, climatic, and chemical information in a pesticide leaching assessment. Journal of Contaminant Hydrology 5:171-194.

McKenna, D.P., and D.A. Keefer. 1991. Potential for Agricultural Chemical Contamination of Aquifers in Illinois. Open File 1991-7R. Champaign: Illinois State Water Survey.

McLean, J.E., R.C. Sims, W.J. Doucette, C.R. Caupp, and W.J. Girenney. 1988. Evolution of mobility of pesticides in soil using U.S. EPA methodology. ASCE. Journal of Environmental Engineering 114(3):689-703.

Mead, D.A. 1982. Assessing data quality in geographic information systems. Pp. 51-62 in

Remote Sensing for Resource Management, C.J. Johansen, and J.L. Sanders, eds. Ankeny, Iowa: Soil Conservation Society of America.

Meeks, Y.J., and J.D. Dean. 1990. Evaluating ground-water vulnerability to pesticides. Journal of Water Resources Planning and Management 116(5):693-707.

Moore, J.S. 1988. SEEPPAGE: A System for Early Evaluation of Pollution Potential of Agricultural Ground Water Environments. Geology Technical Note 5 (Revision 1). Washington, D.C.: U.S. Department of Agriculture, Soil Conservation Service.

Moreau, D.H., and L.E. Danielson. 1990. Agricultural Pesticides and Ground Water in North Carolina: Identification of the Most Vulnerable Areas. North Carolina: Water Resources Research Institute of the University of North Carolina, North Carolina State University.

National Research Council (NRC). 1990. Ground Water Models: Scientific and Regulatory Applications. Washington, D.C.: National Academy Press.

Nelson, D.W., and R.H. Dowdy, eds. 1990. Methods for ground water quality studies. In Proc. National Workshop, Arlington, VA, November 1-3, 1989. Lincoln, Nebraska: University of Nebraska—Lincoln Press.

Nicholls, P.H., R.H. Bromilow, and T.A. Addiscott. 1982a. Measured and simulated behavior of fluometuron, aldoxycarb, and chloride ion in a fallow structured soil. Pesticide Science 12:475-483.

Nicholls, P.H., A. Walker, and R.J. Baker. 1982b. Measurement and simulation of the movement and degradation of atrazine and metribuzin in a fallow soil. Pesticide Science 12:484-494.

Nofziger, D.L., and A.G. Hornsby. 1986. A microcomputer-based management tool for chemical movement. Soil. Appl. Agr. Res. 1:50-56.

Pedroli, B. 1990. Classification of Shallow groundwater types in a dutch covers and landscape. Journal of Hydrology 115:361-375.

Pennell, K.D., A.G. Hornsby, R.E. Jessup, and P.S.C. Rao. 1990. Evaluation of five simulation models for predicting aldicarb and bromide behavior under field conditions. Water Resources Research 26(11):2679-2693.

Pettyjohn, W.A., M. Savoca, and D. Self. 1991. Regional Assessment of Aquifer Vulnerability and Sensitivity in the Conterminous United States. Report EPA-600/2-91/043. Ada, Oklahoma: U.S. Environmental Protection Agency.

Plummer, L.N., R.L. Michel, E.M. Thurman, and P.D. Glynn. 1993. Environmental tracers for age-dating young ground water. Pp. 255-294 in Regional Ground-Water Quality, W.M. Alley, ed. New York: Van Nostrand Reinhold.

Popper, K. 1959. The Logic of Scientific Discovery. New York: Harper and Row.

Puls, R.W., and M.J. Barcelona. 1989a. Filtration of ground water samples for metals analysis. Hazardous Waste & Hazardous Materials 6(4):385-393.

Puls, R.W., and M.J. Barcelona. 1989b. Ground Water Sampling for Metals Analysis. Superfund Ground Water Issue. U.S. Environmental Protection Agency.

Puls, R.W., and R.M. Powell. 1992. Acquisition of representative ground water quality samples for metals. Ground Water Monitoring Reviews 12:167-176.

Rao, P.S.C., A.G. Hornsby, and R.E. Jessup. 1985. Indices for Ranking the Potential for Pesticide Contamination of Groundwater. Soil Crop Science Society Florida Proceedings 44:1-8.

Rawls, W.J., and D.L. Brakensiek. 1985. Prediction of Soil Water Properties for Hydrological Modeling. In Proc. Symposium of Committee of Watershed Management, Irrigation and Drainage Div., ASCE Convention, Denver, CO.

Riley, J.A., R.K. Steinhorst, G.V. Winter, and R.E. Williams. 1990. Statistical analysis of the hydrochemistry of ground waters in Columbia River basalts. Journal of Hydrology 119:245-262.

Robbins, G.A. 1989. Influence of using purged and partially penetrating monitoring wells on contaminant detection, mapping, and modeling. Ground Water 27(2):155-162.

Robbins, G.A., and J.M. Martin-Hayden. 1991. Mass balance evaluation of monitoring well purging: I. Theoretical models and implications for representative sampling. Journal of Contaminant Hydrology 8:203-24.

Robbins, G.A., R.D. Bristol, J.M. Hayden, and J.D. Stuart. 1989. Mass continuity and distribution implications for collection of representative ground water samples from monitoring wells. Pp. 125-140 in Proceedings of the Conference on Petroleum Hydrocarbons and Organic Chemicals in Ground Water: Prevention, Detection, and Restoration. Dublin, Ohio: National Water Well Association.

Robin, M.J.L., and R.W. Gillham. 1987. Field evaluation of well purging procedures. Ground Water Monitoring Review 7:85-93.

Roth, K., W.A. Jury, H. Flüher, and W. Attinger. 1991. Transport of chloride through an unsaturated field soil. Water Resources Research 27(10):2533-2541.

Rupert, M., T. Dace, M. Maupin, and B. Wicherski. 1991. Ground Water Vulnerability Assessment: Snake River Plain, Southern Idaho. Boise: Idaho Department of Health and Welfare.

Ryan, J.N., and P.M. Gschwend. 1990. Colloid mobilization in two Atlantic coastal plain aquifers: Field studies. Water Resources Research 26:307-322.

Sacha, L., D. Fleming, and H. Wysocki. 1987. Survey of Pesticides in Selected Areas Having Vulnerable Ground Waters in Washington State. EPA/910/9-87/169. Seattle, Washington: U.S. Environmental Protection Agency, Region X.

Seyhan, E., A.A. van de Griend, and G.B. Engelen. 1985. Multivariate analysis and interpretation of the Hydrochemistry of a Dolomitic Reef Aquifer, Northern Italy. Water Resources Research 21(7):1010-1024.

Small, M.J., and J.R. Mular. 1987. Long-term pollutant degradation in the unsaturated zone with stochastic rainfall infiltration. Water Resources Research 23:2246-2256.

Smith C.N., R.S. Parrish, R.F. Carsel, A.S. Donigian, Jr., and J.M. Cheplick. 1988. Validation Status of Pesticide Leaching and Groundwater Transport Model. Athens, Georgia: U.S. Environmental Protection Agency, Environmental Research Laboratory.

Steenhuis, T.S., S. Pacenka, and K.S. Porter. 1987. MOUSE: A management model for evaluation groundwater contamination from diffuse surface sources aided by computer graphics. Appl. Agr. Res. 2:277-289.

Teso, R.R., T. Younglove, M.R. Peterson, D.L. Sheeks, III, and R.E. Gallavan. 1988. Soil taxonomy and surveys: Classification of areal sensitivity to pesticide contamination of groundwater. Journal of Soil and Water Conservation 43(4):348-352.

U.S. Army Corps of Engineers. 1988. GRASS, Geographic Resource Analysis Support System Version 3.0. Champaign, Illinois: Construction Engineering Research Laboratory.

U.S. Department of Agriculture (USDA). 1985. User Manual for Interactive Soils Data Bases: National Soil Survey Area Data Base, Soil Interpretations Record Data Base and Plant Name Data Base. Fort Collins, Colorado: USDA, Soil Conservation Service.

U.S. Department of Agriculture (USDA). 1986. Urban Hydrology for Small Watersheds, TR-55. USDA, Soil Conservation Service.

U.S. Environmental Protection Agency (EPA). 1982. Exposure modeling committee report: Testing for the field applicability of chemical exposure models. In Proc. Workshop on Field Applicability Testing. Athens, Georgia: U.S. EPA.

U.S. Environmental Protection Agency (EPA). 1989. Resolution on Use of Mathematical Models by EPA for Regulatory Assessment and Decision-Making. Prepared by the Environmental Engineering Committee of the Science Advisory Board. EPA-SAB-EEC-89-012. Washington, D.C.: U.S. Environmental Protection Agency.

U.S. Environmental Protection Agency (EPA). 1992a. A Review of Methods for Assessing

Aquifer Sensitivity and Ground-Water Vulnerability to Pesticides. Contract No. 68-C0-0083. Raleigh, North Carolina: Geraghty & Miller, Inc.

U.S. Environmental Protection Agency (EPA). 1992b. Another Look: National Survey of Pesticides in Drinking Water Wells Phase II Report. Washington, D.C.: U.S. Environmental Protection Agency.

van Genuchten, M.T. 1978. Calculating the Unsaturated Hydraulic Conductivity with a New Closed-Form Analytical Model. 78-WR-08. Princeton, New Jersey: Water Resources Program, Department of Civil Engineering, Princeton University.

Vieux, B.E., and Y.T. Kang. 1990. GRASS Waterworks: A GIS Toolbox for Watershed Hydrologic Modelling. Proceedings of Application of GIS, Simulation Models, and Knowledge-Based Systems for Land Use Management. November 12-14, 1990. Blacksburg: Virginia Polytechnic and State University.

Villeneuve, J., O. Banton, P. Lafrance, and P.G.C. Cambell. 1987. A new model for the evaluation of groundwater vulnerability to non-point contamination by pesticides. Pp. 1097-1109 in Vulnerability of Soil and Groundwater to Pollutants, W. van Duijvenbooden and H.G. van Waegeningh, eds. The Hague, Netherlands: TNO Committee on Hydrological Research., National Institute of Public Health and Environmental Hygiene.

Wagenet, R.J., and J.L. Hutson. 1987. LEACHM: A Finite-Difference Model for Simulating Water, Salt, and Pesticide Movement in the Plant Root Zone, Continuum 2. Ithaca: New York State Resources Institute, Cornell University.

Wagenet, R.J., and P.S.C. Rao. 1990. Modeling pesticide fate in soil. Pp. 357-399 in Pesticides in the Soil Environment, SSSA Book Series No. 2, H.H. Cheng, ed. Madison, Wisconsin: Soil Science Society of America.

Wisconsin Department of Natural Resources, and Wisconsin Geological and Natural History Survey. 1987. Groundwater Contamination Susceptibility in Wisconsin. Madison: Wisconsin Geological and Natural History Survey.

4

Data and Databases

INTRODUCTION

Basic information on a variety of spatial and nonspatial attributes of the physiographic setting of the area to be evaluated is required to assess ground water vulnerability to contamination. Although the types of data required depend on the specific technique employed, some combination of information will be needed on natural factors, such as topography, soils, weather, hydrogeology, and land cover; and the human factors such as land use and management.

To date most vulnerability assessments have used existing data sources, and have rarely involved new data collection efforts in support of the vulnerability assessment. Since the data available for a particular region are often meager, the attributes of interest are often derived by some type of interpolation of information collected at sparsely distributed locations, sometimes from outside the region of interest, and frequently using data collected at a different spatial scale.

As discussed in Chapter 3, the reliability of an assessment depends on the validity of the approach for the particular application and the quality and currency of the data used. Thus, even if the vulnerability technique selected is *valid*, the use of poor quality data will introduce uncertainty into the results of the assessment. Uncertainties resulting from data quality problems can be reduced by insuring that the variability in the attributes (e.g., physical features and management practices) over the area is accurately reflected in the interpolated values of the spatial and nonspatial attributes.

Dozier (1992) points out the synergism between model development—that is, for the purposes of this discussion, assessment techniques—and data collection efforts. He observes that "Modeling and data collection each drive and direct each other. Better models illuminate the type and quantity of data that are required to test hypotheses. Better data, in turn, permit better and more complete models and new hypotheses." Most research efforts to date have been concerned primarily with the representation of environmental processes involved in contaminant transport and transformations. Considerable progress has been made in development of increasingly sophisticated simulation models. However, less attention has been paid to collection, entry, and management of the data required to estimate the model inputs at the appropriate spatial/temporal scales. The need for appropriate computing environments (i.e., integration of data bases, model computations, display of model outputs) needed in vulnerability assessments has also received little attention. These limitations have resulted in models (or techniques) that may describe relevant processes at a local scale (e.g., field plots), but are impractical to implement at larger spatial scales (e.g., watersheds, regional, national). On the other hand, paucity of data and a lack of understanding of the relevant processes at the requisite spatial and temporal resolution has led to development of models or techniques that may not be appropriate for larger scales at which vulnerability assessments are being conducted.

Since public funds are limited, many federal agencies currently are interested more in maintaining and improving the usefulness, accuracy, and availability of existing databases than in embarking on new programs of data collection. This chapter reviews the status of existing information, and describes several databases, their availability, and their use in ground water vulnerability assessments. The focus here is on federally developed and managed databases, with some reference to state and local databases. Although many state and local databases may be valuable in helping to assess the vulnerability of ground water to contamination for state, county, and watershed areas, no comprehensive listing of state geographic databases exists. The lack of this information makes it impractical for this committee to specifically cite or assess state and local databases. Appendix A contains a listing of sources of digital resource databases.

Federal Data Management Activities

Multiple federal agencies collect and use spatially-referenced attribute and nonattribute data required for vulnerability assessments. Over the past several decades, many scientists with diverse scientific backgrounds were involved in collecting these data for a variety of intended uses. Integration of such diverse databases into an effective and compatible data and information management system is not a trivial task.

In 1982, the General Accounting Office reported concerns that federal agencies involved in digital cartographic data collection were collecting data without regard to the need for standards, were duplicating each others' efforts, and were not coordinating their efforts (GAO 1982). In 1983, the Office of Management and Budget (OMB) established the Federal Interagency Coordination Committee on Digital Cartography (FICCDC). The primary duties of the committee were to facilitate exchange of cartographic data, coordinate activities, develop data standards, determine requirements for data, and report to OMB annually.

Through the 1980s, the federal government's, as well as the nation's, use of geographic information systems and demand for other categories of digital spatial data grew. The OMB and FICCDC recognized this trend, and developed a revised OMB Circular A-16 (OMB 1990) to establish a process to foster the development of a national spatial framework for an information-based society. This framework will include the participation of federal, state, and local governments, and the private sector.

The circular established the Federal Geographic Data Committee (FGDC) to promote the coordinated development, use, sharing, and dissemination of surveying, mapping, and related spatial data. The FGDC's responsibilities include interagency coordination of data collection and sharing, and the establishment of federal standards for geographic data exchange, content, and quality. Fourteen departments and independent agencies are members of the FGDC, and additional agencies participate on FGDC subcommittees and working groups.

The circular also assigns government-wide coordination leadership responsibilities to federal departments for data categories. Agencies within the lead departments chair FGDC subcommittees that assist in coordination and development of national data standards with the participation of the communities interested in those data categories. The categories and lead agencies are listed in Table 4.1. Additional data categories will be added as the need and opportunity arise. In addition, the FGDC works with the Interagency Advisory Committee on Water Data for coordinate spatial water data issues.

The exchange of data between different computer systems is often difficult and sometimes impossible. Thus, the FICCDC and FGDC, in cooperation with the American Congress on Surveying and Mapping, developed a standard for exchange of geographic data (Mollering 1988), which has since been adopted as a federal information processing standard (FIPS 173) (NIST 1992). The Spatial Data Transfer Standard is described in Box 4.1.

Circular A-16 sets a long range objective of developing an integrated

TABLE 4.1 Federal Geographic Data Coordination Responsibilities (OMB 1990)

Geographic Data Category	Lead Agency
Base Cartographic	U.S. Geological Survey, Department of the Interior
Bathymetric	Coast and Geodetic Survey, Department of Commerce
Cadastral	Bureau of Land Management, Department of the Interior
Cultural and Demographic	Census Bureau, Department of Commerce
Elevation	U.S. Geological Survey, Department of the Interior
Geodetic	National Oceanic and Atmospheric Administration, Department of Commerce
Geologic	U.S. Geological Survey, Department of the Interior
Ground Transportation	Federal Highway Administration, Department of Transportation
International Boundaries	Office of the Geographer, Department of State
Soils	Soil Conservation Service, Department of Agriculture
Vegetation	U.S. Forest Service, Department of Agriculture
Wetlands	U.S. Fish and Wildlife Service, Department of the Interior

---

Box 4.1
The Spatial Data Transfer Standard

The Spatial Data Transfer Standard (SDTS) (NIST 1992), also known as the Federal Information Processing Standard 173, is used to transfer spatial data and their attributes between two noncommunicating systems. The standard consists of three parts which together provide criteria for data exchange, including quality and content.

Part I, logical specifications, provides the fundamental definition of digital spatial data, specifies the logical file structure for the data, and describes requirements for reporting data quality. The quality report requires five basic categories of information: data lineage (i.e., history and source of data, how they were compiled and digitized, etc.), positional accuracy, attribute accuracy, logical consistency, and completeness.

Part II, spatial features, defines common geographic features, such as stream, road, aquifer, and their attributes. Currently, these definitions and their included terms define an initial set of entities found on topographic maps and hydrographic charts. The set will be expanded to include soils, wetlands, geology, and other data categories.

Part III, ISO 8211 encoding, explains how to use the International Standards Organization (ISO) 8211 standard to implement Parts I and II. ISO 8211 is a specification for using a descriptive file technique which includes header information for each file being transferred. The standard is media independent, so that the SDTS can be used with any recording media.

national spatial data infrastructure (NSDI), with the participation of state and local governments and the private sector. Several FGDC activities support the development of the NSDI. Town meetings and more direct contacts with groups representing different sectors of the spatial data community provide forums for making the public aware of federal geographic data and discussing roles and opportunities for participating in the NSDI. FGDC members are developing a data clearinghouse, including a draft standard for data documentation, or "metadata." The committee is encouraging the use of the SDTS to ease the problems of transferring and sharing geographic data, and is developing standards for the content of data sets for categories coordinated under Circular A-16. The committee also gathers requirements for geographic data and is forging partnerships for data production.

State and Local Data Management Activities

Many states have established strong programs for collecting, maintaining, analyzing, and distributing topographic, cartographic, natural resource, and attribute information. In several of these states, interagency committees have been created to coordinate data preparation and develop standards for these databases. These standards may, in fact, surpass federal standards owing to the scales and/or attributes required for state applications. In these cases, data tend to be of high quality and collected following a plan and standard.

Minnesota, for example, operates one of the oldest and most extensive state geographic information systems (GIS) in the country. The Minnesota Land Management Information System, established at the University of Minnesota in 1967, later became the Land Management Information Center (LMIC). The LMIC, together with the Department of Natural Resources, serves as the state's repository of geographic resource data and coordinates data collection and management activities within the state. A 1989 inventory identified more than 135 digital databases in Minnesota of which more than half were concerned with hydrology (Warnecke et al. 1992).

Other states have collected geographic information and made it available to users, but in a less organized fashion. In these areas, individual agencies have procured and developed automated systems and the data to support them on an as-needed basis. In many cases, the available digital database may be large, but not managed directly by any one group. Often state data centers act more as clearinghouses than as coordinating agencies, and the data tend to be fragmented, nonstandardized, and of unknown quality. Such data should be used with caution in conformance with standards, and within the sensitivity of the model to the data. Some of these states may have made some commitment to automating data collection and analysis and may be in the process of formulating data requirements for various applications.

In the remaining states, little or no activity has occurred in the automation of geographic information and only limited geographic data are available. Generally, one or two agencies have begun to collect geographic data in digital form on an *ad hoc* basis. Many of these states are watching the development and maturation of information groups in other states before initiating their own process.

Local databases and their associated support systems also vary greatly in their degree of organization and sophistication. To date, cost of establishing digital database systems has been prohibitively large for all but the biggest municipalities. However, as costs decrease and the number of proven applications rises, local usage of these systems can be expected to grow dramatically, as will the amount of local-scale digital information. It is critical that some form of standardization be established early in the development of local systems to insure that adjacent jurisdictions can work cooperatively in the future and that data and applications can be transferred with minimum effort.

The availability and quality of state and local digital databases needed to support ground water vulnerability assessments depend on: (1) the presence of a jurisdictionwide coordination entity, (2) existing laws and mandates that require digital information, (3) multiagency or departmental use of the data, and (4) vision and financial support by senior management. Where these conditions are met, vulnerability assessments are likely to be better supported by data and personnel; where they are not, attempts at assessments will be difficult.

The *State Geographic Information Systems Activities Compendium* (Warnecke 1992) provides anecdotal information about digital database activities as well as a listing of contacts for those seeking additional information about state GIS activities.

TOPOGRAPHY

Topography affects ground water quality primarily through its influence on the hydrologic processes of runoff and infiltration. Slope, slope shape, and aspect information for use in determining runoff characteristics, snow melt patterns, and drainage basin delineation can be derived from raw elevation data. Elevation data can be combined with soil profile information, geophysical data, and well drilling records to produce three dimensional representations of the subsurface hydrogeologic features.

Characteristics and Availability of Data

Topography is represented on traditional paper maps in the form of elevation lines (contours) with the contour interval dependent on the scale of the map and the amount of topographic relief. Contour data can be represented in a digital database as vectors. However, digital elevation is usually maintained in a grid-cell (point samples) format called a digital elevation model (DEM).

The U.S. Geological Survey (USGS) and the Defense Mapping Agency (DMA) have produced most of the topographic contour maps and subsequent DEMs for the United States. The USGS's National Mapping Division distributes DEM information at scales of 1:24,000 and 1:250,000. These two product lines differ in topographic detail and positional accuracies. The 1:250,000 scale DEMs are available nationwide, while the 1:24,000 scale DEMs are available for approximately 20 percent of the country, primarily in the western part. A status map of 1:24,000 scale DEM coverage is shown in Figure 4.1. Digital elevation data are distributed on nine-track tape and soon will be distributed on CD-ROM disks by the U.S. Geological Survey. Some additional digital elevation data are collected as part of operational programs or specialized research projects in other federal, state, and local agencies, and may be available from these sources.

Discussion

Digital terrain data, which might be used in regional or national ground water vulnerability assessments, are not currently accessible on a nationwide basis with uniform spatial and attribute characteristics. Data at map scales of 1:100,000 and 1:250,000 could be used for regional analysis. Because of the significant problems encountered in matching the boundaries of existing maps for adjoining subareas, often it is not possible to produce a *seamless* map of the larger area or region of interest. It is difficult to derive meaningful slope information from these data since the distance between sample points is orders of magnitude larger than the vertical component.

The 1:24,000 scale data provide high definition land surface information, however, complete elevation data are rarely available at this scale. Also, in certain instances, such as urban and forested areas, terrain data may be influenced by features above the actual terrain. Caution should be exercised when using such data for precise elevation analysis.

The utility of digital elevation data for ground water vulnerability studies would be enhanced by several actions:

• Complete the 1:24,000 scale Digital Elevation Models series to provide continuous and uniform data.

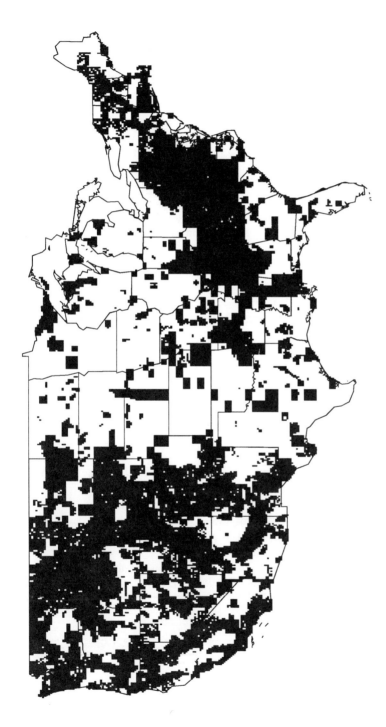

FIGURE 4.1 Status of 1:24,000 scale Digital Elevation Model (DEM) coverage. (Map provided by the U.S. Geological Survey)

• Change the data preparation standards or develop algorithms to reduce the errors associated with nonterrain factors (e.g., trees, buildings) affecting elevation data.

• Develop effective edge matching routines to eliminate errors along quadrangle boundaries at all scales.

• Provide users with elevation point data sets rather than the rasterized averages in a DEM. Digital elevation data values are the average elevation of a number of sample points found in a resolution cell. Delivering the source point information would allow the user to sample or reclass the data in any fashion suitable for the application.

• Develop new data collection methods for preparing digital elevation data. Stereo remote sensing, global positioning system technology, and other innovations may be useful in speeding up the data collection efforts and may perhaps result in a higher resolution product.

• Develop standards for high resolution, large scale elevation models that are based on available technology and not on historic standards and procedures.

SOILS

Soil can be one of the most important factors affecting the transport of contaminants from the earth's surface to ground water. Various soil properties will affect the rates of contaminant transport, retardation, and sometimes degradation. Most vulnerability assessment techniques require soils information.

Characteristics and Availability of Data

The Soil Conservation Service (SCS) of the U.S. Department of Agriculture, through the National Cooperative Soil Survey (NCSS) program, is responsible for mapping the soils of the nation. Surveys have been completed for more than 75 percent of these soils, including most cropland. This mapping has been done on aerial photobases at scales of 1:15,840 to 1:31,680 and line maps at a scale of 1:250,000. SCS has established standards for creation of digital soil geographic databases and begun adding to these databases (Reybold and TeSelle 1989). Box 4.2 describes how soils are mapped.

Geographic Databases

Three digital geographic databases of different scales have been established for use in conjunction with other geographically referenced information: the Soil Survey Geographic Database (SSURGO), the State Soil Geo-

---

**Box 4.2
Soil Mapping**

Soil is defined as the unconsolidated mineral and organic matter on the surface of the earth that has been subjected to and influenced by genetic and environmental factors: parent material, climate (including water and temperature effects), macro- and microorganisms, and topography, all acting over time and producing a product—soil—that differs from its parent material in many physical, chemical, biological, and morphological properties, and characteristics (SSSA 1987). Soils, within a landscape, are a continuum and hence are spatially variable. Most soil properties used for predicting the vulnerability of ground water to contamination vary in time and space (Wilding 1985), which allows the pedologist to partition the landscape into areas with greater homogeneity and to delineate and display these areas on maps as mapping units as shown in Figure 4.2.

Mapping units are named for the dominant soil series within the mapped polygon (USDA 1975). Series are the lowest level of soil classification (Lytle and Mausbach 1991). Phases of series (e.g., eroded) constitute components within map units and allow for more precise definition. Once the mapping unit has been delineated, vertical and horizontal components are described, and physical, chemical, and biological properties recorded. These characterizations are based on corings and/or excavations at various points within the map unit, referred to as soil pedons. A pedon is the smallest sample—a minimum of one cubic meter in size—used for describing and classifying soils. This information and data are published collectively in a Soil Survey Report, usually on a county basis.

---

graphic Database (STATSGO), and the National Soil Geographic Database (NATSGO). The soil map unit boundaries in each geographic database are linked with soil attribute data to give the extent and properties of the dominant soil series phase in each mapping unit.

SSURGO is the digitized version of county soil surveys designed for farm, township, and county level resource planning and management. Soil map unit boundaries are delineated on orthophotographs or 7.5 minute quadrangles at scales ranging from 1:20,000 to 1:31,680 (Lytle and Mausbach 1991). In a typical soil survey (1:24,000), a map unit may vary from 1 to 5 hectares (2.5 to 12.5 acres) in size. These soil maps are digitized in vector format suitable for use in vector based GIS or conversion to raster format for raster analysis systems. SSURGO map units, such as that shown in Figure 4.2, contain one to three components (e.g., soil series, eroded phase) with up to 60 component/site properties (e.g., slope) and 1 to 28 layer

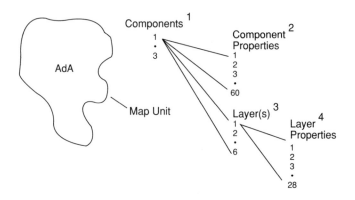

1 *SSURGO map units consist of 1 to 3 components.*

2 *Component properties are 60 soil properties and interpretations in 84 different data elements (component tables); for example, flooding potential for each component.*

3 *Each component consists of 1 to 6 soil layers.*

4 *Layer consists of 28 soil properties for each layer and 53 different data elements (layer table); for example, clay percent.*

FIGURE 4.2 A conceptual diagram of a soil geographic database (SSURGO) map unit. (Adapted from Lytle and Mausbach 1991. Reprinted, with permission, from *Proceedings: Resource Technology 90* copyright 1991, by the American Society for Photogrammetry and Remote Sensing: "Interpreting Soil Geographic Databases," D.J. Lytle and M.J. Mausbach, pp. 469-476.)

properties (e.g., percent organic matter). Attribute data for SSURGO are derived from the Map Unit Interpretation Record (MUIR) database.

The STATSGO database is designed for regional and statewide natural resource monitoring, planning, and management. It is an aggregation of SSURGO soil survey information at a scale of 1:250,000, using U.S. Geological Survey topographic quadrangle base maps. Since STATSGO map unit delineations, such as that shown in Figure 4.3, are generalized from SSURGO databases, each map unit can have up to 21 phases of soil series as components. For each STATSGO map unit, the area of each soil series phase present is recorded and can be associated with appropriate attribute data from MUIR for more precise analyses than would be suggested by the map scale (Bliss and Reybold 1989).

The NATSGO database is designed for multi-state and national resource assessment and planning. It is the digitized Major Land Resource Area (MLRA) map of the United States on a scale of 1:7,500,000 (USDA 1981).

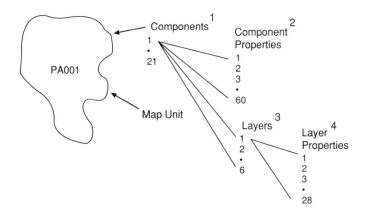

1 *STATSGO map units consist of 1 to 21 components.*

2 *Component properties are 60 soil properties and interpretations in 84 different data elements (component tables); for example, flooding potential for each component.*

3 *Each component consists of 1 to 6 soil layers.*

4 *Layer is comprised of 28 soil properties for each layer and 53 different data elements (layer table); for example, clay percent.*

FIGURE 4.3 A conceptual diagram of a state soil geographic database (STATSGO) map unit. (Adapted from Lytle and Mausbach 1991. Reprinted, with permission, from *Proceedings: Resource Technology 90* copyright 1991, by the American Society for Photogrammetry and Remote Sensing: "Interpreting Soil Geographic Databases," D.J. Lytle and M.J. Mausbach, pp. 469-476.)

Map units, such as that shown in Figure 4.4, were developed from generalized state soil maps using land use, elevation, topography, climate, water, and natural vegetation information independent of state boundaries. Soil components in each map unit were determined by field investigations at three Primary Sampling Units (PSUs) selected by stratified random sampling procedures (Figure 4.5) as a part of the 1982 National Resource Inventory (USDA 1979). Soil properties for each of the soil series phases occurring in a NATSGO mapping unit are derived through a linkage with the Soil Interpretation Record database.

NATSGO coverage is complete for the country. The status of SSURGO and STATSGO mapping efforts is shown in Figures 4.6 and 4.7, respectively.

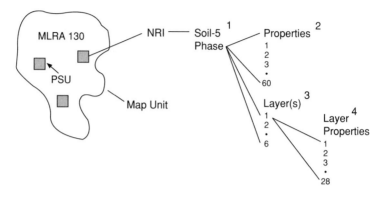

1   *NATSGO map units are linked thru NRI to Soil-5
    Phase at 3 points in each Primary Sampling Unit (PSU).*

2   *There are 60 soil properties and interpretations for
    each Soil-5 data elements; for example, flooding potential.*

3   *Each Soil-5 Phase consists of 1 to 6 layers.*

4   *There are 28 soil properties for each layer;
    for example, clay percent.*

FIGURE 4.4   A conceptual diagram of a national soil geographic database (NATS-GO) map unit (Adapted from Lytle and Mausbach 1991. Reprinted, with permission, from *Proceedings: Resource Technology 90* copyright 1991, by the American Society for Photogrammetry and Remote Sensing: "Interpreting Soil Geographic Databases," D.J. Lytle and M.J. Mausbach, pp. 469-476.)

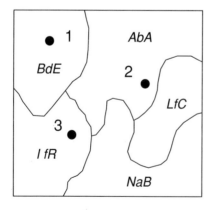

FIGURE 4.5   A conceptual diagram of a 1982 national resources inventory primary sampling unit (PSU) (Lytle and Mausbach 1991. Reprinted, with permission, from *Proceedings: Resource Technology 90* copyright 1991, by the American Society for Photogrammetry and Remote Sensing: "Interpreting Soil Geographic Databases," D.J. Lytle and M.J. Mausbach, pp. 469-476.)

Three PSU points in a 160 acre PSU
overlayed on a SSURGO soil map.

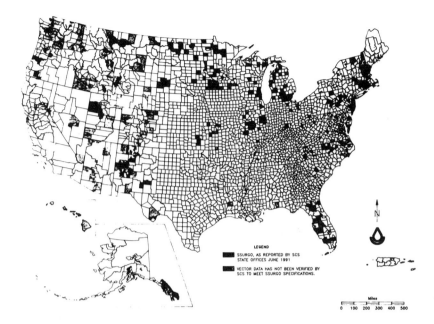

FIGURE 4.6   The June 1991 status map of the soil survey geographic databases (SSURGO) (USDA 1991a).

Attribute Databases

The Soil Interpretation Record (SIR or SOIL-5) database contains estimated values for more than 25 properties of more than 30,000 soil series and phases of soil series in the United States. These property or attribute values define the expected range of values for the site and major layer (horizon) of a soil series. The properties included are site characteristics including mean annual air temperature, precipitation, elevation, frost free days, and drainage; and horizon attributes including particle size distribution, bulk density, permeability, organic matter, available water capacity, soil reaction, salinity, cation exchange capacity, sodium absorption ratio, gypsum, and calcium carbonate equivalent. Estimates of flooding potential, water table depth, depth to bedrock, shrink-swell, and potential frost action characteristics are also listed.

Soil property data are recorded in SIR as an estimated range of values because soils in the landscape occur naturally in a continuum, not as discrete entities. Hence, all map units have inclusions of other soil series with similar and/or dissimilar properties. Soil survey guidelines (USDA 1983) specify that no more than 25 percent of a mapping unit should be comprised of dissimilar soils. Wilding (1988) and colleagues attempted to quantify the spatial variability of a number of soil properties within mapping units of

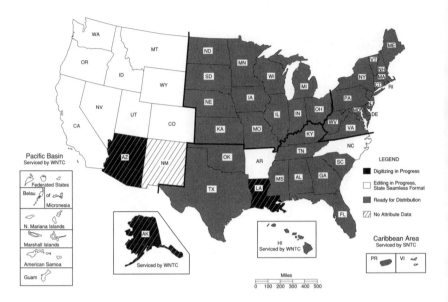

FIGURE 4.7   Status map of the state soil geographic database (STATSGO) (Map provided by the U.S. Department of Agriculture).

soil surveys. Their findings are recorded in Table 4.2 as the mean and range in coefficients of variation observed for various soil properties included in SIR. The section on uncertainty analysis in Chapter 3 contains information on other approaches to estimating uncertainty associated with soil properties.

A subset of SIR that contains most of the soil properties applicable for ground water vulnerability assessments is being compiled in ASCII formatted direct access files as the soil database used in the NLEAP model (Shaffer et al. 1991). Soil attributes have been depth weighted for the top 0.3 meter of soil (layer 1) and the rest of the profile (layer 2). This database contains a complete set of data for all soil series entries, and has been subjected to numerous internal checks of the data to assure consistency between various soil attributes, added missing data, and corrected erroneous entries. Significant attention was devoted to improved estimates for *in situ* permeability, water holding capacity, and water content at 15 kPa, including adjustments based on soil mineralogical composition as manifested through soil cation exchange capacity. The data are single valued and linked to SSURGO map units through the soil name and identification number of SIR. This database contains approximately 80 percent (most cropland) of SIR and all sand-textured soils exceeding 800 ha in area.

The Map Unit Use File (MUUF) database includes the name and sym-

TABLE 4.2 Relative Variability of Selected Soil Properties Sampled
Within Mapping Units of Soil Series (Adapted from Wilding 1988)

Soil Property	Coefficient of Variability (CV), % Mean	Range	Relative Order of Soil Variability
Bulk density	7	5-13	Least variable (CVs
Soil pH	10	5-15	commonly less than 15%)
A horizon thickness	18	8-31	
Water retention (1/3 bar)	18	10-31	
Base saturation	25	17-33	Moderately variable (CVs
Total sand content	25	8-46	commonly between 16-35%)
Total clay content	25	10-61	
Calcium carbonate equivalent	28	20-30	
Depth to carbonates	30	20-49	
Cation exchange capacity	32	20-40	
Depth to mottling	35	20-50	
Organic matter content	39	20-61	
Soil thickness	43	25-58	
Exchangeable Ca	48	30-73	Most variable (CVs
Exchangeable K	57	7-160	commonly between 36-70%)
Exchangeable Mg	58	31-121	
Estimated hydraulic conductivity	75	13-150	

Note: The coefficient of variability (CV) values represent variations for equivalent horizons and/or depths.

bol of each soil map unit in more than 2,600 soil survey areas. In addition, where available, acreage, percent composition of different taxonomic units, and SIR numbers to link SIR data with map unit components are included. When the MUUF database is combined with subsets of estimated soil properties from SIR, the resulting Map Unit Interpretation Record (MUIR) forms a database specific to phases of soil series in a given survey area. The Official Soil Series Description (OSED) database contains the narrative description of each soil series, while the Soil Classification File (SC) stores the taxonomic classification of the more than 18,000 soil series. Collectively, data in OSED, SC, and SIR define a soil series.

Site-Specific Databases

Site-specific or point data, often called hard data (Mausbach et al. 1989), are generated by field sampling of pedons for laboratory characterization and morphological description in support of soil surveys. These data are used for definition of soil series in OSED and SIR databases. However, these data seldom represent the entire suite of properties embodied in the central concept of a soil series (Mausbach et al. 1989). Currently, a National Soil Characterization Database (NSCDB) is being designed to house pedon data collected by SCS at the national level and by cooperating land grant universities at the state level.

Discussion

Collectively, SSURGO, STATSGO, and NATSGO, and their associated databases can be useful in many methods available for assessing ground water vulnerability. SSURGO data are typically used at scales from the farm field level to multicounty level; STATSGO data may be useful at the multicounty to state level; and NATSGO data are intended for use at the multistate to national level. Primary limitations of these databases for vulnerability assessments can be characterized as follows: (1) soil attribute data in SIR are presented as ranges of soil properties rather than as measures of central tendency and associated variance, (2) SSURGO is not linked with digital elevation data, (3) contribution of macropores to water flow through the soil profile is difficult to evaluate, (4) location of appropriate sampling sites for characterization of a given soil parameter may not be related to soil taxonomy, and (5) the validity of transforming from field to state and national scale has not been demonstrated for either data or models.

Several efforts are currently under way to address some of these limitations. The NSCDB, which, in part, will replace SIR database, will incorporate site-specific, experimental data, including data means, variances, and associated uncertainties. The development of NSCDB will require the identification of the specific pedon that best describes the dominant soil series phase of each soil map unit. These data, compiled in NSCDB and linked to SSURGO, will represent the landscape more accurately and give planners and managers a better appraisal of the vulnerability of ground water to contamination in specific areas.

A listing of additional data needs would be endless if it reflected the needs of every potential assessment technique. However, particularly important soil parameters for assessing vulnerability are the *in situ* hydraulic properties of the soil profile and the soil organic carbon content. When these and other data are not available, empirical functions are used to approximate these properties based on other soil parameters (e.g., soil pH, bulk density). Inclusion of these properties in NSCDB will improve the reliability of assessments requiring these data.

The linkage of SSURGO to digital elevation data would allow for a better understanding of water movement across and into soil. This linkage would also enhance the accuracy of soil maps generated during field mapping. In addition, incorporation of the location, extent, and description of inclusions within a given soil map unit in SSURGO would improve the utility of these data for vulnerability assessments. This task could be partially achieved by soil survey at a scale of 1:12,000. Vulnerability assessments at the field and watershed scale must consider land use and spatial and temporal variability of the land surface as they affect water movement across and into soil.

The development of digital soil geographic databases has not kept pace with demand. One major obstacle to automating the soil map, especially in the Midwest and the South, is that most current soil surveys were mapped and published on aerial photobases that do not meet National Map Accuracy Standards, now required by SCS. These maps must be meticulously recompiled to 7.5 minute topographic quadrangles or orthophotoquads before digitizing. This process must assure that line placement and data integrity are maintained. SCS has no active program to digitize detailed soil surveys for inclusion in SSURGO. Emphasis has been on digitizing ongoing surveys, with limited resources directed toward recompiling and digitizing published surveys, which are often the most critical for automated resource planning and analysis.

HYDROGEOLOGY

The properties of materials in the porous media below the soil zone, coupled with differences in the elevation of the water table, which is time-dependent, control movement of contaminants in the subsurface once they pass through the soil zone. Hydrogeologic databases incorporate details on water table configuration, subsurface geology, and hydraulic properties of saturated consolidated and unconsolidated geologic units. Often information in hydrogeologic databases is synthesized into a series of maps showing the areal and vertical extent of geologic units having similar hydraulic properties (e.g., hydraulic conductivity, porosity, and storage properties), the ability of geologic units to deliver water to wells, and directions of ground water flow.

Characteristics and Availability of Data

Currently, there is no national compilation of hydrogeologic data that can be used easily as a database or map. The U.S. Geological Survey, as part of its ongoing Regional Aquifer-System Analysis (RASA) program, produces maps showing basic hydrogeologic data at variuos scales. A *Ground Water Atlas of the United States* is being developed as part of the RASA program; the first of 13 planned multistate sections of the atlas has been published (Miller 1990). The Geological Society of America recently started to develop hydrostratigraphic (Maxey 1964) nomenclature for the United

States (Seaber 1988) at a regional scale that may have limited use in practice (NRC 1988). Several states, such as Minnesota and Wisconsin, have prepared statewide and larger scale hydrogeologic maps. A major product of most of these efforts is a generalized hydrogeologic map showing areal variability in aquifer material properties in the context of well yield or well capacity. Statewide hydrogeologic assessments of this type were used extensively by Pettyjohn et al. (1991) in their national assessment of ground water vulnerability and can be obtained by inquiries to individual state departments of natural resources or similar agencies.

Discussion

The establishment of a more useful hydrogeologic database at a national level is in its infancy, mostly because of the lack of good geologic mapping; the areal coverage of geologic maps at large map scales in the United States is scant at best (NRC 1988). Less than 20 percent of the continental United States has been mapped geologically at a standard scale of 1:24,000 or larger (NRC 1988)—one of the proportionally smallest national geological map bases in the developed world (Haney 1991). Although the U.S. Geological Survey and state geologic surveys are mandated to prepare geologic maps, these efforts have received low priority due to funding limitations. For example, USGS mapping in the 1980s was only a quarter of that done in the 1960s.

Geologic maps at sufficiently large scales provide the lithologic and structural data from which the information found in SCS soil maps can be placed in a larger context, particularly if lithologic facies are identified (e.g., Anderson 1989). Geologic and hydrogeologic maps, however, are only progress reports, whose accuracy depends on scale and the expertise of the scientist doing the mapping. State line and regional differences in nomenclature confound synthesis of some maps, whereas in some parts of the country (e.g., Canadian shield and glacial drift in parts of the midwestern United States), geologic units and surficial deposits are mapped as undifferentiated.

While the accessibility and national coverage of large scale geologic maps are poor, that of the national and state databases for basic hydrogeologic and subsurface information are even more scant, especially where there is no active mineral or hydrocarbon exploration history. Subsurface and hydraulic information must be compiled from individual well logs or soil boring data, usually found in state environmental agencies or geologic survey offices. The quality of these data and the extent to which such files are maintained are highly variable. Some states, such as Minnesota, require that all drillers submit to the state all well logs, measured water levels, and other hydraulic data, which are then digitized and stored as readily accessible computer files. From a synthesis of these data and geologic maps, high quality large scale hydrogeologic maps are being prepared (e.g., Kanivetsky 1989a, b; Piaget 1989). In contrast, some states keep no systematic record of well logs, although subsurface data are available in consulting reports and published literature.

Finally, little attention has been paid to development of a national or regional effort to characterize the stratigraphic column between the upper 1.5 meters, which is investigated by soil scientists, and the water table. Although research in vadose zone hydrology is expanding, most studies are highly site-specific and no regional compilation of data has been made. In places like the Southwest, the vadose zone can be hundreds to thousands of meters thick, and its properties arguably will have a large effect on whether contaminants reach the water table.

WEATHER AND CLIMATE

Weather and climate can have significant influence on the transport of materials from the soil surface to the water table. Water from precipitation or irrigation is the main transport agent for most pollutants that affect ground water quality. Weather and climate elements important to water quality are: (1) precipitation, including intensities and timing of precipitation events, (2) solar radiation, (3) wind speed, (4) air temperature, (5) relative humidity, (6) potential evaporation, and (7) air quality variables.

Characteristics and Availability of Data

The National Weather Service (NWS) is the federal agency responsible for coordinating, collecting, maintaining, and distributing climate data. It operates a data collection network of some 8,000 weather stations producing the daily and monthly precipitation and temperature information that forms the backbone of our nation's climate database. This information was initially collected to evaluate climate in populated areas, and also used for weather prediction and flood warnings. Later, weather stations were placed in areas around airports to assist in aviation control. This arrangement has served the country well except in the less populated western third which has been sparsely covered with weather stations in mountain areas, which are natural water supply producing areas. As a result, several natural resource oriented agencies, such as the Forest Service, SCS, National Park Service, Bureau of Land Management, Bureau of Reclamation, and Bureau of Indian Affairs, and similar state government and university entities have developed climate data collection systems and databases to suit their own needs in their areas of jurisdiction. Also, agency coordination in climate data collection and management has increased as a result of a more integrated approach to environmental and natural resource planning.

Existing climate databases are limited in terms of geographic coverage of climate data, data formats, data homogeneity, data quality, period of record, data record serial completeness, computerized availability, and/or timeliness. Many long term NWS data records in urban areas are largely unadjusted for the dramatic urban and industrial growth during this century. Of the 8,000 currently active U.S. weather stations, only 492 have been checked for instrument and location changes and adjusted for population (Hughes et al. 1991). Data from other stations are not representative of larger, more rural regions, complicating comprehensive spatial climate analysis. Urbanization has been most dramatic in affecting temperatures (particularly summer minimums) and to some extent precipitation, although urban effects on precipitation are more difficult to quantify.

Precipitation data have high spatial variability and are needed not just in daily increments but in hourly and 15 minute intervals to fully evaluate pollutant transport through the soil profile. Wintertime precipitation in cold regions of the country and particularly in the western U.S. in the form of ice or snow is very important in the evaluation of airborne dry or storm deposited pollutants. The mountain snowpack delays release of airborne pollutants accumulated in its layers until spring when the snowpack profiles become isothermal or otherwise have free water passing through. This situation creates significant short-term high concentrations of the pollutants (Sommerfeld et al. 1990). Since more than 70 percent of the water that flows in the West comes from melting mountain snows, this phenomenon is critical to subsequent water quality.

Solar radiation, relative humidity, and wind information are collected sparsely, mostly at aviation centers. For other areas this information requires considerable estimation and extrapolation for spatial analysis. Potential evaporation information also is collected sparsely, usually in areas where irrigation water management has required the data to guide water use and maximize crop production. Air quality data, except in populous areas, are scant, providing an inadequate database for spatial analysis.

Although not necessarily part of a climate database, soil moisture and soil temperature, important factors in chemical fate and transport, are sparsely observed nationwide. A 1991 SCS pilot project monitoring global climatic change identified more than 300 separate collection efforts for these two soil parameters. This information is in a variety of formats, specifications, and quality (USDA 1991b). However, much of this data collection is driven by irrigation water management needs, which do not necessarily match the data needs for ground water vulnerability assessments.

Several regional and national efforts are attempting to index climate information available from many sources for common use. A catalog of

215 U.S. Department of Commerce climate data sets has been prepared by the NWS (NOAA 1988), most of which are available either as microfiche or nine-track tape. The most extensive of these efforts is the Historical Climate Network (HCN) archived by the National Climatic Data Center (NCDC). It contains monthly values for precipitation and maximum/minimum temperature for 1,219 U.S. weather stations active in 1987 with at least 80 years of data record. The HCN contains both unadjusted and adjusted data, where the adjustments are for station moves and instrument or recording changes. An elaborate set of missing data and error codes are provided to aid in the interpretation and use of these data. The HCN is generally believed to be the most accurate database describing U.S. climate.

Several companies and government agencies have edited the NWS data and repackaged it for sale or their own use. EarthInfo Incorporated of Boulder, Colorado, has produced a CD-ROM version of Historical Climate Network which includes a user interface for the personal computer. WeatherDisc Associates of Seattle, Washington has produced a CD-ROM called World WeatherDisc which includes monthly average weather data for 5,511 NWS and cooperative stations from 1951 to 1980, as well as ten other climate data sets. IBM's Watson Research Laboratory (Wallis et al. 1991) has produced a CD-ROM containing the unadjusted daily and monthly values for 1,036 HCN sites from 1948 to 1988. This data set is serially complete, with missing data filled by correlation; obvious errors and missing values are flagged, and HCN codes and monthly differences from HCN values are recorded.

An on-line interactive operational database of all the snow survey data archived over the past 70 years for the western United States is available through the SCS. These data include snow depth, water equivalent, and associated precipitation and temperature.

During the 1980s, the NOAA National Climate Program established six Regional Climate Centers (RCCs) to provide services tailored to regional climate requirements. Many climate information providers collect climate data from RCC established networks or from agencies under RCC contract or data archiving services.

Three other major efforts are under way to develop better climate databases for the United States. The Climatic Data Access Facility (CDAF) was established by SCS in 1990 to assess, obtain, evaluate, manage, and disseminate climatic data and analyses needed to support the agency's water management and environmental modeling activities. One of the CDAF's goals is to provide error free, serially complete, spatially representative, and timely data through a network of climatic data liaisons to the nearly 3,000 SCS field offices nationwide. Currently the NCDC TD-3200 daily data set and SCS's Snow Telemetry (SNOTEL) data set are on-line and accessible through the CDAF's Centralized Database System (CDBS). The CDBS now contains corrected daily temperature and precipitation data (Reek et al. 1992) and is expected to begin inclusion of spatial estimates of missing data to create serially complete data in 1993.

The U.S. Environmental Protection Agency (EPA) Global Change Database Program is producing a Global Ecosystem Data Set on a CD-ROM. The disc will contain locational data on soils, slope, aspect, elevation, vegetative cover, and climate, including monthly minimum and maximum temperature and precipitation. The data set has 10 minute resolution (approximately 13 by 18 km spacing), although the original resolution of some data was 0.5 degree.

The NWS's new Advanced Weather Information Processing System (AWIPS) uses state-of-the-art computer work stations to process information from Next Generation Radar (NEXRAD) sites and automated data networks. AWIPS will provide a highly sophisticated tool for weather forecasting as well as integrated spatial analysis and modeling of climatic data associated with specific storms. The system is expected to be a significant new source of computer derived spatial information for use in calibration of spatial data extrapolation models. Over the next decade AWIPS and NEXRAD will be implemented nationwide.

Discussion

Currently no U.S. climate database has adequate elevational and spatial coverage to define the great variability of climatic factors that exist, provides information consistent in format and quality, and makes it widely accessible to users by telecommunications and other means. However, this situation is receiving significant attention from the many agencies involved, and serious attempts are being made to improve data collection and archiving.

LAND USE AND LAND COVER

Land use and land cover (LULC) descriptions are used to provide insight on ground water vulnerability to contamination. LULC designations provide general descriptions of the natural and cultural activities taking place at the Earth's surface, and are broadly indicative of the kinds of contaminants likely to be available for leaching, including naturally occurring ones. For example, a cropland land use designation would indicate the potential for agrichemical use. An urban classification would suggest a different set of potential contaminants. The type of land cover affects how much precipitation and irrigation water infiltrates the ground, and how much water, nutrients, and other chemicals are taken up by plants.

Characteristics and Availability of Data

LULC data are usually represented as either mapped areas with associated attributes, or statistical indices for given areas such as a county or state. In both instances, data are collected using a standardized classification scheme. Most land use or land cover mapping projects manually interpret areas from remotely sensed imagery and then digitize class boundaries.

The classification scheme applied to LULC data is perhaps the most critical factor in determining the value of this information for ground water vulnerability assessment. For example, classes that are useful for forestry applications may not be appropriate for hydrologic investigations and vice versa. The spatial resolution of LULC data is also critical to use of these data. Large polygons generally will be more heterogeneous than smaller ones, and it is therefore more difficult to estimate meaningful average values for large polygons.

Land use and land cover are important data elements for many agencies of the federal government (USGS 1992). These data are used to evaluate current status, changing conditions, and resources over large areas in support of agency initiatives and planning operations. Many agencies have been digitizing existing and collecting new LULC data for their specific purposes, resulting in a mixture of data formats, LULC classification systems, and scales and accuracies.

The USGS is producing LULC maps and associated files for the entire United States. Most of the available files have been digitized using the Geographic Information Retrieval and Analysis System (GIRAS) format, and are available as either vector or raster files. The data are distributed in 1 degree of latitude by 2 degrees of longitude corresponding to the standard 1:250,000 topographic mapping series. The minimum resolution for GIRAS data is 4 hectares in urban and built-up lands and 16 hectares in other areas. The GIRAS digital data provide LULC information using the Level II Anderson classification (Anderson et al. 1976). Digital LULC data are distributed by the USGS/NMD on nine-track tape and will be distributed soon on CD-ROM disks.

Many other federal agencies, such as the Forest Service, Bureau of Land Management, Tennessee Valley Authority, and Fish and Wildlife Service, have collected their own LULC data or have modified existing GIRAS files. Many state and local government agencies also have extensive LULC data collection programs, primarily at the 1:24,000 scale.

Discussion

LULC data are by nature transitional—each file provides only a snapshot of the environment at one point in time. Vulnerability assessment methods may require LULC information at discrete times to analyze the environment properly. Currently, the USGS has available comprehensive LULC data for the United States. As currently planned, future LULC data collection will be user driven and not collected on a routine repeat basis. In the past, USGS acquisition of LULC data has been slow, and the data for adjacent quadrangles may have been collected years apart and by differing interpreters using different collection techniques. In these circumstances, the resulting data are variable in their spatial accuracy and attribute quality. For these reasons, users of vulnerability assessment methods may need to seek additional sources of LULC data (e.g., interpretation of synoptic satellite data).

The Level II Anderson classification scheme used by the USGS is detailed enough for simple applications and provides the framework for more specific information where additional detail is needed. However, data requirements for more complex or comprehensive methods may quickly outdistance the attribute characteristics of this scheme. For example, Anderson Level II does not distinguish pasture land from cropland or irrigated from nonirrigated lands, yet these factors may affect vulnerability significantly.

The 1987 Agricultural Census and 1987 National Resources Inventory (NRI) are additional sources of land use information for state and national assessments. The data collection techniques and classification schemes differ between the Agricultural Census and the NRI, making comparisons of data difficult. The Agricultural Stabilization and Conservation Service (ASCS) and SCS land use and land cover data collected at the farm and ranch level are valuable because of their level of detail and currency, however, they lack a digital geographic reference.

The utility of digital LULC data for ground water vulnerability studies and other applications could be enhanced by the development of a standard LULC classification scheme to achieve consistency in data at the national scale. The development of such a classification scheme will require cooperation among scientists, other user groups, and image interpretation specialists. The scheme should include hydrologically significant land use classes developed to support vulnerability assessments and other ground water investigations.

In addition, much more thought should be given to mapping land cover as a mutually exclusive data category, with land use attributes added to the cover polygons as appropriate. The existing Anderson classification scheme intermixes land use and land cover categories so that a single land use or single land cover classification is not possible. Ancillary land use and land cover attributes would enhance the utility of the simple classification scheme now in use. Examples might include estimates of surface roughness, amount of impermeable surface, and type of cultural features present.

Since land use and land cover are dynamic attributes (agricultural cropping practices change annually and seasonally), data collection programs should be completed quickly to create a database that is, ideally, specific to a given year.

MANAGEMENT FACTORS

Ideally, management factors such as plant growth, tillage and other soil disturbances with their associated ground cover conditions, irrigation, drainage, conservation practices, grazing, and agrichemical applications should be considered when conducting a ground water vulnerability assessment (USDA 1992). Not all these factors are described in national or regional databases; however, several databases are worthy of note because they address some of these factors, including the National Resources Inventory, the National Agricultural Census of 1987, the Irrigation Water Use Survey of 1988, and several pesticide databases.

Characteristics and Availability of Data

National Resources Inventory

The National Resources Inventory (NRI) is a multiresource inventory conducted at five-year intervals by the SCS. Data are collected at approximately 800,000 points on nonfederal lands and include information on soils, land cover, land use, cropping history, conservation practices, conservation treatment needs, potential cropland, prime farmland, highly erodible cropland, water and wind erosion, wetlands, wildlife habitat, vegetative cover conditions, irrigation, and flood susceptibility. In 1982 and 1992, sufficient sample information was collected to characterize major land resource areas (MLRAs). In 1987, however, fewer areas were sampled allowing for good characterization at the state level. For nonfederal lands, the NRI is one of the most comprehensive and consistent databases for national resource analysis and is one of the few that links soil type with management factors such as conservation practices, land use, land cover condition, and irrigation.

Agricultural Census of 1987

The Bureau of the Census conducts an agricultural census every five years. The 1987 census includes statistical information by county about farm numbers, farm value, farm size, market value of agricultural products, farm income, farm expenses, farm land use, farm irrigation, agricultural chemical use, livestock and poultry operations, crops and vegetables harvested, fruits, nuts, and berry production, and nursery and greenhouse crops.

Farm and Ranch Irrigation Survey

The 1987 Agricultural Census has been supplemented by a special survey of irrigators, which contains tabulations of irrigation data on U.S. farms and ranches in 1988. It provides county level data that relate water use to crops produced, sources of the water, and the technology used to apply irrigation water (USDC 1990).

Pesticide Databases

The EPA's Pesticides in Ground Water Database identifies the pesticides that have been looked for in ground water, the areas monitored, and the pesticides detected. The EPA is using this database to identify areas where pesticide use has been a problem in order to evaluate the need for restricted usage. This database may be made available in the future in electronic form from EPA's Pesticide Information Network.

An agrichemical use database compiled by Resources For The Future, Inc., is called the National Herbicide Use Database of 1989-90. It summarizes use of 96 herbicides on 84 crops on a county basis.

The USDA National Agricultural Statistics Service (NASS) has recently initiated a survey of the type and quantity of pesticides used on major crops. Initial data were gathered for pesticides on cotton in 1989. NASS has expanded the survey to corn, soybeans, sorghum, wheat, rice, peanuts, potatoes, vegetables, and fruits for 1990 and 1991.

The Pesticide Properties Database compiled by the SCS, Agricultural Research Service, and Extension Service (ES) describes the fate and transport characteristic of about 300 pesticides by crop and soil type. This database has been linked to the SCS soil databases to assist SCS and others in assessing pesticide leaching potential past the root zone.

Field Level Databases

Two agencies in the USDA, the Agriculture Stabilization and Conservation Service (ASCS) and the SCS, collect land information such as land cover and use, irrigation, drainage, crop history, crop yield, erosion rates, and conservation practices such as terracing and residue management for farmers and ranchers who participate in USDA farm programs. This information is collected on a farm field or ranch pasture basis and exists in digital tabular form for much of the country's private croplands. Field or pasture boundaries are drawn on aerial photographs at scales from 1:7,920 to 1:12,000, but are not available in digital form.

The extensive farm field and ranch pasture boundaries collected by ASCS and SCS need to be geo-referenced to be useful in a digital domain.

If this is done and a standard classification system is adopted, this database would no doubt be one of the most valuable available for ground water vulnerability assessment of private lands at the county, watershed, and field levels. An accurate photo-image base, such as an orthophotograph, would need to be used instead of an aerial photograph in order to meet national standards and permit effective sharing of these data with others.

CONCLUSION

Assessment of ground water vulnerability to contamination is a complex task requiring information contained in a variety of geographic databases maintained by federal, state, and local agencies. Early efforts in compiling spatially-referenced data resulted in analog outputs (i.e., paper maps), but more recent efforts have led increasingly to data stored in digital formats. Currently, such databases are used routinely in a wide range of applications, including vulnerability assessments, to produce thematic maps for policy makers and resource management. The production of thematic maps, and similar decision aids, requires retrieval, transfer, manipulation, interpretation, and analysis of the digital information.

Since these data and information have been collected and maintained by a number of entities and for differing purposes, a myriad of problems have been encountered in their use. The National Research Council's Mapping Science Committee (MSC) recently reported that lack of coordination has resulted in duplicative efforts among the federal agencies, at significant cost to the public, and that existing spatial data may not always be compatible or reliable (NRC 1993). On this basis, the MSC report argued for the development of the National Spatial Data Infrastructure (NSDI), which is defined as the "total ensemble of geographic information at our disposal" as well as all the other resources required to use such information. The MSC concluded that "unless a vision for the National Spatial Data Infrastructure exists and the spatial data bases, policies, and standards are in place to facilitate the access and use of the spatial data on a national scale, opportunities in areas from environment to development will be lost."

The MSC report also recommends that federal efforts expand beyond the compilation of various types of spatial databases and development of standards for data exchange to include "more specific measures and standards of content, quality, currency, and performance of various components" of the proposed NSDI. It is not enough to have easy access to existing spatial data; it is important to know how good is the information contained in these databases. The MSC also recommends that base data (also referred to as minimum data sets in some modeling literature) required for small-, medium-, and large-scale applications of spatial data be identified. Base data requirements for vulnerability assessments are clearly needed.

Increasing use of thematic maps, and other decision aids, based on existing spatial databases has begun to point the need for additional data or for data of better quality. However, allocation of additional federal funds is unlikely for collection of new spatial databases, at least not for traditional approaches used in the past to collect the existing spatial databases. Thus, our attention must be focused on innovative, cost-effective techniques for gathering new spatial data. For example, Engman and Gurney (1991) and Dozier (1992) have reviewed the use of a broad spectrum of remote sensing techniques for gathering data required for describing hydrologic processes over a wide range of spatial and temporal scales. They discuss the more established remote sensing techniques based on earth-orbiting satellites, as well as the emerging remote sensing techniques (e.g., ground-penetrating radar and tomographic reconstruction) for the local-scale characterizations of subsurface hydrogeologic features. In addition, there exists a wealth of analog maps and photographs that could be converted to the more useful digital format.

The collection and synthesis of existing spatial databases has involved the extraordinary efforts of a large number of technical experts. The challenge is to meet the present and future spatial data needs without having to expend similarly tremendous efforts. Meeting this challenge will require close coordination among those who generate the spatial databases and those who use them for a variety of policy and management purposes.

REFERENCES

Anderson, M.P. 1989. Hydrogeologic facies models to delineate large-scale spacial trends in glacial and glaciofluvial sediments. Geological Society America Bulletin 101:501-511.

Anderson, J.R., E.E. Hardy, J.T. Roach, and R.E. Witmer. 1976. A Land Use and Land Cover Classification System for Use with Remote Sensor Data. Professional Paper 964. U.S. Geological Survey.

Bliss, N.B., and W.U. Reybold. 1989. Small-scale digital soil maps for interpreting natural resources. Journal of Soil Water Conservation 44:30-34.

Dozier, J. 1992. Opportunities to improve hydrologic data. Reviews of Geophysics 30(4):315-331.

Engman, E.T., and R.J. Gurney. 1991. Remote Sensing in Hydrology. London: Chapman and Hall.

Haney, D. 1991. Geologic Mapping—a National Issue. GSA Today, Geological Society of America, July, 1991, p. 143-1344.

Hughes, P.Y., E.H. Mason, T.R. Karl, and W.A. Brower. 1991. United States Historical Climatology Network Daily (HCN/D) Temperature and Precipitation Data. ORNL/CDIAC-50, NDP-042. Oak Ridge, Tennessee: Carbon Dioxide Information Analysis Center, Oak Ridge National Laboratory.

Kanivetsky, R. 1989a. Quaternary Hydrogeology. Geologic Atlas Hennepin County, Minnesota. N.H. Balaban, ed. County Atlas Series Atlas C-4. St. Paul: Minnesota Geological Survey.

Kanivetsky, R. 1989b. Bedrock Hydrogeology. Geologic Atlas Hennepin County, Minnesota.

N.H. Balaban, ed. County Atlas Series Atlas C-4. St. Paul: Minnesota Geological Survey.

Lytle, D.J., and M.J. Mausbach. 1991. Interpreting soil geographic databases. Pp. 469-476 in Proc. Resource Tech. 90, Second Intern. Sym. Adv. Tech. in Nat'l. Resource Manag., Washington, D.C., Nov. 12-15, 1990. Bethesda, Maryland: Amer. Soc. Photo. and Remote Sensing.

Mausbach, M.J., D.L. Anderson, and R.W. Arnold. 1989. Soil survey databases and their uses. Pp. 659-664 in Proc. Computer Simulation Conf., Austin, TX. July 24-27, 1989. San Diego, California: Soc. Computer Simul.

Maxey, G.B. 1964. Hydrostratigraphic units. Journal of Hydrology 2:124-129.

Miller, J.A. 1990. Ground Water Atlas of the United States: Segment 6—Alabama, Florida, Georgia, and South Carolina. Hydrologic Investigations Atlas 730-G. Reston, Virginia: U.S. Geological Survey.

Mollering, H., ed. 1988. Proposed standard for digital cartographic data. The American Cartographer 15(1):11-140.

National Research Council (NRC). 1988. Geologic Mapping: Future Needs. Washington D.C.: National Academy Press. 84 p.

National Research Council (NRC). 1993. Towards a Coordinated Spatial Data Infrastructure for the Nation. Washington, D.C.: National Academy Press.

National Institute of Standards and Technology (NIST). 1992. Federal Information Data Processing Standard 173. Gaithersburg, Maryland: National Institute of Standards and Technology.

National Oceanic and Atmospheric Administration (NOAA). 1988. Selective Guide to Climatic Data Sources. National Environmental Satellite and Data Information Service, National Climatic Data Center. Washington D.C.: U.S. Department of Commerce.

Office of Management and Budget (OMB). 1990. Circular A-16. Washington, D.C.: Office of Management and Budget.

Pettyjohn, W.A., M. Savoca, and D. Self. 1991. Regional Assessment of Aquifer Vulnerability and Sensitivity in the Conterminous United States. EPA-600/RSKERL-Ada-9141. Washington, D.C.: U.S. Environmental Protection Agency.

Piaget, J. 1989. Sensitivity of Ground-Water Systems to Pollution. Geologic Atlas Hennepin County, Minnesota. N.H. Balaban, ed. County Atlas Series Atlas C-4.

Reek, T., S. Doty, and T. Owen. 1992. A deterministic approach to validation of historical daily temperature and precipitation data from the cooperative network. Bulletin of the American Meteorological Society 73:753-762.

Reybold, W.U., and G.W. TeSelle. 1989. Soil geographic databases. Journal of Soil and Water Conservation 44:28-29.

Seaber, P.R. 1988. Hydrostratigraphic units. Pp. 9-14 (Chapter 2) in The Geology of North America, Vol. 0-2, W. Back, J.S. Rosensehein, and P.R. Seaber, eds. Boulder, Colorado: Geological Society of America.

Shaffer, M.J., A.D. Halvorson, and F.J. Pierce. 1991. Nitrate leaching and economic analysis package (NLEAP): Model description and application. Pp. 285-322 in Managing Nitrogen for Groundwater Quality and Farm Profitability, R.F. Follett, D.R. Keeney, and R.M. Cruse, eds. Madison, Wisconsin: Soil Science Society America.

Soil Science Society of America (SSSA). 1987. Glossary of Soil Science Terms. Madison, Wisconsin: Soil Science Soc. Amer.

Sommerfeld, R.A., D.G. Fox, and R.C. Musselman. 1990. Snow in Mountain Watersheds: Connection to Climate and Ecosystem Health. Fort Collins, Colorado: Rocky Mountain Forest Experiment Station.

U.S. Department of Agriculture (USDA). 1975. Soil Taxonomy: A Basic System of Soil

Classification for Making and Interpreting Soil Surveys. Soil Conservation Service. Agric. Handbook No. 436. Washington, D.C.: U.S. Government Printing Office.

U.S. Department of Agriculture (USDA). 1979. National Resources Inventory Instructions. 1981-82. Washington, D.C.: USDA, Soil Conservation Service.

U.S. Department of Agriculture (USDA). 1981. Land Resource Regions and Major Land Resource Areas of the United States. Agriculture Handbook No. 296. Washington, D.C.: USDA, Soil Conservation Service.

U.S. Department of Agriculture (USDA). 1983. National Soils Handbook. Soil Conservation Service. Washington, D.C.: U.S. Government Printing Office.

U.S. Department of Agriculture (USDA). 1991a. Digital Soil Data. Washington, D.C.: USDA, Soil Conservation Service.

U.S. Department of Agriculture (USDA). 1991b. A National Inventory of Soil Moisture and Temperature Data Sets. USDA Soil Conservation Service Global Climate Change Pilot Project. Portland, Oregon: U.S. Department of Agriculture.

U.S. Department of Agriculture (USDA). 1992. Water Quality Modeling User Requirements. Draft 4.0 June 1992. Washington, D.C.: Agricultural Research Service, Extention Source, and Soil Conservation Service.

U.S. Department of Commerce (USDC). 1990. 1987 Census of Agriculture; Volume 3: Related Surveys; Part 1: Farm and Ranch Irrigation Survey (1988). Washington, D.C.: U.S. Department of Commerce.

U.S. General Accounting Office (GAO). 1982. Duplicative Federal Computer-Mapping Programs: A Growing Problem. GAO/RCED-83-19. Gaithersburg, Maryland: U.S. General Accounting Office.

U.S. Geological Survey (USGS). 1992. Forum on Land Use & Land Cover: Summary Report. Reston, Virginia: U.S. Geological Survey.

Wallis, J.R., D.P. Lettenmaier, and E.F. Wood. 1991. A daily hydroclimatological data set for the continental United States. Water Resources Research 27(7):1657-1663.

Warnecke, L., J.M. Johnson, K. Marshall, and R.S. Brown. 1992. State Geographic Information Systems Activities Compendium. Lexington, Kentucky: The Council of State Governments.

Wilding, L.P. 1985. Spatial variability: Its documentation, accommodation and implication to soil surveys. Pp. 166-167 in Soil Spatial Variability, D.R. Nielsen, and J. Bouma, eds. Wageningen, The Netherlands: Pudoc. Publishers.

Wilding, L.P. 1988. Improving our understanding of the composition of the soil landscape. Pp. 13-35 in Proceedings of the International Interactive Workshop on Soil Resources: Their Inventory, Analysis and Interpretation for Use in the 1990's, H.R. Finney, ed. St. Paul: Minn. Extension Service, Univ. of Minnesota.

5

Case Studies

INTRODUCTION

This chapter presents six case studies of uses of different methods to assess ground water vulnerability to contamination. These case examples demonstrate the wide range of applications for which ground water vulnerability assessments are being conducted in the United States. While each application presented here is directed toward the broad goal of protecting ground water, each is unique in its particular management requirements. The intended use of the assessment, the types of data available, the scale of the assessments, the required resolution, the physical setting, and institutional factors all led to very different vulnerability assessment approaches. In only one of the cases presented here, Hawaii, are attempts made to quantify the uncertainty associated with the assessment results.

IOWA

Introduction

Ground water contamination became an important political and environmental issue in Iowa in the mid-1980s. Research reports, news headlines, and public debates noted the increasing incidence of contaminants in rural and urban well waters. The *Iowa Groundwater Protection Strategy* (Hoyer et al. 1987) indicated that levels of nitrate in both private and municipal wells were increasing. More than 25 percent of the state's population was served by water with concentrations of nitrate above 22 milligrams per liter (as NO_3). Similar increases were noted in detections of pesticides in public water supplies; about 27 percent of the population was periodically consuming low concentrations of pesticides in their drinking water. The situation in private wells which tend to be shallower than public wells may have been even worse.

Defining the Question

Most prominent among the sources of ground water contamination were fertilizers and pesticides used in agriculture. Other sources included urban use of lawn chemicals, industrial discharges, and landfills. The pathways of ground water contamination were disputed. Some interests argued that contamination occurs only when a natural or human generated condition, such as sinkholes or agricultural drainage wells, provides preferential flow to underground aquifers, resulting in local contamination. Others suggested that chemicals applied routinely to large areas infiltrate through the vadose zone, leading to widespread aquifer contamination.

Mandate, Selection, and Implementation

In response to growing public concern, the state legislature passed the Iowa Groundwater Protection Act in 1987. This landmark statute established the policy that further contamination should be prevented to the "maximum extent practical" and directed state agencies to launch multiyear programs of research and education to characterize the problem and identify potential solutions.

The act mandated that the Iowa Department of Natural Resources (DNR) assess the vulnerability of the state's ground water resources to contamination. In 1991, DNR released *Groundwater Vulnerability Regions of Iowa*, a map developed specifically to depict the intrinsic susceptibility of ground water resources to contamination by surface or near-surface activities. This assessment had three very limited purposes: (1) to describe the physical setting of ground water resources in the state, (2) to educate policy makers and the public about the potential for ground water contamination, and (3) to provide guidance for planning and assigning priorities to ground water protection efforts in the state.

Unlike other vulnerability assessments, the one in Iowa took account of factors that affect both ground water recharge and well development. Ground water recharge involves issues related to aquifer contamination; well development involves issues related to contamination of water supplies in areas where sources other than bedrock aquifers are used for drinking water. This approach considers jointly the potential impacts of contamination on the water resource in aquifers and on the users of ground water sources. The basic principle of the Iowa vulnerability assessment involves the travel time of water from the land surface to a well or an aquifer. When the time is relatively short (days to decades), vulnerability is considered high. If recharge occurs over relatively long periods (centuries to millennia), vulnerability is low. Travel times were determined by evaluating existing contaminants and using various radiometric dating techniques. The large reliance on travel time in the Iowa assessment likely results in underestimation of the potential for eventual contamination of the aquifer over time.

The most important factor used in the assessment was thickness of overlying materials which provide natural protection to a well or an aquifer. Other factors considered included type of aquifer, natural water quality in an aquifer, patterns of well location and construction, and documented occurrences of well contamination. The resulting vulnerability map (Plate 1) delineates regions having similar combinations of physical characteristics that affect ground water recharge and well development. Qualitative ratings are assigned to the contamination potential for aquifers and wells for various types and locations of water sources. For example, the contamination potential for wells in alluvial aquifers is considered high, while the potential for contamination of a variable bedrock aquifer protected by moderate drift or shale is considered low.

Although more sophisticated approaches were investigated for use in the assessment, ultimately no complex process models of contaminant transport were used and no distinction was made among Iowa's different soil types. The DNR staff suggested that since the soil cover in most of the state is such a small part of the overall aquifer or well cover, processes that take place in those first few inches are relatively similar and, therefore, insignificant in terms of relative susceptibilities to ground water contamination. The results of the vulnerability assessment followed directly from the method's assumptions and underlying principles. In general, the thicker the overlay of clayey glacial drift or shale, the less susceptible are wells or aquifers to contamination. Where overlying materials are thin or sandy, aquifer and well susceptibilities increase. Vulnerability is also greater in areas where sinkholes or agricultural drainage wells allow surface and tile water to bypass natural protective layers of soil and rapidly recharge bedrock aquifers.

Basic data on geologic patterns in the state were extrapolated to determine the potential for contamination. These data were supplemented by databases on water contamination (including the Statewide Rural Well-Water Survey conducted in 1989-1990) and by research insights into the transport, distribution, and fate of contaminants in ground water. Some of the simplest data needed for the assessment were unavailable. Depth-to-bedrock information had never been developed, so surface and bedrock topographic maps were revised and integrated to create a new statewide depth-to-bedrock map. In addition, information from throughout the state was compiled to produce the first statewide alluvial aquifer map. All new maps were checked against available well-log data, topographic maps, outcrop records, and soil survey reports to assure the greatest confidence in this information.

While the DNR was working on the assessment, it was also asked to integrate various types of natural resource data into a new computerized geographic information system (GIS). This coincident activity became a significant contributor to the assessment project. The GIS permitted easier construction of the vulnerability map and clearer display of spatial information. Further, counties or regions in the state can use the DNR geographic data and the GIS to explore additional vulnerability parameters and examine particular areas more closely to the extent that the resolution of the data permits.

The Iowa vulnerability map was designed to provide general guidance in planning and ranking activities for preventing contamination of aquifers and wells. It is not intended to answer site-specific questions, cannot predict contaminant concentrations, and does not even rank the different areas of the state by risk of contamination. Each of these additional uses would require specific assessments of vulnerability to different activities, contaminants, and risk. The map is simply a way to communicate qualitative susceptibility to contamination from the surface, based on the depth and type of cover, natural quality of the aquifer, well location and construction, and presence of special features that may alter the transport of contaminants.

Iowa's vulnerability map is viewed as an intermediate product in an ongoing process of learning more about the natural ground water system and the effects of surface and near-surface activities on that system. New maps will contain some of the basic data generated by the vulnerability study. New research and data collection will aim to identify ground water sources not included in the analysis (e.g., buried channel aquifers and the "salt and pepper sands" of western Iowa). Further analyses of existing and new well water quality data will be used to clarify relationships between aquifer depth and ground water contamination. As new information is obtained, databases and the GIS will be updated. Over time, new vulnerability maps may be produced to reflect new data or improved knowledge of environmental processes.

CAPE COD

Introduction

The Cape Cod sand and gravel aquifer is the U.S. Environmental Protection Agency (EPA) designated sole source of drinking water for Barnstable County, Massachusetts (ca. 400 square miles, winter population 186,605 in 1990, summer population ca. 500,000) as well as the source of fresh water for numerous kettle hole ponds and marine embayments. During the past 20 years, a period of intense development of open land accompanied by well-reported ground water contamination incidents, Cape Cod has been the site of intensive efforts in ground water management and analysis by many organizations, including the Association for the Preservation of Cape Cod, the U.S. Geological Survey, the Massachusetts Department of Environmental Protection (formerly the Department of Environmental Quality Engineering), EPA, and the Cape Cod Commission (formerly the Cape Cod Planning and Economic Development Commission). An earlier NRC publication, *Ground Water Quality Protection: State and Local Strategies* (1986) summarizes the Cape Cod ground water protection program.

Defining the Question

The *Area Wide Water Quality Management Plan for Cape Cod* (CCPEDC 1978a, b), prepared in response to section 208 of the federal Clean Water Act, established a management strategy for the Cape Cod aquifer. The plan emphasized wellhead protection of public water supplies, limited use of public sewage collection systems and treatment facilities, and continued general reliance on on-site septic systems, and relied on density controls for regulation of nitrate concentrations in public drinking water supplies. The water quality management planning program began an effort to delineate the zones of contribution (often called contributing areas) for public wells on Cape Cod that has become increasingly sophisticated over the years. The effort has grown to address a range of ground water resources and ground water dependent resources beyond the wellhead protection area, including fresh and marine surface waters, impaired areas, and water quality improvement areas (CCC 1991). Plate 2 depicts the water resources classifications for Cape Cod.

Selection and Implementation of Approaches

The first effort to delineate the contributing area to a public water supply well on Cape Cod came in 1976 as part of the initial background studies for the *Draft Area Wide Water Quality Management Plan for Cape*

Cod (CCPEDC 1978a). This effort used a simple mass balance ratio of a well's pumping volume to an equal volume average annual recharge evenly spread over a circular area. This approach, which neglects any hydrogeologic characteristics of the aquifer, results in a number of circles of varying radii that are centered at the wells.

The most significant milestone in advancing aquifer protection was the completion of a regional, 10 foot contour interval, water table map of the county by the USGS (LeBlanc and Guswa 1977). By the time that the Draft and Final Area Wide Water Quality Management Plans were published (CCPEDC 1978a, b), an updated method for delineating zones of contribution, using the regional water table map, had been developed. This method used the same mass balance approach to characterize a circle, but also extended the zone area by 150 percent of the circle's radius in the upgradient direction. In addition, a water quality watch area extending upgradient from the zone to the ground water divide was recommended. Although this approach used the regional water table map for information on ground water flow direction, it still neglected the aquifer's hydrogeologic parameters.

In 1981, the USGS published a digital model of the aquifer that included regional estimates of transmissivity (Guswa and LeBlanc 1981). In 1982, the CCPEDC used a simple analytical hydraulic model to describe downgradient and lateral capture limits of a well in a uniform flow field (Horsley 1983). The input parameters required for this model included hydraulic gradient data from the regional water table map and transmissivity data from the USGS digital model. The downgradient and lateral control points were determined using this method, but the area of the zone was again determined by the mass balance method. Use of the combined hydraulic and mass balance method resulted in elliptical zones of contribution that did not extend upgradient to the ground water divide. This combined approach attempted to address three-dimensional ground water flow beneath a partially penetrating pumping well in a simple manner.

At about the same time, the Massachusetts Department of Environmental Protection started the Aquifer Lands Acquisition (ALA) Program to protect land within zones of contribution that would be delineated by detailed site-specific studies. Because simple models could not address three-dimensional flow and for several other reasons, the ALA program adopted a policy that wellhead protection areas or Zone IIs (DEP-WS 1991) should be extended upgradient all the way to a ground water divide. Under this program, wells would be pump tested for site-specific aquifer parameters and more detailed water table mapping would often be required. In many cases, the capture area has been delineated by the same simple hydraulic analytical model but the zone has been extended to the divide. This method has resulted in some 1989 zones that are 3,000 feet wide and extend 4.5

miles upgradient, still without a satisfactory representation of three-dimensional flow to the well.

Most recently the USGS (Barlow 1993) has completed a detailed subregional, particle-tracking three-dimensional ground water flow model that shows the complex nature of ground water flow to wells. This approach has shown that earlier methods, in general, overestimate the area of zones of contribution (see Figure 5.1).

In 1988, the public agencies named above completed the Cape Cod Aquifer Management Project (CCAMP), a resource-based ground water protection study that used two towns, Barnstable and Eastham, to represent the more and less urbanized parts of Cape Cod. Among the CCAMP products were a GIS-based assessment of potential for contamination as a result of permissible land use changes in the Barnstable zones of contribution (Olimpio et al. 1991) and a ground water vulnerability assessment by Heath (1988) using DRASTIC for the same area. Olimpio et al. characterized land uses by ranking potential contaminant sources without regard to differences in vulnerability within the zones. Heath's DRASTIC analysis of the same area, shown in Figure 5.2, delineated two distinct zones of vulnerability based on hydrogeologic setting. The Sandwich Moraine setting, with deposits of silt, sand and gravel, and depths to ground water ranging from 0 to more than 125 feet, had DRASTIC values of 140 to 185; the Barnstable Outwash Plain, with permeable sand and fine gravel deposits with beds of silt and clay and depths to ground water of less than 50 feet, yielded values of 185 to 210. The DRASTIC scores and relative contributions of the factors are shown in Tables 5.1 and 5.2. Heath concluded that similar areas of Cape Cod would produce similar moderate to high vulnerability DRASTIC scores. The CCAMP project also addressed the potential for contamination of public water supply wells from new land uses allowable under existing zoning for the same area. The results of that effort are shown in Plate 4.

Results

In summary, circle zones were used initially when the hydrogeologic nature of the aquifer or of hydraulic flow to wells was little understood. The zones improved with an understanding of ground water flow and aquifer characteristics, but in recognition of the limitations of regional data, grossly conservative assumptions came into use. Currently, a truer delineation of a zone of contribution can be prepared for a given scenario using sophisticated models and highly detailed aquifer characterization. However, the area of a given zone still is highly dependent on the initial assumptions that dictate how much and in what circumstances a well is pumped. In the absence of ability to specify such conditions, conservative assump-

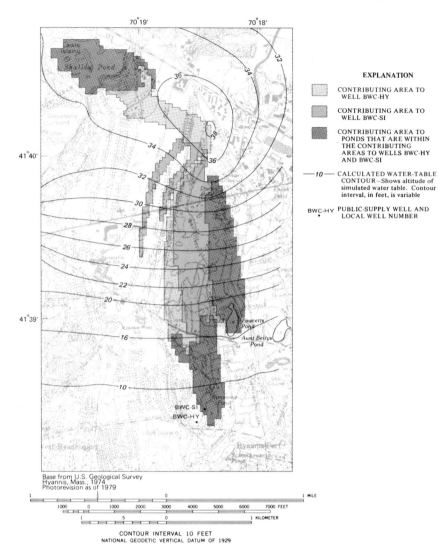

FIGURE 5.1 Contributing areas of wells and ponds in the complex flow system determined by using the three-dimensional model with 1987 average daily pumping rates. (Barlow 1993)

tions, such as maximum prolonged pumping, prevail, and, therefore, conservatively large zones of contribution continue to be used for wellhead protection.

The ground water management experience of Cape Cod has resulted in a better understanding of the resource and the complexity of the aquifer

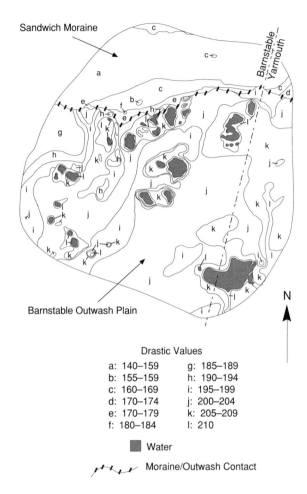

Drastic Values

a: 140–159   g: 185–189
b: 155–159   h: 190–194
c: 160–169   i: 195–199
d: 170–174   j: 200–204
e: 170–179   k: 205–209
f: 180–184   l: 210

■ Water

ⁱ⁺ᵗᵘᵘ Moraine/Outwash Contact

FIGURE 5.2 DRASTIC contours for Zone 1, Barnstable-Yarmouth, Massachusetts.

system, as well as the development of a more ambitious agenda for resource protection. Beginning with goals of protection of existing public water supplies, management interests have grown to include the protection of private wells, potential public supplies, fresh water ponds, and marine embayments. Public concerns over ground water quality have remained high and were a major factor in the creation of the Cape Cod Commission by the Massachusetts legislature. The commission is a land use planning and regulatory agency with broad authority over development projects and the ability to create special resource management areas. The net result of 20 years of effort by many individuals and agencies is the application of

TABLE 5.1 Ranges, Rating, and Weights for DRASTIC Study of
Barnstable Outwash Plain Setting (NOTE: gpd/ft^2 = gallons per day per
square foot) (Heath 1988)

Factor	Range	Rating	Weight	Number
Depth to Water	0-50+ feet	5-10	5	25-50
Net Recharge Per Year	10+ inches	9	4	36
Aquifer Media	Sand & Gravel	9	3	27
Soil Media	Sand	9	2	18
Topography	2-6%	9	1	9
Impact of Vadose Zone	Sand & Gravel	8	5	40
Hydraulic Conductivity	2000+ gpd/ft^2	10	3	30

Total = 185-210

TABLE 5.2 Ranges, Rating, and Weights for DRASTIC Study of
Sandwich Moraine Setting (NOTE: gpd/ft^2 = gallons per day per square
foot) (Heath 1988)

Factor	Range	Rating	Weight	Number
Depth to Water	0-100+ feet	1-10	5	5-50
Net Recharge Per Year	10+ inches	9	4	36
Aquifer Media	Sand & Gravel	8	3	24
Soil Media	Sandy Loam	6	2	12
Topography	6-12%	5	1	5
Impact of Vadose Zone	Sand & Gravel	8	5	40
Hydraulic Conductivity	700-1000 gpd/ft^2	6	3	18

Total = 140-185

higher protection standards to broader areas of the Cape Cod aquifer. With
some exceptions for already impaired areas, a differentiated resource protection approach in the vulnerable aquifer setting of Cape Cod has resulted
in a program that approaches universal ground water protection.

Color Plates

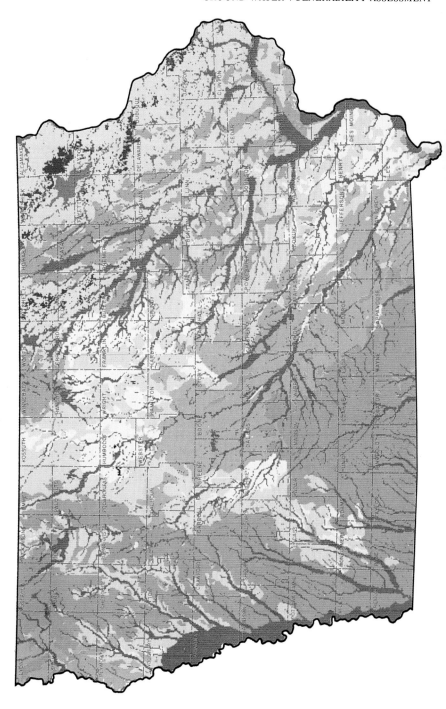

GROUND WATER VULNERABILITY ASSESSMENT

WATER SOURCE	CONTAMINATION POTENTIAL	
	aquifers	wells
ALLUVIAL AQUIFERS	high	high
GOOD BEDROCK AQUIFERS protected by:		
Thin drift	high	high
Moderate drift	low	low
Shale	moderate	moderate
VARIABLE BEDROCK AQUIFERS Protected by:		
Thin drift	moderate to high	moderate to high
Moderate drift	low	low: bedrock wells / high: drift wells
Shale	low	moderate: bedrock wells / high: drift wells
DRIFT GROUNDWATER SOURCE	low	high
special features:		
SINKHOLES		enhance transport of contaminants
AG-DRAINAGE WELLS		
LAKES / RESERVOIRS		

PLATE 1 Ground water vulnerability regions of Iowa. (Hoyer 1991. Reprinted, by permission, from Iowa Department of Natural Resources, 1991.) A more detailed version of this map is available from the Iowa Department of Natural Resources, Geological Survey Bureau, Iowa City, Iowa.

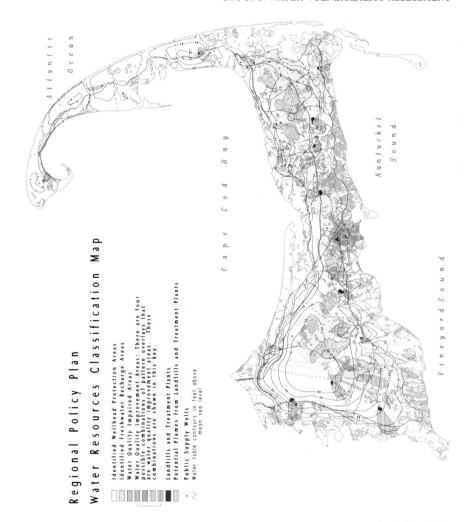

Regional Policy Plan

Water Resources Classification Map

Identified Wellhead Protection Areas
Identified Freshwater Recharge Areas
Water Quality Impaired Areas
Water Quality Improvement Areas: There are four
possible combinations of pattern overlays that
are water quality improvement areas. These
combinations are shown in this key.

Landfills and Treatment Plants
Potential Plumes from Landfills and Treatment Plants

Public Supply Wells
Water table contours in feet above
mean sea level

Atlantic Ocean

Cape Cod Bay

Nantucket Sound

Vineyard Sound

PLATE 2 Water resources classification map for Cape Cod, Massachusetts. (Adapted from CCC
1991. Reprinted, by permission,
from Cape Cod Commission, 1991.)

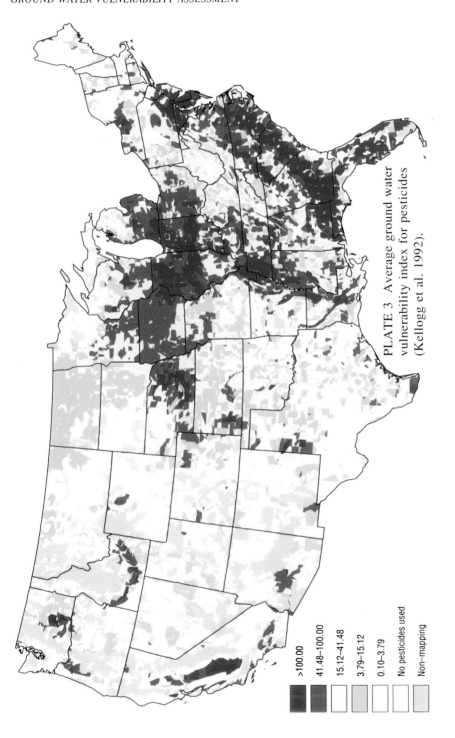

PLATE 3 Average ground water vulnerability index for pesticides (Kellogg et al. 1992).

>100.00

41.48–100.00

15.12–41.48

3.79–15.12

0.10–3.79

No pesticides used

Non–mapping

BEFORE LAND-USE CHANGE

A

EXPLANATION

INCREASING RISK

Open land
Undevelopable land
Developable residential
Developable commercial
Developable industrial
Entertainment
Residential, single and multifamily
Hotels, motels, inns, and restaurants
Offices and public services
Retail
Storage, warehouse and distribution
Industrial storage
Auto related
Industrial
Waste disposal
Publicly owned land (variable risk)
Zone of contribution boundary
Town boundary
Public water-supply wells

1 MILE
1 KILOMETER
0
0

B

AFTER
LAND-USE
CHANGE

N

PLATE 4 Risk to public-supply wells from land use in the Barnstable zone of contribution. (Olimpio et al. 1991.)

FLORIDA

Introduction

Florida has 13 million residents and is the fourth most populous state (U.S. Bureau of the Census 1991). Like several other sunbelt states, Florida's population is growing steadily, at about 1,000 persons per day, and is estimated to reach 17 million by the year 2000. Tourism is the biggest industry in Florida, attracting nearly 40 million visitors each year. Ground water is the source of drinking water for about 95 percent of Florida's population; total withdrawals amount to about 1.5 billion gallons per day. An additional 3 billion gallons of ground water per day are pumped to meet the needs of agriculture—a $5 billion per year industry, second only to tourism in the state. Of the 50 states, Florida ranks eighth in withdrawal of fresh ground water for all purposes, second for public supply, first for rural domestic and livestock use, third for industrial/commercial use, and ninth for irrigation withdrawals.

Most areas in Florida have abundant ground water of good quality, but the major aquifers are vulnerable to contamination from a variety of land use activities. Overpumping of ground water to meet the growing demands of the urban centers, which accounts for about 80 percent of the state's population, contributes to salt water intrusion in coastal areas. This overpumping is considered the most significant problem for degradation of ground water quality in the state. Other major sources of ground water contaminants include: (1) pesticides and fertilizers (about 2 million tons/year) used in agriculture, (2) about 2 million on-site septic tanks, (3) more than 20,000 recharge wells used for disposing of stormwater, treated domestic wastewater, and cooling water, (4) nearly 6,000 surface impoundments, averaging one per 30 square kilometers, and (5) phosphate mining activities that are estimated to disturb about 3,000 hectares each year.

The Hydrogeologic Setting

The entire state is in the Coastal Plain physiographic province, which has generally low relief. Much of the state is underlain by the Floridan aquifer system, largely a limestone and dolomite aquifer that is found in both confined and unconfined conditions. The Floridan is overlain through most of the state by an intermediate aquifer system, consisting of predominantly clays and sands, and a surficial aquifer system, consisting of predominantly sands, limestone, and dolomite. The Floridan is one of the most productive aquifers in the world and is the most important source of drinking water for Florida residents. The Biscayne, an unconfined, shallow, limestone aquifer located in southeast Florida, is the most intensively used aquifer and the sole source of drinking water for nearly 3 million residents in the Miami-Palm Beach coastal area. Other surficial aquifers in southern Florida and in the western panhandle region also serve as sources of ground water.

Aquifers in Florida are overlain by layers of sand, clay, marl, and limestone whose thickness may vary considerably. For example, the thickness of layers above the Floridan aquifer range from a few meters in parts of west-central and northern Florida to several hundred meters in south-central Florida and in the extreme western panhandle of the state. Four major groups of soils (designated as soil orders under the U.S. Soil Taxonomy) occur extensively in Florida. Soils in the western highlands are dominated by well-drained sandy and loamy soils and by sandy soils with loamy subsoils; these are classified as Ultisols and Entisols. In the central ridge of the Florida peninsula, are found deep, well-drained, sandy soils (Entisols) as well as sandy soils underlain by loamy subsoils or phosphatic limestone (Alfisols and Ultisols). Poorly drained sandy soils with organic-rich and clay-rich subsoils, classified as Spodosols, occur in the Florida flatwoods. Organic-rich muck soils (Histosols) underlain by muck or limestone are found primarily in an area extending south of Lake Okeechobee.

Rainfall is the primary source of ground water in Florida. Annual rainfall in the state ranges from 100 to 160 cm/year, averaging 125 cm/year, with considerable spatial (both local and regional) and seasonal variations in rainfall amounts and patterns. Evapotranspiration (ET) represents the largest loss of water; ET ranges from about 70 to 130 cm/year, accounting for between 50 and 100 percent of the average annual rainfall. Surface runoff and ground water discharge to streams averages about 30 cm/year. Annual recharge to surficial aquifers ranges from near zero in perennially wet, lowland areas to as much as 50 cm/year in well-drained areas; however, only a fraction of this water recharges the underlying Floridan aquifer. Estimates of recharge to the Floridan aquifer vary from less than 3 cm/year to more than 25 cm/year, depending on such factors as weather patterns (e.g., rainfall-ET balance), depth to water table, soil permeability, land use, and local hydrogeology.

Defining the Question

Permeable soils, high net recharge rates, intensively managed irrigated agriculture, and growing demands from urban population centers all pose considerable threat of ground water contamination. Thus, protection of this valuable natural resource while not placing unreasonable constraints on agricultural production and urban development is the central focus of environmental regulation and growth management in Florida.

Along with California, Florida has played a leading role in the United

States in development and enforcement of state regulations for environmental protection. Detection in 1983 of aldicarb and ethylene dibromide, two nematocides used widely in Florida's citrus groves, crystallized the growing concerns over ground water contamination and the need to protect this vital natural resource. In 1983, the Florida legislature passed the Water Quality Assurance Act, and in 1984 adopted the State and Regional Planning Act. These and subsequent legislative actions provide the legal basis and guidance for the Ground Water Strategy developed by the Florida Department of Environmental Regulation (DER).

Ground water protection programs in Florida are implemented at federal, state, regional, and local levels and involve both regulatory and nonregulatory approaches. The most significant nonregulatory effort involves more than 30 ground water studies being conducted in collaboration with the Water Resources Division of the U.S. Geological Survey. At the state level, Florida statutes and administrative codes form the basis for regulatory actions. Although DER is the primary agency responsible for rules and statutes designed to protect ground water, the following state agencies participate to varying degrees in their implementation: five water management districts, the Florida Geological Survey, the Department of Health and Rehabilitative Services (HRS), the Department of Natural Resources, and the Florida Department of Agriculture and Consumer Services (DACS). In addition, certain interagency committees help coordinate the development and implementation of environmental codes in the state. A prominent example is the Pesticide Review Council which offers guidance to the DACS in developing pesticide use regulation. A method for screening pesticides in terms of their chronic toxicity and environmental behavior has been developed through collaborative efforts of the DACS, the DER, and the HRS (Britt et al. 1992). This method will be used to grant registration for pesticide use in Florida or to seek additional site-specific field data.

Selecting an Approach

The emphasis of the DER ground water program has shifted in recent years from primarily enforcement activity to a technically based, quantifiable, planned approach for resource protection.

The administrative philosophy for ground water protection programs in Florida is guided by the following principles:

• Ground water is a renewable resource, necessitating a balance between withdrawals and natural or artificial recharge.

• Ground water contamination should be prevented to the maximum degree possible because cleanup of contaminated aquifers is technically or economically infeasible.

•   It is impractical, perhaps unnecessary, to require nondegradation standards for all ground water in all locations and at all times.

•   The principle of "most beneficial use" is to be used in classifying ground water into four classes on the basis of present quality, with the goal of attaining the highest level protection of potable water supplies (Class I aquifers).

Part of the 1983 Water Quality Assurance Act requires Florida DER to "establish a ground water quality monitoring network designed to detect and predict contamination of the State's ground water resources" via collaborative efforts with other state and federal agencies. The three basic goals of the ground water quality monitoring program are to:

•   Establish the baseline water quality of major aquifer systems in the state,

•   Detect and predict changes in ground water quality resulting from the effects of various land use activities and potential sources of contamination, and

•   Disseminate to local governments and the public, water quality data generated by the network.

Results

The ground water monitoring network established by DER to meet the goals stated above consists of two major subnetworks and one survey (Maddox and Spicola 1991). Approximately 1,700 wells that tap all major potable aquifers in the state form the Background Network, which was designed to help define the background water quality. The Very Intensively Studied Area (VISA) network was established to monitor specific areas of the state considered highly vulnerable to contamination; predominant land use and hydrogeology were the primary attributes used to evaluate vulnerability. The DRASTIC index, developed by EPA, served as the basis for statewide maps depicting ground water vulnerability. Data from the VISA wells will be compared to like parameters sampled from Background Network wells in the same aquifer segment. The final element of the monitoring network is the Private Well Survey, in which up to 70 private wells per county will be sampled. The sampling frequency and chemical parameters to be monitored at each site are based on several factors, including network well classification, land use activities, hydrogeologic sensitivity, and funding. In Figure 5.3, the principal aquifers in Florida are shown along with the distribution of the locations of the monitoring wells in the Florida DER network.

The Preservation 2000 Act, enacted in 1990, mandated that the Land Acquisition Advisory Council (LAAC) "provide for assessing the impor-

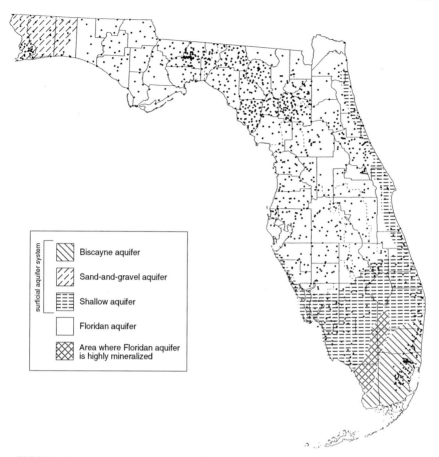

FIGURE 5.3 Principal aquifers in Florida and the network of sample wells as of March 1990 (1642 wells sampled). (Adapted from Maddox and Spicola 1991, and Maddox et al. 1993.)

tance of acquiring lands which can serve to protect or recharge ground water, and the degree to which state land acquisition programs should focus on purchasing such land." The Ground Water Resources Committee, a subcommittee of the LAAC, produced a map depicting areas of ground water significance at regional scale (1:500,000) (see Figure 5.4) to give decision makers the basis for considering ground water as a factor in land acquisition under the Preservation 2000 Act (LAAC 1991). In developing maps for their districts, each of the five water management districts (WMDs) used the following criteria: ground water recharge, ground water quality, aquifer vulnerability, ground water availability, influence of existing uses on the resource, and ground water supply. The specific approaches used by

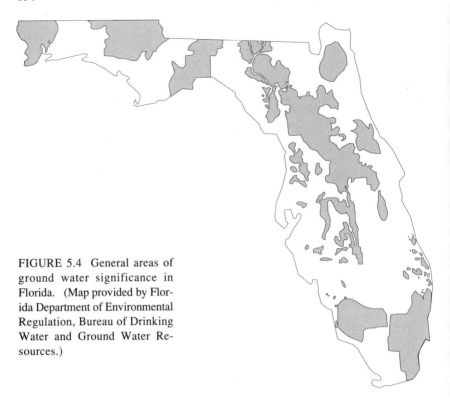

FIGURE 5.4 General areas of
ground water significance in
Florida. (Map provided by Florida Department of Environmental
Regulation, Bureau of Drinking
Water and Ground Water Resources.)

the WMDs varied, however. For example, the St. Johns River WMD used a
GIS-based map overlay and DRASTIC-like numerical index approach that
rated the following attributes: recharge, transmissivity, water quality, thickness
of potable water, potential water expansion areas, and spring flow capture
zones. The Southwest Florida WMD also used a map overlay and index
approach which considered four criteria, and GIS tools for mapping. Existing databases were considered inadequate to generate a DRASTIC map for
the Suwannee River WMD, but the map produced using an overlay approach was considered to be similar to DRASTIC maps in providing a
general depiction of aquifer vulnerability.

In the November 1988, Florida voters approved an amendment to the
Florida Constitution allowing land producing high recharge to Florida's
aquifers to be classified and assessed for *ad valorem* tax purposes based on
character or use. Such recharge areas are expected to be located primarily
in the upland, sandy ridge areas. The Bluebelt Commission appointed by
the 1989 Florida Legislature, studied the complex issues involved and recommended that the tax incentive be offered to owners of such high recharge
areas if their land is left undeveloped (SFWMD 1991). The land eligible

for classification as "high water recharge land" must meet the following criteria established by the commission:

•   The parcel must be located in the high recharge areas designated on maps supplied by each of the five WMDs.
•   The high recharge area of the parcel must be at least 10 acres.
•   The land use must be vacant or single-family residential.
•   The parcel must not be receiving any other special assessment, such as Greenbelt classification for agricultural lands.

Two bills related to the implementation of the Bluebelt program are being considered by the 1993 Florida legislation.

THE SAN JOAQUIN VALLEY

Introduction

Pesticide contamination of ground water resources is a serious concern in California's San Joaquin Valley (SJV). Contamination of the area's aquifer system has resulted from a combination of natural geologic conditions and human intervention in exploiting the SJV's natural resources. The SJV is now the principal target of extensive ground water monitoring activities in the state.

Agriculture has imposed major environmental stresses on the SJV. Natural wetlands have been drained and the land reclaimed for agricultural purposes. Canal systems convey water from the northern, wetter parts of the state to the south, where it is used for irrigation and reclamation projects. Tens of thousands of wells tap the sole source aquifer system to supply water for domestic consumption and crop irrigation. Cities and towns have sprouted throughout the region and supply the human resources necessary to support the agriculture and petroleum industries.

Agriculture is the principal industry in California. With 1989 cash receipts of more than $17.6 billion, the state's agricultural industry produced more than 50 percent of the nation's fruits, nuts, and vegetables on 3 percent of the nation's farmland. California agriculture is a diversified industry that produces more than 250 crop and livestock commodities, most of which can be found in the SJV.

Fresno County, the largest agricultural county in the state, is situated in the heart of the SJV, between the San Joaquin River to the north and the Kings River on the south. Grapes, stone fruits, and citrus are important commodities in the region. These and many other commodities important to the region are susceptible to nematodes which thrive in the county's coarse-textured soils.

While agricultural diversity is a sound economic practice, it stimulates the growth of a broad range of pest complexes, which in turn dictates greater reliance on agricultural chemicals to minimize crop losses to pests, and maintain productivity and profit. Domestic and foreign markets demand high-quality and cosmetically appealing produce, which require pesticide use strategies that rely on pest exclusion and eradication rather than pest management.

Hydrogeologic Setting

The San Joaquin Valley (SJV) is at the southern end of California's Central Valley. With its northern boundary just south of Sacramento, the Valley extends in a southeasterly direction about 400 kilometers (250 miles) into Kern County. The SJV averages 100 kilometers (60 miles) in width and drains the area between the Sierra Nevada on the east and the California Coastal Range on the west. The rain shadow caused by the Coastal Range results in the predominantly xeric habitat covering the greater part of the valley floor where the annual rainfall is about 25 centimeters (10 inches). The San Joaquin River is the principal waterway that drains the SJV northward into the Sacramento Delta region.

The soils of the SJV vary significantly. On the west side of the valley, soils are composed largely of sedimentary materials derived from the Coastal Range; they are generally fine-textured and slow to drain. The arable soils of the east side developed on relatively unweathered, granitic sediments. Many of these soils are wind-deposited sands underlain by deep coarse-textured alluvial materials.

Defining the Question

From the mid-1950s until 1977, dibromochloropropane (DBCP) was the primary chemical used to control nematodes. DBCP has desirable characteristics for a nematocide. It is less volatile than many other soil fumigants, such as methylbromide; remains active in the soil for a long time, and is effective in killing nematodes. However, it also causes sterility in human males, is relatively mobile in soil, and is persistent. Because of the health risks associated with consumption of DBCP treated foods, the nematocide was banned from use in the United States in 1979. After the ban, several well water studies were conducted in the SJV by state, county and local authorities. Thirteen years after DBCP was banned, contamination of well waters by the chemical persists as a problem in Fresno County.

Public concern over pesticides in ground water resulted in passage of the California Pesticide Contamination Prevention Act (PCPA) of 1985. It is a broad law that establishes the California Department of Pesticide Regulation as the lead agency in dealing with issues of ground water contamination by pesticides. The PCPA specifically requires:

1. pesticide registrants to collect and submit specific chemical and environmental fate data (e.g., water solubility, vapor pressure, octanol-water partition coefficient, soil sorption coefficient, degradation half-lives for aerobic and anaerobic metabolism, Henry's Law constant, hydrolysis rate constant) as part of the terms for registration and continued use of their products in California,

2. establishment of numerical criteria or standards for physical-chemical characteristics and environmental fate data to determine whether a pesticide can be registered in the state that are at least as stringent as those standards set by the EPA,

3. soil and water monitoring investigations be conducted on:

   a. pesticides with properties that are in violation of the physical-chemical standards set in 2 above, and

   b. pesticides, toxic degradation products or other ingredients that are:

   1. contaminants of the state's ground waters, or

   2. found at the deepest of the following soil depths:

      a. 2.7 meters (8 feet) below the soil surface,

      b. below the crop root zone, or

      c. below the microbial zone, and

4. creation of a database of wells sampled for pesticides with a provision requiring all agencies to submit data to the California Department of Pesticide Regulation (CDPR).

Difficulties associated with identifying the maximum depths of root zone and microbial zone have led to the establishment of 8 feet as a somewhat arbitrary but enforceable criterion for pesticide leaching in soils.

Selection and Implementation of an Approach

Assessment of ground water vulnerability to pesticides in California is a mechanical rather than a scientific process. Its primary goal is compliance with the mandates established in the PCPA. One of these mandates requires that monitoring studies be conducted in areas of the state where the contaminant pesticide is used, in other areas exhibiting high risk portraits (e.g., low organic carbon, slow soil hydrolysis, metabolism, or dissipation), and in areas where pesticide use practices present a risk to the state's ground water resources.

The numerical value for assessments was predetermined by the Pesticide Use Report (PUR) system employed in the state. Since the early

1970s, California has required pesticide applicators to give local authorities information on the use of restricted pesticides. This requirement was extended to all pesticides beginning in 1990. Application information reported includes names of the pesticide(s) and commodities, the amount applied, the formulation used, and the location of the commodity to the nearest section (approximately 1 square mile) as defined by the U.S. Rectangular Coordinate System. In contrast to most other states that rely on county pesticide sales in estimating pesticide use, California can track pesticide use based on quantities applied to each section. Thus, the section, already established as a political management unit, became the basic assessment unit.

The primary criteria that subject a pesticide to investigation as a ground water pollutant are:

- detection of the pesticide or its metabolites in well samples, or
- its failure to conform to the physical-chemical standards set in accordance with the PCPA, hence securing its position on the PCPA's Ground Water Protection List of pesticides having a potential to pollute ground water.

In either case, relatively large areas surrounding the original detection site or, in the latter case, high use regions are monitored via well surveys. Positive findings automatically increase the scope of the surveys, and since no tolerance levels are specified in the PCPA, any detectable and confirmed result establishes a pesticide as a contaminant.

When a pesticide or its degradation products is detected in a well water sample and the pesticide is judged to have contaminated the water source as a result of a legal agricultural use, the section the well is in is declared a Pesticide Management Zone (PMZ). Further application of the detected pesticide within PMZ boundaries may be prohibited or restricted, depending on the degree of contamination and subject to the availability of tried and tested modifications in management practices addressing environmental safety in use of the pesticide. PMZs are pesticide-specific—each contaminant pesticide has its own set of PMZs which may or may not overlap PMZs assigned another pesticide. Currently, consideration is being given to the extension of PMZs established for one chemical to other potential pesticide pollutants. In addition to monitoring activities in PMZs, protocols have been written to monitor ground water in sections adjacent to a PMZ. Monitoring of adjacent sections has resulted in many new PMZs. Currently, California has 182 PMZs involving five registered pesticides.

California has pursued this mechanical approach to assessing ground water vulnerability to pesticides for reasons that cover a spectrum of political, economic, and practical concerns. As noted earlier, the scale of the assessment unit was set at the section level because it is a well-defined geopolitical unit used in the PUR system. Section boundaries frequently are marked by roads and highways, which allows the section to be located readily and makes enforcement of laws and regulations more practical. California law also requires that well logs be recorded by drillers for all wells in the state. Well-site information conforms to the U.S. Rectangular Coordinate System's township, range, and section system.

The suitability and reliability of databases available for producing vulnerability assessments was a great concern before passage of the PCPA in 1985. Soil survey information holds distinct advantages for producing assessments and developing best management practices strategies, but it was not available in a format that could work in harmony with PUR sections. To date, several areas of the SJV are not covered by a modern soil survey; they include the western part of Tulare County, which contains 34 PMZs. Other vadose zone data were sparse, if available at all.

The use of models was not considered appropriate, given the available data and because no single model could cope with the circumstances in which contaminated ground water sources were being discovered in the state. While most cases of well contamination were associated with the coarse-textured soils of the SJV and the Los Angeles Basin, several cases were noted in areas of the Central Valley north of the SJV, where very dense fine-textured soils (vertisols and other cracking clays) were dominant.

The potential vagaries and uncertainties associated with more scientific approaches to vulnerability assessment, given the tools available when the PCPA was enacted, presented too large a risk for managers to consider endorsing their use. In contrast, the basic definition of the PMZ is difficult to challenge (pesticide contamination has been detected or not detected) in the legal sense. And the logic of investing economic resources in areas immediately surrounding areas of acknowledged contamination are relatively undisputable. The eastern part of the SJV contains more than 50 percent of the PMZs in the state. Coarse-textured soils of low carbon content are ubiquitous in this area and are represented in more than 3,000 sections. The obvious contamination scenario is the normal scenario in the eastern SJV, and because of its size it creates a huge management problem. While more sophisticated methods for assessing ground water vulnerability have been developed, a question that begs to be asked is "How would conversion to the use of enhanced techniques for evaluating ground water vulnerability improve ground water protection policy and management in the SJV?"

HAWAII

Introduction

More than 90 percent of the population of Hawaii depends on ground water (nearly 200 billion gallons per day) for their domestic supply (Au 1991). Ground water contamination is of special concern in Hawaii, as in other insular systems, where alternative fresh water resources are not readily available or economically practical. Salt water encroachment, caused by pumping, is by far the biggest source of ground water contamination in Hawaii; however, nonpoint source contamination from agricultural chemicals is increasingly a major concern. On Oahu, where approximately 80 percent of Hawaii's million-plus population resides, renewable ground water resources are almost totally exploited; therefore, management action to prevent contamination is essential.

Each of the major islands in the Hawaiian chain is formed from one or more shield volcanoes composed primarily of extremely permeable thin basaltic lava flows. On most of the Hawaiian islands the margins of the volcanic mountains are overlapped by coastal plain sediments of alluvial and marine origin that were deposited during periods of volcanic quiescence. In general, the occurrence of ground water in Hawaii, shown in Figure 5.5, falls into three categories: (1) basal water bodies floating on and displacing salt water, (2) high-level water bodies impounded within compartments formed by impermeable dikes that intrude the lava flows, and (3) high-level water bodies perched on ash beds or soils interbedded with

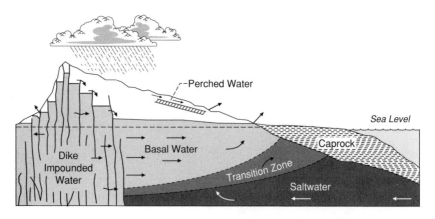

FIGURE 5.5   Cross section of a typical volcanic dome showing the occurrence of ground water in Hawaii (After Peterson 1972.   Reprinted, by permission, from Water Well Journal Publishing Company, 1972.)

thin lava flows on unconformities or on other relatively impervious lava flows (Peterson 1972).

A foundation of the tourist industry in Hawaii is the pristine environment. The excellent quality of Hawaii's water is well known. The public has demanded, and regulatory agencies have adopted, a very conservative, zero-tolerance policy on ground water contamination. The reality, however, is that past, present, and future agricultural, industrial, and military activities present potentially significant ground water contamination problems in Hawaii.

Since 1977 when 1,874 liters of ethylene dibromide (EDB) where spilled within 18 meters of a well near Kunia on the island of Oahu, the occurrence and distribution of contaminants in Hawaii's ground water has been carefully documented by Oki and Giambelluca (1985, 1987) and Lau and Mink (1987). Before 1981, when the nematocide dibromochloropropane (DBCP) was found in wells in central Oahu, the detection limit for most chemicals was too high to reveal the low level of contamination that probably had existed for many years.

Concern about the fate of agriculture chemicals led the Hawaii State Department of Agriculture to initiate a large sampling program to characterize the sources of nonpoint ground water contamination. In July 1983, 10 wells in central Oahu were closed because of DBCP and EDB contamination. The public has been kept well informed of possible problems through the publication of maps of chemicals detected in ground water in the local newspaper. Updated versions of these maps are shown in Figures 5.6a, b, c, and d.

In Hawaii, interagency committees, with representation from the Departments of Health and Agriculture, have been formed to address the complex technical and social questions associated with ground water contamination from agricultural chemicals. The Hawaii legislature has provided substantial funding to groups at the University of Hawaii to develop the first GIS-based regional scale chemical leaching assessment approach to aid in pesticide regulation. This effort, described below, has worked to identify geographic areas of concern, but the role the vulnerability maps generated by this system will play in the overall regulatory process is still unclear.

Defining the Question

Agrichemicals are essential to agriculture in Hawaii. It is not possible to maintain a large pineapple monoculture in Hawaii without nematode control using pesticides. Pineapple and sugar growers in Hawaii have generally employed well controlled management practices in their use of fertilizers, herbicides, and insecticides. In the early 1950s, it was thought that organic chemicals such as DBCP and EDB would not leach to ground water

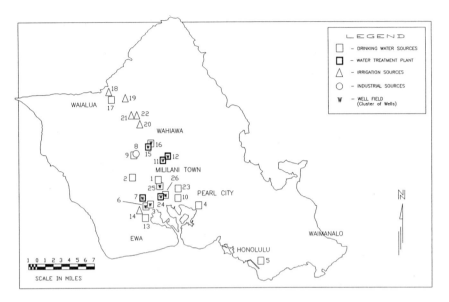

FIGURE 5.6a The occurrence and distribution of ground water contamination on the Island of Oahu. (Map provided by Hawaii State Department of Health.)

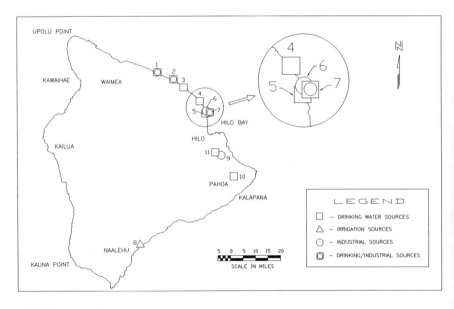

FIGURE 5.6b The occurrence and distribution of ground water contamination on the Island of Hawaii. (Map provided by Hawaii State Department of Health.)

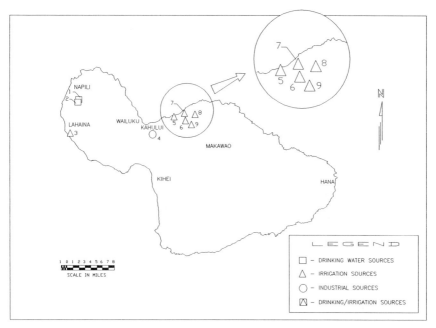

FIGURE 5.6c The occurrence and distribution of ground water contamination on the Island of Maui. (Map provided by Hawaii State Department of Health.)

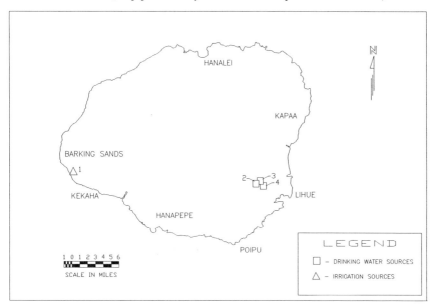

FIGURE 5.6d The occurrence and distribution of ground water contamination on the Island of Kauai. (Map provided by Hawaii State Department of Health.)

because (1) the chemicals are highly sorbed in soils with high organic carbon contents, (2) the chemicals are highly volatile, and (3) the water table is several hundred meters below the surface. Measured concentrations of DBCP and EDB down to 30 meters at several locations have shown the original assessment to be wrong. They have resulted in an urgent need to understand processes such as preferential flow better and to predict if the replacement chemicals used today, such as Telon II, will also leach to significant depths.

Leaching of pesticides to ground water in Hawaii could take decades. This time lag could lead to a temporary false sense of security, as happened in the past and potentially result in staggering costs for remedial action. For this reason, mathematical models that permit the user to ask "what if" questions have been developed to help understand what the future may hold under certain management options. One needs to know what the fate of chemicals applied in the past will be and how to regulate the chemicals considered for use in the future; models are now being developed and used to help make these vulnerability assessments.

Approaches

Researchers have embarked on several parallel approaches to quantitatively assess the vulnerability of Hawaii's ground water resources, including: (1) sampling, (2) physically-based numerical modeling, and (3) vulnerability mapping based on a simple chemical leaching index. Taken together these approaches have provided insight and guidance for work on a complex, spatially and temporally variable problem.

The sampling programs (Wong 1983 and 1987, Peterson et al. 1985) have shown that the chemicals applied in the past do, in fact, leach below the root zone, contrary to the original predictions, and can eventually reach the ground water. Experiments designed to characterize the nuances of various processes, such as volatilization, sorption, and degradation, have been conducted recently and will improve the conceptualization of mathematical models in the future.

The EPA's Pesticide Root Zone Model (PRZM), a deterministic-empirical/conceptual fluid flow/solute transport model, has been tested by Loague and co-workers (Loague et al. 1989a, b; Loague 1992) against measured concentration profiles for DBCP and EDB in central Oahu. These simulations illustrate that the chemicals used in the past can indeed move to considerable depths. Models of this kind, once properly validated, can be used to simulate the predicted fate of future pesticide applications. One must always remember, however, that numerical simulations must be interpreted in terms of the limiting assumptions associated with model and data errors.

Ground water vulnerability maps and assessments of their uncertainty were pioneered at the University of Hawaii in the Department of Agriculture Engineering (Khan and Liang 1989, Loague and Green 1990a). These pesticide leaching assessments were made by coupling a simple mobility index to a geographic information system. Loague and coworkers have investigated the uncertainty in these maps owing to data and model errors (Loague and Green 1988; Loague et al. 1989c, 1990; Loague and Green 1990b, 1990c; Loague 1991; Kleveno et al. 1992; Yost et al. 1993). The Hawaiian database on soils, climate, and chemicals is neither perfect nor poor for modeling applications; it is typical of what exists in most states—major extrapolations are required to estimate the input parameters required for almost any chemical fate model.

Results

Sampling from wells in Hawaii has shown the concentrations of various chemicals, both from agriculture and industrial sources, which have leached to ground water in Hawaii. These concentrations, in general, are low compared to the levels detected in other states and for the most part are below health advisory levels established by EPA. In some instances contamination has not resulted from agriculture, but rather from point sources such as chemical loading and mixing areas and possibly from ruptured fuel lines. The widespread presence of trichloropropane (TCP) in Hawaii's ground water and deep soil cores at concentrations higher than DBCP was totally unexpected. TCP was never applied as a pesticide, but results from the manufacture of the fumigant DD, which was used until 1977 in pineapple culture. The occurrence of TCP illustrates that one must be aware of the chemicals applied as well as their components and transformation products.

Wells have been closed in Hawaii even though the measured contaminant concentrations have been below those considered to pose a significant health risk. At municipal well locations in central Oahu, where DBCP, EDB, and/or TCP have been detected, the water is now passed through carbon filters before it is put into the distribution system. The cost of this treatment is passed on to the water users, rather than to those who applied the chemicals.

The pesticide leaching assessment maps developed by Khan and Liang (1989) are intended for incorporation into the regulatory process. Decisions are not made on the basis of the red and green shaded areas for different chemicals (see Plate 3), but this information is considered. The uncertainty analysis by Loague and coworkers has shown some of the limitations of deterministic assessments in the form of vulnerability maps and provided initial guidance on data shortfalls.

APPLICATION OF A VULNERABILITY INDEX FOR
DECISION-MAKING AT THE NATIONAL LEVEL

Need for a Vulnerability Index

A vulnerability index for ground water contamination by pesticides has been developed and used by USDA as a decision aid to help attain the objectives of the President's Water Quality Initiative (see Box 1.1). A vulnerability index was needed for use in program management and to provide insight for policy development. Motivation for the development of the vulnerability index was provided by two specific questions:

1. Given limited resources and the geographic diversity of the water quality problems associated with agricultural production, what areas of the country have the highest priority for study and program implementation?
2. What policy implications emerge from the spatial patterns of the potential for contamination from a national perspective, given information currently available about farming practices and chemical use in agriculture?

Description of the Vulnerability Index

A vulnerability index was derived to evaluate the likelihood of shallow ground water contamination by pesticides used in agriculture in one area compared to another area. Because of the orientation of Initiative policies to farm management practices, it was necessary that the vulnerability measure incorporate field level information on climate, soils, and chemical use. It also needed to be general enough to include all areas of the country and all types of crops grown.

A Ground Water Vulnerability Index for Pesticides (GWVIP) was developed by applying the Soil-Pesticide Interaction Screening Procedure (SPISP) developed by the Soil Conservation Service to the National Resource Inventory (NRI) land use database for 1982 and the state level pesticide use database created by Resources for the Future (Gianessi and Puffer 1991). Details of the computational scheme and databases used are described by Kellogg et al. (1992). The 1982 NRI and the associated SOIL-5 database provide information on soil properties and land use at about 800,000 sample points throughout the continental United States. This information is sufficient to apply the SPISP to each point and thus obtain a relative measure of the soil leaching potential throughout the country. The RFF pesticide use database was used to infer chemical use at each point on the basis of the crop type recorded in the NRI database. By taking advantage of the statistical properties of the NRI database, which is based on a statistical survey sampling design, the GWVIP score at each of the sample points can be statistically aggregated for making comparisons among regions.

Since the GWVIP is an extension of a screening procedure, it is designed to minimize the likelihood of incorrectly identifying an area as having a low potential for contamination—that is, false negatives are minimized and false positives are tolerated. The GWVIP is designed to classify an area as having a potential problem even if the likelihood is small.

GWVIP scores were graphically displayed after embedding them in a national cartographic database consisting of 13,172 polygons created by overlaying the boundaries of 3,041 counties, 189 Major Land Resource Areas (MLRAs), 2,111 hydrologic units, and federal lands.

Three caveats are especially important in using the GWVIP and its aggregates as a decision aid:

1. Land use data are for 1982 and do not represent current cropping patterns in some parts of the country. Although total cropland acreage has remained fairly stable over the past 10 years, there has been a pronounced shift from harvested cropland to cropland idled in government programs.

2. The approach uses a simulation model that predicts the amount of chemical that leaches past the root zone. In areas where the water table is near the surface, these predictions relate directly to shallow ground water contamination. In other areas a time lag is involved. No adjustment was made for areas with deep water tables.

3. No adjustment in chemical use is made to account for farm management factors, such as chemical application rates and crop rotations. The approach assumes that chemical use is the same for a crop grown as part of a rotation cropping system as for continuous cropping. Since the chemical use variable in the GWVIP calculation is based on acres of land treated with pesticides, application rates are also not factored into the analysis.

Application to Program Management

By identifying areas of the country that have the highest potential for leaching of agrichemicals, the GWVIP can serve as a basis for selecting sites for implementation of government programs and for more in-depth research on the environmental impact of agrichemical use. These sites cannot be selected exclusively on the basis of the GWVIP score, however, because other factors, such as surface water impacts and economic and demographic factors, are also important.

For example, the GWVIP has been used as a decision aid in selecting sites for USDA's Area Study Program, which is designed to provide chemical use and farming practice information to aid in understanding the relationships among farming activities, soil properties, and ground water quality. The National Agricultural Statistics Service interviews farm operators in 12 major watersheds where the U.S. Geological Survey is working to measure the quality of surface and ground water resources under its National Water Quality Assessment Program. At the conclusion of the project, survey information will be combined with what is learned in other elements of the President's Water Quality Initiative to assess the magnitude of the agriculture-related water quality problem for the nation as a whole and used to evaluate the potential economic and environmental effects of Initiative policies of education, technical assistance, and financial assistance if implemented nationwide.

To meet these objectives, each Area Study site must have a high potential for ground water contamination relative to other areas of the country. A map showing the average GWVIP for each of the 13,172 polygons comprising the continental United States, shown in Plate 3, was used to help select the sites. As this map shows, areas more likely to have leaching problems with agrichemicals than other areas of the country occur principally along the coastal plains stretching from Alabama and Georgia north to the Chesapeake Bay area, the corn belt states, the Mississippi River Valley, and the irrigated areas in the West. Sites selected for study in 1991 and 1992 include four from the eastern coastal plain (Delmarva Peninsula, southeastern Pennsylvania, Virginia and North Carolina, and southern Georgia), four from the corn belt states (Nebraska, Iowa, Illinois, and Indiana), and two from the irrigated areas in the West (eastern Washington and southeastern Idaho). Four additional sites will be selected for study in 1993.

Application to Policy Analysis and Development

The GWVIP has also been used by USDA to provide a national perspective on agricultural use of pesticides and the potential for ground water contamination to aid in policy analysis and development.

The geographic distribution of GWVIP scores has shown that the potential for ground water contamination is diverse both nationally and regionally. Factors that determine intrinsic vulnerability differ in virtually every major agricultural region of the country. Whether an impact is realized in these intrinsically vulnerable areas depends on the activities of producers—such as the type of crop planted, chemical use, and irrigation practices—which also vary both nationally and regionally. High vulnerability areas are those where a confluence of these factors is present. But not all cropland is vulnerable to leaching. About one-fourth of all cropland has GWVIP scores that indicate very low potential for ground water contamination from the use of agrichemicals. Nearly all agricultural states have significant acreage that meets this low vulnerability criterion. Areas of the country identified as being in a high vulnerability group relative to potential for agrichemical leaching also have significant acreages that appear to have low vulnerability.

This mix of relative vulnerabilities both nationally and regionally has important policy implications. With the potential problem so diverse, it is not likely that simple, across-the-board solutions will work. Simple policies—such as selective banning of chemicals—may reduce the potential for ground water contamination in problem areas while imposing unnecessary costs on farming in nonproblem areas. The geographic diversity of the GWVIP suggests that the best solutions will come from involvement of both local governments and scientists with their state and national counterparts to derive policies that are tailored to the unique features of each problem area.

In the future, USDA plans to use vulnerability indexes, like the GWVIP, in conjunction with economic models to evaluate the potential for solving agriculture-related water quality problems with a nationwide program to provide farmers with the knowledge and technical means to respond voluntarily to water quality concerns.

SUMMARY

These six case studies illustrate how different approaches to vulnerability assessment have evolved under diverse sets of management requirements, data constraints, and other technical considerations. In addition, each of these examples shows that vulnerability assessment is an ongoing process through which information about a region's ground water resources and its quality can be organized and examined methodically.

In Iowa, the Iowa DNR staff elected to keep their vulnerability characterization efforts as simple as possible, and to use only properties for which data already existed or could be easily checked. They assumed that surficial features such as the soil are too thin and too disrupted by human activities (e.g., tillage, abandoned wells) to provide effective ground water protection at any particular location and sought to identify a surrogate measure for average travel time from the land surface to the aquifer. Thus, a ground water vulnerability map was produced which represents vulnerability primarily on the basis of depth to ground water and extent of overlying materials. Wells and sinkholes are also shown. The results are to be used for informing resource managers and the public of the vulnerability of the resource and to determine the type of information most needed to develop an even better understanding of the vulnerability of Iowa's ground water.

The Cape Cod approach to ground water vulnerability assessment is perhaps one of the oldest and most sophisticated in the United States. Driven by the need to protect the sole source drinking water aquifer underlying this sandy peninsula, the vulnerability assessment effort has focused on the identification and delineation of the primary recharge areas for the major aquifers. This effort began with a simple mass balance approach which assumed even recharge within a circular area around each drinking water well. It has since evolved to the development of a complex, particle-tracking three-dimensional model that uses site-specific data to delineate zones of contribution. Bolstered by strong public concern, Cape Cod has been able to pursue an ambitious and sophisticated agenda for resource protection, and now boasts a sophisticated differential management ground water protection program.

In Florida, ground water resource managers rely on a combination of monitoring and vulnerability assessment techniques to identify high recharge areas and develop the state ground water protection program. Overlay and index methods, including several modified DRASTIC maps were produced to identify areas of ground water significance in support of decision making in state land acquisition programs aimed at ground water protection. In addition, several monitoring networks have been established to assess background water quality and monitor actual effects in areas identified as highly vulnerable. The coupling of ground water vulnerability assessments with monitoring and research efforts, provides the basis of an incremental and evolving ground water protection program in Florida.

The programs to protect ground water in California's intensely agricultural San Joaquin Valley are driven largely by compliance with the state Pesticide Contamination Prevention Act. The California Department of Pesticide Regulation determined that no model would be sufficient to cover their specific regulatory needs and that the available data bases were neither suitable nor reliable for regulatory purposes. Thus, a ground water protection program was built on the extensive existing pesticide use reporting system and the significant ground water monitoring requirements of the act. Using farm sections as management units, the state declares any section in which a pesticide or its degradation product is detected as a pesticide management zone and establishes further restrictions and monitoring requirements. Thus, the need to devise a defensible regulatory approach led California to pursue a mechanistic monitoring based approach rather than a modeling approach that would have inherent and difficult to quantify uncertainties.

In contrast, the approach taken in Hawaii involves an extensive effort to understand the uncertainty associated with the assessment models used. The purpose of this is to provide guidance to, but not the sole basis for, the pesticide regulation program. The combined use of sampling, physically-based numerical modeling, and a chemical leaching index has led to extensive improvements in the understanding of the fate of pesticides in the subsurface environment. Uncertainty analyses are used to determine where additional information would be most useful.

Finally, USDA's Ground Water Vulnerability Index for Pesticides illustrates a national scale vulnerability assessment developed for use as a decision aid and analytical tool for national policies regarding farm management and water quality. This approach combines nationally available statistical information on pesticide usage and soil properties with a simulation model to predict the relative likelihood of contamination in cropland areas. USDA has used this approach to target sites for its Area Study Program which is designed to provide information to farmers about the relationships between farm management practices and water quality. The results of the GWVIP have also indicated that, even at the regional level, there is often an mix of high and low vulnerability areas. This result suggests that effective ground water policies should be tailored to local conditions.

REFERENCES

Au, L.K.L. 1991. The Relative Safety of Hawaii's Drinking Water. Hawaii Medical Journal 50(3):71-80.

Barlow, P.M. 1993. Particle-Tracking Analysis of Contributing Areas of Public-Supply Wells in Simple and Complex Flow Systems, Cape Cod, Massachusetts. USGS Open File Report 93-159. Marlborough, Massachusetts: U.S. Geological Survey.

Britt, J.K., S.E. Dwinell, and T.C. McDowell. 1992. Matrix decision procedure to assess new pesticides based on relative groundwater leaching potential and chronic toxicity. Environ. Toxicol. Chem. 11:721-728.

Cape Cod Commission (CCC). 1991. Regional Policy Plan. Barnstable, Massachusetts: Cape Cod Commission.

Cape Cod Planning and Economic Development Commission (CCPEDC). March 1978a. Draft Area Wide Water Quality Management Plan for Cape Cod. Barnstable, Massachusetts: Cape Cod Commission.

Cape Cod Planning and Economic Development Commission (CCPEDC). September 1978b. Final Area Wide Water Quality Management Plan for Cape Cod. Barnstable, Massachusetts: Cape Cod Commission.

Department of Environmental Protection, Division of Water Supply (DEP-WS). 1991. Guidelines and Policies for Public Water Supply Systems. Massachusetts Department of Environmental Protection.

Gianessi, L.P., and C.A. Puffer. 1991. Herbicide Use in the United States: National Summary Report. Washington, D.C.: Resources for the Future.

Guswa, J.H., and D.R. LeBlanc. 1981. Digital Models of Groundwater Flow in the Cape Cod Aquifer System, MA. USGS Water Supply Paper 2209. U.S. Geological Survey.

Heath, D.L. 1988. DRASTIC mapping of aquifer vulnerability in eastern Barnstable and western Yarmouth, Cape Cod, Massachusetts. In Appendix D, Cape Cod Aquifer Management Project, Final Report, G.A. Zoto and T. Gallagher, eds. Boston: Massachusetts Department of Environmental Quality Engineering.

Horsely, S.W. 1983. Delineating zones of contribution of public supply wells to protect ground water. In Proceedings of the National Water Well Association Eastern Regional Conference, Ground-Water Management, Orlando, Florida.

Hoyer, B.E. 1991. Groundwater vulnerability map of Iowa. Pp. 13-15 in Iowa Geology, no. 16. Iowa City, Iowa: Iowa Department of Natural Resources.

Hoyer, B.E., J.E. Combs, R.D. Kelley, C. Cousins-Leatherman, and J.H. Seyb. 1987. Iowa Groundwater Protection Strategy. Des Moines: Iowa Department of Natural Resources.

Kellogg, R.L., M.S. Maizel, and D.W. Goss. 1992. Agricultural Chemical Use and Ground Water Quality: Where Are the Potential Problems? Washington, D.C.: U.S. Department of Agriculture, Soil Conservation Service.

Khan, M.A., and T. Liang. 1989. Mapping pesticide contamination potential. Environmental Management 13(2):233-242.

Kleveno, J.J., K. Loague, and R.E. Green. 1992. An evaluation of a pesticide mobility index: Impact of recharge variation and soil profile heterogeneity. Journal of Contaminant Hydrology 11(1-2):83-99.

Land Acquisition Advisory Council (LAAC). 1991. Ground Water Resources Committee Final Report: Florida Preservation 2000 Needs Assessment. Tallahassee, Florida: Department of Environmental Regulation. 39 pp.

Lau, L.S., and J.F. Mink. 1987. Organic contamination of ground water: A learning experience. J. American Water Well Association 79(8):37-42.

LeBlanc, D.R., and J.H. Guswa. 1977. Water-Table Map of Cape Cod, MA. May 23-27, 1976, USGS Open File Report 77-419, scale 1:48,000.

Loague, K. 1991. The impact of land use on estimates of pesticide leaching potential: Assessments and uncertainties. Journal of Contaminant Hydrology 8: 157–175.

Loague, K. 1992. Simulation of organic chemical movement in Hawaii soils with PRZM: 3. Calibration. Pacific Science 46(3):353-373.

Loague, K.M., and R.E. Green. 1988. Impact of data-related uncertainties in a pesticide leaching assessment. Pp. 98-119 in Methods for Ground Water Quality Studies, D.W. Nelson and R.H. Dowdy, eds. Lincoln, Nebraska: Agricultural Research Division, University of Nebraska.

Loague, K., and R.E. Green. 1990a. Comments on "Mapping pesticide contamination potential," by M.A. Khan and T. Liang. Environmental Management 4:149-150.

Loague, K., and R.E. Green. 1990b. Uncertainty in Areal Estimates of Pesticide Leaching Potential. Pp. 62-67 in Transactions of 14th International Congress of Soil Science. Kyoto, Japan: International Soil Science Society.

Loague, K., and R.E. Green. 1990c. Criteria for evaluating pesticide leaching models. Pp. 175-207 in Field-Scale Water and Solute Flux in Soils, K. Roth, H. Flühler, W.A. Jury, and J.C. Parker, eds. Basel, Switzerland: Birkhauser Verlag.

Loague, K.M., R.E. Green, C.C.K. Liu, and T.C. Liang. 1989a. Simulation of organic chemical movement in Hawaii soils with PRZM: 1. Preliminary results for ethylene dibromide. Pacific Science 43(1):67-95.

Loague, K., T.W. Giambelluca, R.E. Green, C.C.K. Liu, T.C. Liang, and D.S. Oki. 1989b. Simulation of organic chemical movement in Hawaii soils with PRZM: 2. Predicting deep penetration of DBCP, EDB, and TCP. Pacific Science 43(4):362-383.

Loague, K.M., R.S. Yost, R.E. Green, and T.C. Liang. 1989c. Uncertainty in a pesticide leaching assessment for Hawaii. Journal of Contaminant Hydrology 4:139-161.

Loague, K., R.E. Green, T.W. Giambelluca, T.C. Liang, and R.S. Yost. 1990. Impact of uncertainty in soil, climatic, and chemical information in a pesticide leaching assessment. Journal of Contaminant Hydrology 5:171-194.

Maddox, G., and J. Spicola. 1991. Ground Water Quality Monitoring Network. Tallahassee, Florida: Florida Department of Environmental Regulation. 20 pp.

Maddox, G., J. Lloyd, T. Scott, S. Upchurch, and R. Copeland, eds. 1993. Florida's Ground Water Quality monitoring Program: Background Hydrogeochemistry. Florida Geological Survey Special Publication #34. Tallahassee, Florida: Florida Department of Environmental Regulation in cooperation with Florida Geological Survey.

National Research Council (NRC). 1986. Ground Water Quality Protection: State and Local Strategies. Washington, D.C.: National Academy Press.

Oki, D.S., and T.W. Giambelluca. 1985. Subsurface Water and Soil Quality Data Base for State of Hawaii: Part 1. Spec. Rept. 7. Manoa, Hawaii: Water Resources Research Center, University of Hawaii at Manoa.

Oki, D.S., and T.W. Giambelluca. 1987. DBCP, EDB, and TCP contamination of ground water in Hawaii. Ground Water 25:693-702.

Olimpio, J.C., E.C. Flynn, S. Tso, and P.A. Steeves. 1991. Use of a Geographic Information System to Assess Risk to Ground-Water Quality at Public-Supply Wells, Cape Cod, Massachusetts. Boston, Massachusetts: U.S. Geological Survey.

Peterson, F.L. 1972. Water development on tropic volcanic islands—Type example: Hawaii. Ground Water 5:18-23.

Peterson, F.L., K.R. Green, R.E. Green, and J.N. Ogata. 1985. Drilling program and pesticide analysis of core samples from pineapple fields in central Oahu. Water Resources Research Center, University of Hawaii at Manoa, Special Report 7.5. Photocopy.

Southwest Florida Water Management Districts (SFWMD). 1991. The Bluebelt Commission. Brooksville, Florida: Southwest Florida Water Management Districts.

U.S. Bureau of the Census. 1991. Statistical Abstracts of the United States: 1991, 111th edition. Washington, D.C.: U.S. Government Printing Office.

Wong, L. 1983. Preliminary report on soil sampling EDB on Oahu. Pesticide Branch, Div. of Plant Industry, Department of Agriculture, State of Hawaii. Photocopy.

Wong, L. 1987. Analysis of ethylene dibromide distribution in the soil profile following shank injection for nematode control in pineapple culture. Pp. 28-40 in Toxic Organic Chemicals in Hawaii's Water Resources, P.S.C. Rao and R.E. Green, eds. Ser. 086. Honolulu: Hawaii Inst. Trop Agric. Hum. Resources Res. Exten. University of Hawaii.

Yost, R.S., K. Loague, and R.E. Green. 1993. Reducing variance in soil organic carbon estimates—soil classification and geostatistical approaches. Geoderma 57(3):247-262

6

Conclusions and Recommendations

"Of course there must be subtleties.
Just make sure you make them clear."
—Billy Wilder

This final chapter of the report revisits two of the laws of ground water vulnerability and addresses the most important findings of the preceding chapters. The chapter includes advice to policy makers and managers seeking to apply vulnerability assessments in ground water protection programs and a research agenda that suggests promising directions for improved understanding of the process of ground water contamination and the prediction of vulnerability to contamination.

First Law of Ground Water Vulnerability:
All ground water is vulnerable.

Second Law of Ground Water Vulnerability:
Uncertainty is inherent in all vulnerability assessments.

The First Law says, in effect, that ground water vulnerability is a relative rather than an absolute concept. That is, an aquifer or portion of an aquifer can only be judged to be more or less vulnerable to contamination than other aquifers or other portions of a given aquifer. Furthermore, it may be necessary to consider effects on ground water quality over longer time spans and greater distances than is commonly done in vulnerability assessments. The Second Law says that both natural variability in spatial attributes and inability to specify attribute values accurately at all spatial scales of interest over a given region will impart uncertainty, often undetermined, to all assessments of ground water vulnerability. These laws should caution users of vulnerability assessments that ignoring uncertainty can lead to considerable error. Careful attention should be paid to the effects of these potential errors on decisions that will be informed by a vulnerability assessment. If the decisions would not change if the uncertainty were considered, then users of the assessment should have increased confidence in using its results. If the decision would change in the face of uncertainty, then the use of the assessment in making decisions would have to be viewed with caution.

This pervasive, inherent uncertainty led the committee to a probabilistic, rather than deterministic, definition of ground water vulnerability: *The tendency or likelihood for contaminants to reach a specified position in the ground water system after introduction at some location above the uppermost aquifer.* Ground water vulnerability is not a measurable property, but a probability statement about future contamination that must be inferred from surrogate measurements. Such information, in its simplest form, may be a single parameter, such as depth to ground water. Like a weather forecast, vulnerability to contamination is best expressed as a probability of an event (e.g., 30 percent chance of rain). Yet very few of the vulnerability assessment methods discussed in Chapter 3 produce results in the form of probabilities. This report distinguishes between two types of ground water vulnerability: *intrinsic vulnerability*, which reflects properties that are a function of the natural setting and does not consider the attributes and behavior of particular contaminants, and *specific vulnerability*, which reflects factors that relate to the properties of the specific constituent(s) of concern, and possibly specific circumstances of land and chemical use (Chapter 1).

Using vulnerability assessments currently available, it is fairly easy to delineate many areas of high vulnerability, difficult to say for certain that an area has very low vulnerability, and not possible to make fine gradations in between.

MANAGEMENT IMPLICATIONS

Ground water vulnerability assessment is a dynamic, iterative, and interactive process that must involve the cooperative efforts of policy makers, resource managers, and technical experts. Figure 1.3, Chapter 1, illustrates the dynamic interactions among the four major components of an assessment: intended purpose, approaches, required data, and management actions. Chapter 2 describes the uses of vulnerability assessments and the technical and institutional considerations that should be addressed in planning a vulnerability assessment as a tool for management. The case studies (Chapter 5) illustrate how the vulnerability assessment process is being approached across the country. Clearly, the case studies demonstrate that information gained is fed back to improve and refine the resulting actions.

The value of educating people must be emphasized. For example, the main purpose of the Iowa vulnerability assessment process was to inform the state's residents of the need for better pesticide and nutrient management practices to protect ground water from potential contamination. The case studies show that structured, quantitative vulnerability assessments do not necessarily fill a direct decisionmaking role, but contribute to the understanding of the scope of the problem and help create a consensus for action. Vulnerability assessments should be refined as experience grows. For this reason, models, indices, or other approaches should not be chosen without careful consideration of the factors discussed in Chapter 2 that should influence the selection and use of vulnerability assessments.

Although maps are only a small component of the vulnerability assessment process, they are an inevitable, and the most visible, product and often can impart a false sense of security to the user who accepts them uncritically. For example, a user may conclude with false confidence that areas identified by assessments as having low vulnerability will provide reliably acceptable sites for land uses or activities likely to be potential sources of ground water contamination. A false negative vulnerability rating—areas shown on the map as low vulnerability that are in reality high—could result in serious contamination and related management problems. Also, false positive errors—high vulnerability areas on the map that are actually low— can lead to overly restrictive, costly, and unpopular land use requirements. Again, the consequences of false positives or false negatives, as they affect management decisions, need to be thought through before action is taken.

Analysis further suggests that even if a region can be partitioned into safe and vulnerable areas, subdividing it into areas having intermediate vulnerabilities will be difficult. More categories of vulnerability in the assessment may suggest to managers an ability to construct a zoning system or site screening process of greater discrimination, but the ultimate utility of these devices is limited by both uncertainty in the vulnerability assessment and uncertainty in the evaluation of contamination risk by the land use or activity. Chapter 3 contains further discussion of the inability of existing techniques to support such discrimination. This finding departs from the expectations of both regulatory policy makers and the regulated community, who idealistically may prefer a finer discrimination among safe and vulnerable areas.

In the context of differential management of ground water—with its goal of efficient use of resources—policy makers, resource managers, and land users, would use vulnerability assessments as a tool in adjusting regulatory requirements and management practices for different areas and allocating program resources. For example, regulatory requirements and management practices aimed at potential ground water contaminants, such as agricultural pesticides, could vary from area to area with the results of the vulnerability assessment as displayed on a multicategory map. This strategy for ground water management allows limited resources and/or personnel to be directed toward particular areas or activities with a higher likelihood of contamination, or higher vulnerability. That is not to say, however, that other areas should not be managed; less vulnerable areas still demand some level of management.

APPROACHES

The vulnerability assessment methods discussed in Chapter 3 range from simple overlay approaches, to index and statistical methods, to process-based modeling approaches. A rule of thumb for currently available techniques is that the more complex and data intensive the method, the smaller the area that can be assessed. For example, detailed process-based models are often used for field and small hydrologic unit scales; overlay and indexing methods have often been applied at the larger regional and national levels. This rule of thumb, however, does not suggest the appropriate use of methods; it simply suggests how cost considerations and data availability have led to methodological preferences based on the scale of application. Statistical methods can be applied at all levels consistent with the spatial resolution of the data.

In theory, chemical movement through the soil and vadose zone could be described by a model of contaminant transport and fate, but current models are not good enough for predicting where, when, and at what concentration a constituent will appear. This situation is due to spatial variability in characteristics of the landscape and properties of the media, uncertainties associated with the modeling techniques, and uncertainties involved in estimation of attributes based on available data. These difficulties are discussed extensively in Chapters 3 and 4. On a regional scale, index methods are in some sense conceptually appropriate in that they deal explicitly with the multivariate nature of the problem; however, one set of weights is not sufficient for all situations.

None of these methods, even process-based models, can be validated in the usual scientific sense for vulnerability assessments because of spatial and temporal variability. This uncertainty in the ability to estimate the likelihood of future contamination will persist in the absence of noninvasive techniques for characterizing soil and ground water systems in three dimensions with respect to the parameters that affect contaminant movement through soil and the vadose zone.

Despite these difficulties, inferences about the accuracy of a regional vulnerability assessment can be made through several lines of inquiry. The process of testing and evaluating vulnerability assessments may involve a hierarchical approach that evolves over several stages. In fact, the most sensible applications of vulnerability assessment techniques may include explicit plans to test, review, and refine the assessment over time.

Those who generate vulnerability assessments must ensure that users are aware of the uncertainties associated with the modeling scheme and data used. Policy and decision makers are left with the responsibility of making informed choices using uncertain scientific assessments. Scientists must accept the responsibility of assisting decision makers in correctly interpreting the sources of uncertainty and increasing their confidence in the results of vulnerability assessments.

DATA AND DATABASES

Databases and their characteristics, content, scale, limitations, deficiencies, and availability are discussed in Chapter 4. Only nationally available databases are discussed, but many states have data and machine retrievable databases that are valuable for vulnerability assessments. The appropriateness of the various databases for different levels of assessment are discussed.

One of the committee's original goals was to develop a single set of parameters that are important for a national level assessment for vulnerability. However, the complexity and local nature of conditions leading to ground water vulnerability make it impossible to establish a set of parameters important in all cases. The important parameters differ in different parts of the country and in different conditions.

A major constraint on vulnerability assessments is the different scales of data in the various databases. A second, serious deficiency is the uncertainty of the data in the databases. These limitations are being addressed by the Federal Geographic Data Committee and the new Spatial Data Transfer Standard; however, more emphasis on these and other similar efforts is needed. Standard national databases of good quality and understandable content are essential to ground water resource assessment and protection. The other major constraint on assessment of ground water vulnerability is the lack of digital spatial databases, particularly at the county, watershed, and field levels. Although soils and topography are mapped for most of the country, less than 10 percent are digitized. Geologic mapping at scales useful for many vulnerability assessments is limited in many areas. Good climatic data are also lacking for much of the western United States. Databases on chemical properties and chemical use continue to expand and improve, but are still lacking.

The uncertainty of the data involved in the vulnerability assessment, and the uncertainty of the assessment method itself, are often not well represented in assessment products. In most cases, the major product is the map of the area that portrays the results of the assessment. Often, these maps oversimplify the results of an assessment or include too much information and, therefore, confuse or mislead the user. The ineffective use of maps to portray the results of assessments is due to a combination of poor definition of the purpose of the map, poor assessment of the knowledge of the user, poor cartographic skills of the preparer of the map, and the amount of time and effort it takes to prepare the complex and often multiple maps required to represent the data. If a ground water vulnerability assessment is to be useful, the map must present the results in a clear, understandable fashion so that the user can reach appropriate conclusions. Also, users must commit to vulnerability assessments the time and attention necessary for informed decision-making. By carefully reviewing each of these factors and making suitable choices, the responsible specialists can prepare effective vulnerability assessment maps.

With the availability of geographic information systems (GIS) software in recent years, digital information arising from vulnerability assessments can be easily displayed on a very sophisticated map without displaying the actual quality of the assessment. Innovation by the user and GIS industry, associated with improved assessment methodologies and uncertainty analyses, will prove most useful for depicting uncertainties associated with the vulnerability assessments portrayed on these same maps.

RESEARCH AGENDA

The committee's evaluation of vulnerability assessments led to identification of a body of research needs, many of which are specified here in general terms. This research agenda is divided into four categories: fundamental understanding of transport and fate processes, database improvements, geoprocessing and display improvements, and improvements in assessment methods. No order of priority or relative need is reflected in the following.

Fundamental Transport and Fate Processes

Develop a better understanding of all processes that affect the transport and fate of contaminants. A vulnerability assessment is only as good as the information/knowledge available at the time. Lack of understanding of the factors that affect the transport and fate of the contaminant in the environment decreases the certainty associated with an assessment.

Establish simple, practical, and reliable methods for measuring *in situ* hydraulic conductivities of the soil and the unsaturated and saturated zones. Develop simple, practical, and reliable methods for mea-

suring *in situ* degradation rates (e.g., hydrolysis, methylation, biodegradation), and develop methods for characterizing changes in degradation
rate as a function of other physical parameters (e.g., depth in soil).
Develop methods for scaling measurements that sample different volumes of porous material to provide equivalent measures. This information is of primary importance in determining contaminant fate and transport
in the soil. Emphasis should be placed on developing methods that are
relatively inexpensive.

Develop improved approaches to obtaining information on the residence time of water along flow paths and identifying recharge and discharge areas. It is important to protect recharge zones from contamination.
Additional research into methods that provide the necessary information
should be encouraged. For example, methods that use environmental isotopes may be useful and, therefore, should be developed further and evaluated in this context.

Databases

Develop unified ways to combine soils and geologic information in
vulnerability assessments. A tendency exists to consider only soil or only
geologic information in vulnerability assessments. Both are important and
need to be integrated in assessing vulnerability.

Improve the chemical databases which are currently the source of
much uncertainty in vulnerability assessments. It has been shown that
for some measures of ground water vulnerability, the largest component of
uncertainty involves the chemical aspects of transport. For example, the
sorption process (expressed by "chemical" as K_{oc} and "soil" as f_{oc}) has been
found to produce large uncertainty in vulnerability assessments using the
Attenuation or Retardation Factor approaches. The uncertainty in f_{oc} could
be reduced by incorporating this parameter more systematically into current
soil survey sampling.

Determine the circumstances in which the properties of the intermediate vadose zone are critical to vulnerability assessments and develop methods for characterizing the zone for assessments. Research is
needed to identify environmental situations where the reference or compliance surface must be below the root zone and where the base of the root
zone is adequate. At present, soil surveys contain large amounts of information that can be used in vulnerability assessments, but very few data
exist on the hydrologic, geochemical, and microbial properties of the intermediate vadose zone (the unsaturated zone below the root zone). Criteria
need to be developed that can help to establish when the properties of the
intermediate vadose zone will have little effect on vulnerability. For situations where the intermediate vadose zone cannot be ignored, methods should

be developed that allow systematic and inexpensive measurement of the properties of the zone required in vulnerability assessments. Perhaps in these instances, these data could be incorporated into a database consistent with the soils database of the Soil Conservation Service. One reviewer of this report commented that "Until we have a better quantitative handle on the biological processes, I think we have to assume that everything that escapes the root zone is going to ground water."

Establish in the soil mapping standards of USDA's Soil Conservation Service an efficient soil sampling scheme for acquiring accurate soil attribute data in soil mapping unit polygons and documenting the uncertainty in these data. A need exists to better characterize the inclusions of other soil types in soil mapping units, including fractional area of included soil and distribution of inclusions. The quality of a vulnerability assessment is very dependent on the data employed. The uncertainty or variability of soil attribute data is critical in determining the uncertainty of the assessment. Equally important is the location and quantity of inclusions of material of differing types. In some settings, this knowledge may be as important as knowledge of preferential flow paths. For example, if a coarse sandy soil is included in a soil mapping unit (polygon) dominated by silty loam, the ground water vulnerability may depend more on the included sandy soil than on the dominant soil in the area.

Establish reliable transfer functions for estimating *in situ* hydraulic properties, using available soil attribute data (e.g., bulk densities, particle-size distributions, etc.). Develop ways to determine the additional uncertainty arising from the use of transfer functions in ground water vulnerability assessments. Since the cost of sampling is large, methods that allow other, easy-to-obtain data to be used as surrogates for the required information are desirable. At some locations, such methods may be used to provide additional information when the required parameter has been measured. When these methods are developed, the uncertainty of using them should be determined. It may also be possible that using surrogate information, in comparison with using only the primary data, would reduce the overall uncertainty of results.

Geoprocessing and Display

Develop methods for merging data obtained at different spatial and temporal scales into a common scale for vulnerability assessment. It is highly unlikely that all data will be collected at the same spatial or temporal scale, especially data collected by different agencies for differing purposes. Therefore, it is very important to develop methods that permit data collected at one scale to be transformed to a scale appropriate for a given vulnerability assessment.

Improve analytical tools in GIS to facilitate the integration of assessment methods with spatial and attribute databases and the computing environment.

Establish more meaningful categories of vulnerability for assessment methods. The issue of vulnerability classifications must be addressed before colors can be placed on a map in any meaningful way. The committee doubts such classifications can be used effectively unless the scheme used to develop them has some relevance to the assessment objective and they provide a valid measure of differences in the vulnerability of ground water.

Assessment Methods

Determine which processes are most important to incorporate into vulnerability assessments at different spatial scales. To determine ground water vulnerability accurately, the dominant processes at a given scale need to be identified and methods developed for characterizing them that can be used in modeling approaches.

Obtain more information on the uncertainty associated with vulnerability assessments and develop ways to display this uncertainty. Methods are needed that can identify and differentiate among more sources of uncertainty. It is vital to provide information on the uncertainty of a vulnerability assessment. Current methods, however, only provide lower bounds on the uncertainty since they only take account of uncertainty from specific sources. As more effort is directed toward reducing uncertainty from known sources (e.g., sparse data), other uncertainties (e.g., model uncertainty) need to be evaluated. The task may prove formidable, since determining absolute uncertainty implicitly assumes some knowledge of absolute truth.

Develop methods for accounting for soil macropores and other preferential flow pathways that can affect vulnerability. These investigations should include evaluations of the uncertainty in methods and measurements as they affect the assessment. Routes of transport that circumvent the porous media have a profound effect on transport and are difficult to quantify. Knowledge of these types of pathways could drastically alter the interpretation of an assessment made with traditional methods. Currently, an extensive research effort is devoted to the development of methods for characterizing and modeling the preferential flow process. However, there is no satisfactory method for predicting the effects of this mechanism. Because the ramifications of preferential flow are so large, additional research in this area is highly recommended.

Develop methods for incorporating process-based, statistical, and qualitative information into an integrated or hybrid assessment. Efforts should focus on developing rigorous approaches for making use of all available information so as to decrease uncertainty.

Identify counterintuitive situations leading to a greater true vulnerability than commonly perceived. For example, develop greater understanding of the circumstances in which low-permeability materials that overlay aquifers can transmit contaminants to ground water. Some geohydrologic systems have characteristics that make them appear to have low vulnerability to contamination. Changes in management, however, may circumvent these characteristics, increasing the system's vulnerability. Likewise, some low-permeability materials overlying aquifers may transmit contaminants more easily than commonly perceived because of interconnected fracture systems. These counterintuitive situations typically would not be explicitly characterized in vulnerability assessments, generally because of the simplicity of current methods. Therefore, it would be helpful to document some common counterintuitive situations to warn decision makers and analysts of potential errors in assessing vulnerability.

A

Sources for Digital Resource Databases

GENERAL SOURCE INFORMATION

Earth Science Information Center
U.S. Geological Survey
507 National Center
Reston, Virginia 22092
(703) 860-6045

National Geographical Data Center
National Oceanic and Atmospheric
  Administration
325 Broadway
Boulder, Colorado 80303
(703) 487-4650

National Technical Information
  Service
U.S. Department of Commerce
5285 Port Royal Road
Springfield, Virginia 22161
(703) 487-4660

International GIS Sourcebook
GIS World, Inc.
2629 Redwing Road, Suite 280
Fort Collins, Colorado 80525
(303) 223-4848

State Geographic Information
  Activities Compendium
Council of State Government
Iron Works Pike
P.O. Box 11910
Lexington, Kentucky 40578
(800) 800-1910

Federal Geographic Data Committee
Manual of Federal Geographic Data
  Products
U.S. Geological Survey
507 National Center
Reston, Virginia 22092
(703) 860-6045

CLIMATE

National Databases

National Climatic Data Center
Federal Building
Asheville, North Carolina 28801
(704) CLI-MATE

Climate Data Access Facility
Soil Conservation Service
511 Broadway, Room 248
Portland, Oregon 97209-3489
(503) 326-4098

Regional Databases

Western Regional Climate Center
Desert Research Institute
P.O. Box 60220
Reno, Nevada 89506
(702) 677-3103

High Plains Regional Climate Center
237 Chase Hall (0728)
Center for Agriculture, Meteorology,
  & Climatology
University of Nebraska
Lincoln, Nebraska 68583-0728
(402) 472-6706

Southern Regional Climate Center
Department of Geography
  & Anthropology
Louisiana State University
Baton Rouge, Louisiana 70803
(504) 388-6870

Midwestern Regional Climate Center
Illinois State Water Survey
2204 Griffith Drive
Champaign, Illinois 61820
(217) 244-8226

Southeastern Regional Climate
  Center
1201 Main Street, Suite 1100
  Capital Center
Columbia, South Carolina 29201
(803) 737-0811

Northeast Regional Climate Center
1111 Bradfield Hall
Cornell University
Ithaca, New York 14853
(607) 255-1751

Climate Analysis Center
5200 Auth Road
Washington, D.C. 20233
(301) 763-8167

HYDROGEOLOGY

U.S. Geological Survey
507 National Center
Reston, Virginia 22042
(703) 860-6045

LAND USE AND LAND COVER

U.S. Geological Survey
507 National Center
Reston, Virginia 22042
(703) 860-6045

MANAGEMENT FACTORS

National Resources Inventory
  Database
Resource Inventory and GIS
  Division
U.S. Department of Agriculture,
  Soil Conservation Service
P.O. Box 2890
Washington, D.C. 20013
(202) 720-5420

Agricultural Irrigation and Water
  Use Publication
U.S. Department of Agriculture,
  Economic Research Service
P.O. Box 1608
Rockville, Maryland 20849

National Herbicide Use Database
Resources for the Future
1616 P Street, NW
Washington, D.C. 20036
(202) 328-5000

Pesticide Properties Database
U.S. Department of Agriculture,
Soil Conservation Service
Ecological Sciences Division
P.O. Box 2890
Washington, D.C. 20013
(202) 720-2587

Agricultural Chemical Usage
  Database
U.S. Department of Agriculture,
National Agricultural Statistics
  Service
P.O. Box 1608
Rockville, Maryland 20849
(800) 999-6779

1987 Census of Agriculture
Data User Services Division
Customer Service
U.S. Bureau of the Census
Washington, D.C. 20233
(301) 763-1113

SOILS

National Cartography and GIS
  Center
U.S. Department of Agriculture,
  Soil Conservation Service
P.O. Box 6567
Fort Worth, Texas 76115
(817) 334-5559

SSSA Headquarters Office
677 South Segoe Road
Madison, Wisconsin 53711-1086
Attention: Book Order Department

TOPOGRAPHY

Earth Science Information Center
U.S. Geological Survey
507 National Center, Room 1C402
Reston, Virginia 22092
(703) 860-6045

B

Biographical Sketches

COMMITTEE MEMBERS

ARMANDO J. CARBONELL, *Chair*, is Executive Director of the Cape Cod Commission. Currently he is on leave as a Loeb Fellow in Advanced Environmental Studies at Harvard University (1992-1993). On Cape Cod he has overseen the development of programs in strategic regional planning, ground water and marine resources protection, environmental design, geographic information systems, and land use control during the past eight years. He received his A.B. in Geography from Clark University and was a Doctoral Fellow in the Department of Geography and Environmental Engineering of Johns Hopkins University.

HUGO F. THOMAS, *Chair* (through 3/22/91), holds a Ph.D. in geology from the University of Missouri and is the state geologist of Connecticut. Previously he was on the faculty of the University of Connecticut. He is interested in the study and implementation of new techniques for using natural resources data in land and water decision making. For example, his agency is in the forefront of the use of Geographic Information Systems for planning. Dr. Thomas is a former member of the Water Science and Technology Board.

WILLIAM M. ALLEY is a research hydrologist with the U.S. Geological Survey in Reston, Virginia. He received a B.S. from Colorado School of Mines, an M.S. from Stanford University, and a Ph.D. in Geography and Environmental Engineering from Johns Hopkins University. From

186 GROUND WATER VULNERABILITY ASSESSMENT

1986 to 1990, Dr. Alley was ground-water coordinator for the pilot National Water Quality Assessment Program. His research interests are in regional assessment of ground water quality and surface and ground water interactions.

LAWRENCE G. BATTEN is a Technical Marketing Representative for Environmental Systems Research Institute (ESRI) in Boulder, Colorado, where he is involved in development of GIS applications in a variety of environmental and demographic fields. He has previously held positions at TYDAC Technologies and the U.S. Geological Survey. He received his B.S. in Earth Science from the University of South Dakota. Pertinent areas of research that Mr. Batten has pursued include drainage basin characterization and hydrologic modeling.

CHERYL K. CONTANT is an Associate Professor and Chair of the Graduate Program in Urban and Regional Planning at the University of Iowa. She received her Ph.D. in Civil Engineering from Stanford University. Her current research examines the farm practice and water quality implications of alternative nonpoint pollution policies and effectiveness of field demonstration programs.

PAMELA G. DOCTOR is the Staff Scientist and Manager for the Site Characterization and Assessment Section of Battelle Pacific Northwest Laboratories, where she oversees the work of field geologists and hydrologists and performance and risk assessment modelers doing research in hazardous waste management and remediation. She received her Ph.D. in Statistics from Iowa State University. Areas of interest for Dr. Doctor include environmental sampling and analysis, statistical problems of fatios in environmental radionuclide research, and biological effects studies.

ANTHONY S. DONIGIAN, JR. is President and Principal Engineer of AQUA TERRA Consultants. He received a B.A. in Engineering Sciences and a B.S. in Engineering from Dartmouth College, and an M.S. in Civil Engineering from Stanford University. His recent research and applications studies have concentrated on the movement of contaminants through the vadose zone, ground water contamination by pesticides and hazardous wastes, model validation issues and procedures, and the evaluation of control alternatives such as best management practices, conservation tillage, and remedial actions at waste sites.

ROBERT H. DOWDY received his Ph.D. in Soil Science from Michigan State University, his M.S. in Agronomy from the University of Kentucky, and his B.S. in Agriculture from Berea College. Currently, he is a Soil Scientist with the Agricultural Research Service, USDA, and Professor of Soil Chemistry at the University of Minnesota. Research interests of Dr. Dowdy include ground water quality, plant root development, quantitative analyses of soil clay minerals, and pesticide movement under irrigated potato production.

KEITH LOAGUE (through 4/29/92) received his Ph.D. in Hydrology from the University of British Columbia, Vancouver. Currently he is an Associate Professor of Soil Hydrology at the University of California, Berkeley. Dr. Loague's research has focused on simulating the hydrological response of near-surface systems and model evaluation.

P. SURESH C. RAO received a Ph.D. in Soil Physics in 1974 from the University of Hawaii. Currently, he is a gradaute research professor in the Soil and Water Science Department at the University of Florida. His research interests are in the development and field testing of process-level models for predicting the fate of pollutants in soils and ground water. He has worked with state and federal agencies in providing scientific bases for environmental regulatory policy. Dr. Rao served on the Committee on Ground Water Modeling Assessment, 1987-1988, and as a member of the Water Science and Technology Board, 1988-1991.

DONALD I. SIEGEL is an Associate Professor of Geology at Syracuse University where he teaches graduate courses in hydrogeology and aqueous geochemistry. He holds B.S. and M.S. degrees in geology from the University of Rhode Island and Penn State University, respectively, and a Ph.D. in Hydrogeology from the University of Minnesota. His research interests are in solute transport at both local and regional scales, wetland-ground water interaction, and paleohydrogeology.

GALE W. TESELLE received his M.A. in Geography in 1968 from the University of Nebraska. Currently he is the Director of the Resource Inventory and Geographic Information Systems Division, USDA-Soil Conservation Service. The division is responsible for the development, implementation, and management of national resource inventories, cartography, geographic information systems, and remote sensing technologies. Mr. TeSelle was Chair of the Geographic Data Standards Working Group of the Federal Interagency Coordinating Committee on Digital Cartography from 1983 to 1991.

ROBERTO R. TESO is a Senior Environmental Research Scientist with the California Department of Pesticide Regulation. He received his B.S. in Agriculture and Agronomy and his M.S. in Crop Protection from the University of Arizona, Tucson. Mr. Teso's research endeavors have included field and laboratory investigations of techniques for monitoring pesticide residues in soil and drainage waters, and the development of soil survey, geographic coordinate, and well log databases and their applications to ground water contamination issues.

SCOTT R. YATES received his B.S. in Geology/Hydrology from the University of Wisconsin, Madison; his M.S. in Hydrology from the New Mexico Institute of Mining and Technology; and his Ph.D. in Soil Physics/Mathematics from the University of Arizona. He is currently a Soil Scientist for the U.S. Department of Agriculture—Agricultural Research Service and is an adjunct faculty member in the Department of Soil and Environmental Science at the University of California, Riverside. Some specializations of Dr. Yates include soil physics and hydrology; spatial variability and geostatistical methods; modeling the transport of microorganisms; and analytical and numerical solution methods applied to hydrologic and soil physical problems.

JAMES R. WALLIS (through 10/18/91) received his B.S. in forestry from the University of New Brunswick, his M.S. from Oregon State University, and his Ph.D. in Soil Morphology from University of California, Berkeley. Currently he is a Research Staff Member at the IBM Thomas J. Watson Research Center, where he has been since 1967. Previously, he held positions in hydrology and forestry with the U.S. Forest Service, Montana State University, and elsewhere. His principal interests are in mathematical models applied to hydrology, soils, forestry, and land management. He has lectured at many different universities and has addressed many issues relevant to estimates of extreme floods. He has served on many NRC committees and is a former member of the Water Science and Technology Board.

COMMITTEE STAFF

PATRICIA L. CICERO received her B.A. in Mathematics from Kenyon College. She worked as Senior Project Assistant at the National Research Council's Water Science and Technology Board (WSTB). Currently, she is attending the University of Wisconsin, Madison for her master's in Water Resources Management. Ms. Cicero has worked on a variety of studies at the WSTB, including ones on international soil and water research and development, wastewater management in coastal urban areas, techniques for assessing ground water vulnerability, and the environmental effects of the operations at Glen Canyon Dam on the lower Colorado River.

SARAH CONNICK earned her A.B. in Chemistry from Bryn Mawr College and her M.S. in Environmental Engineering from Stanford University. She is a Senior Staff Officer with the National Research Council's (NRC) WSTB where she directs studies of wastewater management in coastal urban areas, techniques for assessing ground water vulnerability, and Antarctic policy and science. Prior to joining the WSTB staff, Ms. Connick was a Staff Officer for the NRC's Committee to Provide Interim Oversight of the Department of Energy Nuclear Weapons Complex.

Contributors to the Committee's Effort

Joseph Alexander
Research Triangle Institute
Research Triangle Park, North
  Carolina

Bruce Anderson
Hawaii State Department of Health
Honolulu

Jim Ayars
Agricultural Research Service
U.S. Department of Agriculture
Fresno, California

Paul Barlow
U.S. Geological Survey
Marlborough, Massachusetts

Randy Brown
Soil Science Department
University of Florida
Gainesville

Tom Cambareri
Cape Cod Commission
Barnstable, Massachusetts

Larry Carver
National Center for Geographic
  Information and Analysis
University of California
Santa Barbara

Tim Cockrum
Fresno County Department of
  Public Works and Development
  Services
Fresno, California

Stephen Cordle
U.S. Environmental Protection
  Agency
Washington, D.C.

Rodney DeHaan
Bureau of Drinking Water and
  Ground Water Resources
Department of Environmental
  Regulation
Tallahassee, Florida

Doug Edwards
Fresno County Agricultural
  Commission
California

Mike Frimpter
U.S. Geological Survey
Boston, Massachusetts

Tom Giambelluca
Department of Geography
University of Hawaii
Honolulu

Marilyn Ginsberg
U.S. Environmental Protection
  Agency
Washington, D.C.

Niles Glasgow
Soil Conservation Service
U.S. Department of Agriculture
Gainesville, Florida

Don Goss
Soil Conservation Service
U.S. Department of Agriculture
Fort Worth, Texas

Richard Green
Department of Agronomy and Soil
  Science
University of Hawaii
Honolulu

John F. Hackler
U.S. Environmental Protection
  Agency
Boston, Massachusetts

Robert Hirsch
Water Resources Division
U.S. Geological Survey
Reston, Virginia

Ron Hoffer
U.S. Environmental Protection
  Agency
Washington, D.C.

Bernard E. Hoyer
Iowa Department of Natural
  Resources
Iowa City

Berman Hudson
Soil Conservation Service
U.S. Department of Agriculture
Lincoln, Nebraska

Chuck Job
U.S. Environmental Protection
  Agency
Washington, D.C.

Bob Kellogg
Soil Conservation Service
U.S. Department of Agriculture
Washington, D.C.

Chester Lao
Board of Water Supply
Honolulu, Hawaii

Susan Liddle
Research Triangle Institute
Research Triangle Park, North
  Carolina

Karl E. Longley
Department of Civil Engineering
California State University
Fresno

Gary Maddox
Bureau of Drinking Water and
  Ground Water Resources
Department of Environmental
  Regulation
Tallahassee, Florida

Jane Marshall
U.S. Environmental Protection
  Agency
Washington, D.C.

Harry Nightingale
Agricultural Research Service
U.S. Department of Agriculture
Fresno, California

Phil Pasteris
Soil Conservation Service
U.S. Department of Agriculture
Portland, Oregon

Mark Pepple
California Department of Food and
  Agriculture
Sacramento

Claude Phene
Agricultural Research Service
U.S. Department of Agriculture
Fresno, California

Joan M. TeSelle
Mitchellville, Maryland

Lonnie Wass
Regional Water Quality Control
  Board
Fresno, California

Lyle Wong
Hawaii State Department of
  Agriculture
Honolulu

Index

A

Abandoned wells, 22
Advanced Weather Information
Processing System (AWIPS), 126
Age of water, 84
Agricultural Census, 128, 129
Agricultural DRASTIC, 52, 53
Agricultural management, 15, 124
databases, 90, 129-131, 183
in San Joaquin Valley, 151-152
technical assistance, 34-35, 163-164
see also Fertilizers; Pesticides
Agricultural Research Service, 130
Agricultural Stabilization and Conser-
vation Service (ASCS), 128, 130-
131
Air pollution, 123, 124
Aldicarb, 14, 147
Allocation of resources. See Resource
allocation
American Congress on Surveying and
Mapping, 106
Animal wastes, 14
Approaches. See Methods

Aquifer sensitivity assessment methods,
45
Artificial recharge wells, 18
Associative methods. See Statistical
methods
Atrazine, 32
Attenuation Factor (AF), 68, 73-74, 176
Attribute databases, on soil, 117-119
Awareness. See Public education

B

Back-siphoning, 14, 18, 21
Base data, 131
Bayesian methods, 68
Bias, 65
Biochannels, 3, 21
Biodegradation, 2, 42, 43
and water transport time, 2, 19, 43,
48
Bottled water, 14
Brine injection wells, 18
Bureau of Indian Affairs, 123
Bureau of Land Management, 123, 127
Bureau of Reclamation, 123

C

CALF, 58
Calibration, 78, 79
California, 14, 28, 152, 153. *See also*
    San Joaquin Valley
Cape Cod, Massachusetts, 9, 28, 35,
    139-144, 165-166
Cartography. *See* Geographic informa-
    tion systems; Maps and mapping;
    Resolution; Scales and scaling
Case studies
    ground water vulnerablity index for
        pesticides (GWVIP), 162-165
    Cape cod, 139-144
    Florida, 145-151
    Hawaii, 156-161
    Iowa, 135-138
    San Joaquin Valley, 151-155
Cells and polygons, 7, 65, 67, 87, 91
    and geostatistical methods, 62
    in GIS databases, 87, 90
    in land use and cover mapping, 127
    in processed-based models, 59
    in soil mapping, 10, 113, 177
Censored data, 60
Centralized Database System (CDBS),
    125-126
Chemical databases, 10, 176
Chemigation, 18, 21
Circular A-16, 106, 108
Clay in soils, 2, 42-43, 90
    and sampling, 85
Cleanup and control of contamination,
    4, 14, 31, 34
Climate, databases, 9, 91, 123-126, 182
Climatic Data Access Facility, 125-126
Cluster analysis, 60, 61
CMLS, 54, 56, 57, 58
Compliance monitoring, 34
Computers and computing, 22, 39, 40
    environments, 7-8, 86-87
    errors in, 8, 66, 96
    see also Geographic information
        systems; Process-based simula-
        tion models
Concentrations of contaminants, 7, 19,
    80

regulatory limits, 34
    and sampling methods, 85-86
    and statistical methods, 6, 45
Conceptual errors, 66
Conditions on site use, 34
Confidence intervals, and map cells, 7,
    67, 77-78
Confinement over aquifers, 43, 48
Contaminant pathways. *See* Flow paths
Coordination among programs, 5, 39, 40
    Federal, 105-108, 124
    GIS facilitation of, 94
    State and local, 108-109
    weather data, 124-125
Counterintuitive situations, 11, 179
County assessments, 23, 37
    soil databases, 90, 113
Coupled transport models, 6, 45, 53
Cracks, 3, 18, 21, 94
Cross-contamination, 22

D

Data Base Analyzer and Parameter
    Estimator (DBAPE), 90-91
Data collection activity, 7, 9, 27, 38,
    40, 65, 105
    federal, 9, 105-108
    remote sensing, 112, 132
    of states, 9, 108
    see also Monitoring activities and
        data
Data quality and availability, 2-3, 4-5,
    8, 9, 26, 27, 90
    and method selection, 37-38
    and overlay and index methods, 5-6,
        38, 48, 50, 51, 52
    and process-based models, 6, 27, 37-
        38, 53, 56, 94, 105
    processing and storage errors, 7, 66
    and statistical methods, 6, 38, 45,
        60, 63
    uncertainties and errors, 3, 7, 20, 38,
        63-66, 76-77, 104-105
    see also Data collection activity;
        Databases; Monitoring activities
        and data

Databases, 2-3, 9, 32, 87, 104-105, 131-132, 174-175
  agricultural management, 90, 129-131, 183
  automation of, 108-109, 131, 174
  climate, 9, 91, 123-126, 182
  federal coordination, 105-108
  field assessments, 113, 120, 130-131
  hydrogeologic, 2, 9, 63, 121-123, 177, 183
  land use and cover, 2-3, 9, 126-129, 183
  national assessments, 114, 120, 121, 174
  regional assessments, 45, 114
  soil properties, 2, 9, 90-91, 112-121, 177, 184
  sources of, 125, 181-184
  state and local, 108-109
  topography, 9, 109-112, 184
  see also Geographic information systemsDecision making. *See* Land use management; Policy analysis and development
Deep aquifers, 21, 22
Defense Mapping Agency, 110
Definitions
  of soil, 113
  of vulnerability, 1-2, 15-19
Degradation, *in situ* measurement, 10, 175-176
  see also Biodegradation
Delphi approach, 52
Depth to water table, 2, 42, 43.
  in Iowa assessment, 9, 137-138
  in overlay and index methods, 48, 49
  in vulnerability definitions, 17
  see also Flow paths
Derived data, 90, 91, 95
Deterministic models, 9, 57, 79
Development of ground water, 22
  Iowa assessment, 136
Dibromochloropropane (DBCP), 14, 152, 157, 160, 161
Differential geographic assessment, 7, 8, 77-78, 96, 172
  map display of, 36-37, 67

Differential management, 32, 172-173
  Cape Cod, 28, 140-144, 166
  EPA, 16
  Florida, 28, 148-151
Digital Elevation Model (DEM), 110-112
Discharge limits, 34
Discharge zones, 21
  identification of, 10, 50, 176
Discriminant analysis, 60, 61, 62
Dispersion, 19
Display of results. *See* Geographic information systems; Maps and mapping
Distributions of contaminants, 6, 45
DRASTIC, 50, 51, 52, 53, 81, 84
  Cape Cod use, 141, 143, 144
  Florida use, 148, 150, 166
Drinking water, 13, 14, 33
  in Florida, 145-146
  in vulnerability definitions, 17

E

Ecosystems, 13, 33
Education. *See* Public education
Elevation, 109, 110-112, 120, 126
Environmental Protection Agency (EPA), 16, 51
  classification of methods, 44-45
  Data Base Analyzer and Parameter Estimator, 90-91
  databases, 130
  Global Change Database Program, 126
  National Pesticide Survey, 14, 81, 84
  and President's Water Quality Initiative, 15
  PRZM model, 52, 53, 55, 56, 70-72, 90
Equipment, 39, 40
Error. *See* Uncertainty and error
Ethylene dibromide (EDB), 14, 147, 157, 161
Evaluation. *See* Testing and evaluation
Extension Service (ES), 130

F

Farm and Ranch Irrigation Survey, 130
Farms. *See* Agricultural management;
    Fertilizers; Pesticides
Federal Geographic Data Committee
    (FGDC), 9, 106-108, 174, 181
Federal government. *See also* Environ-
    mental Protection Agency; U.S.
    Department of Agriculture; U.S.
    Geologic Survey
    data management, 9, 105-108
    GIS use, 87, 92
    land use management, 33, 127
    water-level information, 48
Federal Information Processing
    Standard 173. *See* Spatial Data
    Transfer Standard
Federal Interagency Coordination
    Committee on Digital Cartogra-
    phy (FICCDC), 106
Fertilizers, 14, 136, 145
Field assessments, 23, 37
    databases, 113, 120, 130-131
    testing of, 7, 8, 78-79
    use of process-based models, 53, 59,
    78-79
First Law of Ground Water Vulnerabil-
    ity, 2, 18-19, 170-171
First-order uncertainty analysis
    (FOUA), 68, 69, 73-75, 77
Fish and Wildlife Service, 127
Florida, 9, 14, 28, 145-151, 166
Flow paths, 3, 20, 21-22. *See also*
    Depth to water table
    preferential, 3, 6, 11, 21-22, 58-59,
    94-95, 177, 178
    travel time, 10, 19, 39, 81, 137, 176
Flow system. *See* Depth to water table;
    Discharge zones; Flow paths;
    Recharge rate; Recharge zones
Forest Service, 123, 127
Fourier Amplitude Sensitivity Test
    (FAST), 71
Fractures, 18

G

Geochemistry, 84
Geographic Information Retrieval and
    Analysis System (GIRAS), 127
Geographic information systems (GIS),
    8, 9, 11, 42, 87-90, 91, 175, 178
    errors in, 63, 66, 67, 92
    Hawaii use of, 157
    Iowa use of, 138
    and modeling, 92-94
    and overlay and index methods, 45,
    52, 94
    uncertainty display, 9, 92, 175
Geographic variation, 38, 170, 173
    and overlay and index methods, 5-6,
    50
    see also Differential geographic
    assessment; Differential manage-
    ment
Geologic Society of America, 121-122
Georgia, 14
Geostatistical analyses, 60, 62-63, 65
GLEAMS, 53, 54, 56
Global Change Database Program, 126
Government. *See* Federal government;
    Local government; Planning
    agencies; Regulation; State
    government
Graphic display. *See* Geographic
    information systems; Maps and
    mapping
GRASS Waterworks, 90, 91
Grid-cell based systems, 8, 87
Groundwater Atlas of the United States,
    121
Ground water vulnerability assessment
    methods, 45
Ground Water Vulnerability Index for
    Nitrates (GWVIN), 52
Ground Water Vulnerability Index for
    Pesticides (GWVIP), 15, 52, 162-
    165, 167

H

Hawaii, 10, 14, 28, 156-161, 166

Hazardous waste disposal, 13
Historical Climate Network (HCN), 125
Horizontal (lateral) movement, 21, 50
Hybrid assessment methods, 11, 45, 60, 165, 167, 179
Hydraulic conductivity, 10, 90, 175
Hydrogeologic (physical) attributes, 37, 43-44. *See also* Depth to water table; Flow paths; Recharge rate; Soil properties; Topography; Unsaturated zone
    and assessment methods, 45
    databases, 2, 9, 63, 121-123, 177, 183
    and degradation rate, 10, 179
    Florida, 145-146
    Iowa, 137-138
    and method selection, 5, 37
    and overlay and index methods, 2, 5-6, 19, 45, 48-53
    and process-based models, 54-55, 56, 57
    San Joaquin Valley, 152
    and statistical methods, 61
    in vulnerability definitions, 17, 18
Hydrologic study units (HSUs), 61
    and scale, 23

I

Illinois, 51, 52
Index methods, 2, 3, 5-6, 19, 45, 46, 48, 62, 95, 173
    GWVIP, 15, 52, 162-165, 167
    Hawaii use of, 160-161, 166
    USDA hybrid approach, 10, 28, 165, 167
    use in Florida, 9, 28, 150, 166
Index value results, 7, 80
Injection wells, 14, 18
In situ measurements
    research needs, 10, 175-176
Integrated assessments. *See* Hybrid assessment methods
Interagency Advisory Committee on Water Data, 106

International Standards Organization (ISO) 8211 standard, 107
Interpretation, errors in, 65
Intrinsic vulnerability, 3, 21, 84, 171
    and assessment method design, 46-47, 48
    Iowa assessment, 9, 136
    in overlay and index methods, 52-53
Ionic composition, 84
Iowa, 9, 22, 35, 52, 135-138, 165
Irrigation, 13, 123, 124, 129, 130
    Florida, 145
    San Joaquin Valley, 151

J

Joints, 3, 21, 94

K

Kriging, 60, 65

L

Land owners, 33
    voluntary behavior changes, 4, 31, 35
Land use and land cover (LULC) databases, 2-3, 9, 126-129, 183
Land use management, 4, 27, 31, 33-35, 40. *See also* Agricultural management; Land use and land cover databases
    maps, 51
    technical assistance, 34-35
Landfills, 13, 16
Lateral transport. *See* Horizontal movement
Law of ground water vulnerability
    First, 2, 18-19, 170-171
    Second, 3, 20, 30, 170-171
    Third, 8, 96
Leaching of contaminants, factors in, 2, 42-43
Leaching Potential Index, 82-83
LEACHM, 53, 55, 56, 58

Linear regression, 62
Loadings of contaminants, 7-8, 51, 80, 81, 97
  in vulnerability definitions, 17
Local differences. *See* Differential geographic assessment; Differential management; Geographic variation
Local government
  data management, 9, 105, 109, 127
  GIS use, 87, 92
  overlay and index methods use, 5, 45

M

Macropores, 11, 120, 178
Major Land Resource Area (MRLA), 114
Management, 4-5, 26, 27
  and process-based models, 56
  see also Agricultural management; Data collection activity; Differential management; Land use decisions; Policy analysis and development; Program management; Public education; Regulation; Resource allocation; Zoning activity
Maps and mapping, 3, 32, 36-37, 131, 132.
  in Cape Cod, 140-141
  errors and uncertainty in, 7, 9, 37, 67, 75-76, 91-92, 96, 172, 175
  in Florida, 149-150
  geologic, 51
  hydrogeologic, 121-123
  technical supplementation, 37
  topographical, 51, 110
  water-level information, 48
  zoning use, 34
  see also Cells and polygons; Geographic information systems; Index methods; Land use and land cover databases; Overlay methods; Resolution; Scales and scaling; Soil maps

Map Unit Interpretation Record (MUIR), 114, 119
Map Unit Use File (MUUF), 118-119
Mathematical models. *See* Process-based simulation models
Methods
  selection of, 4, 5, 26-27, 35-40, 172, 173
  types of, 2-3, 19, 42, 44-48
  see also Hybrid assessment methods; Index methods; Overlay methods; Process-based simulation models; Statistical methods; Testing and evaluation; Uncertainty
Microbial transformation. *See* Biodegradation
Minnesota, 108, 122
Mitigation, 4, 14, 31, 34
Models. *See* Digital Elevation Model; Geographic information systems, and modeling; Process-based simulation models
Monitoring activities and data, 28, 32, 34, 40, 81, 85-86
  in California, 28, 153, 166
  National Pesticide Survey, 14, 81, 84
  and statistical methods, 6, 63
Monte Carlo techniques, 57, 70-72, 77
Multicounty assessments, 23, 37, 120
Multiple-phase transport models, 6, 43, 45
Multiple regression, 62
Multistate assessments, 23, 114, 120
Multivariate statistical techniques, 60, 62

N

National Agricultural Statistics Service (NASS), 130
National Alachlor Well Water Survey, 81, 84
National assessments, 23, 37
  databases, 114, 120, 121, 174
  USDA, 10, 28, 162-165, 167

National Climatic Data Center (NCDC), 125
National Cooperative Soil Survey (NCSS), 112
National Herbicide Use Database, 130
National Oceanic and Atmospheric Administration (NOAA)
 National Climate Program regional centers, 125
 and President's Water Quality Initiative, 15
National Park Service, 123
National Pesticide Survey, 14, 81, 84
National Resource Inventory (NRI), 115, 128, 129, 162-163
National Soil Characterization Database (NSCDB), 120
National Soil Geographic Database (NATSGO), 113, 115, 120
National spatial data infrastructure (NSDI), 106, 108, 131
National Water Quality Assessment Program, 164
National Weather Service (NWS), 123-126
N-dimensional queries, 93
Neighborhood analysis, 93
New York, 14
Next Generation Radar (NEXRAD), 126
Nitrates, 14, 48, 52, 135-136
 travel times, 19
NLEAP, 118
Nonparametric statistical techniques, 61, 62
Nonpoint sources, 14
 in vulnerability definitions, 1, 16, 18
North Carolina, 51
NSSAD/SIRS, 90
Nuclear detonations, 18, 84
Numerical scoring. *See* Index methods

O

Oahu, Hawaii, 10, 156, 157, 158, 160, 161

Office of Management and Budget (OMB), 106
Official Soil Series Description (OSED), 119
Oil, 13, 18
One-dimensional transport models, 6, 28, 45, 53
Organic matter, 2, 42-43, 90, 113
Output. *See also* Maps and mapping; Probability; Uncertainty
 errors in, 67
 presentation of, 36-37
 value of, 39
Overlay methods, 2, 3, 5-6, 22, 45, 46, 48, 62, 95, 173
 use in Florida, 9, 28, 150, 166
 use in Iowa, 9, 22, 28, 137-138, 165
Ownership. *See* Land owners

P

Pedons, 113, 119-120
Percolation, 3, 21
Permits, conditions on, 34
Personnel. *See* Staffing
Pesticide Information Network, 130
Pesticide Management Zones, 28
Pesticide Properties Database, 130
Pesticide-Root Zone Model. *See* PRZM
Pesticides, 14
 assessment methods, 45, 48
 databases, 130
 in Florida, 9, 14, 145, 147
 in Hawaii, 10, 14, 157-161, 166
 in Iowa, 136
 process-based transport models, 53-56
 in San Joaquin Valley, 9-10, 151-155, 166
 transport of, 19, 44, 70-72
 voluntary restrictions, 35
 in vulnerability definitions, 17, 18
 vulnerability index (GWVIP), 15, 52, 162-165, 167
Pesticides and Ground-Water Strategy, 16

Pesticides in Ground Water Database, 130
Physical attributes. *See* Hydrogeologic attributes
Pipelines, 13
Planning agencies
overlay and index methods use, 5, 45
statistical methods use, 61
Point sources, 13-14
in vulnerability definitions, 1, 16, 18
Policy analysis and development, 4, 26-27, 30-32, 40
agricultural management, 164-165, 167
Florida, 147-148
Iowa, 136
maps use in, 131, 132
Polygons. *See* Cells and polygons
Population at risk, 13, 17
in Florida, 145-146
in Hawaii, 156
Postaudit analyses, 78.79
Potential evaporation, 123, 124
Precipitation, 20-21, 124
databases, 2, 91, 123, 125, 126
Florida, 146
Preferential flow paths, 3, 11, 21-22, 94-95, 177, 178
and process-based models, 6, 58-59, 94-95
President's Water Quality Initiative, 15, 162, 164
Probability, 3, 6, 7, 8, 20, 80, 96-97, 171
in statistical methods, 6, 60
in stochastic models, 57
Process-based simulation models, 2, 6, 19, 37, 45, 47, 48, 53-60, 94, 95, 173
Cape Cod use, 9, 28, 140-141, 166
data quality and availability, 6, 27, 37-38, 53, 56, 94, 105
Hawaii use of, 160-161, 166
hybrid methods, 10, 28, 165, 167, 179
and preferential flow paths, 6, 58-59, 94-95
use in Oahu, 10, 28

Program management, 4, 31, 32-33
Protecting the Nation's Ground Water: EPA's Strategy for the 1990s, 16
PRZM, 52, 53, 55, 56, 70-72, 90
Hawaii use of, 160
Pseudospecific vulnerability, 52-53
Public education, 4, 27, 31, 35, 40, 172
in Cape Cod assessment, 35
federal geographic data, 108
in Iowa assessment, 35, 136, 172
Pumping, 18, 22, 81, 86
Cape Cod, 140, 141-142
Florida, 145
Purging, 86
Purposeful placement, 1, 16, 18

R

Recharge rate, 2, 42, 43
Iowa assessment, 136
in overlay and index methods, 48, 49, 50
and uncertainty analysis, 73
Recharge zones, 20-21
Cape Cod, 141-142, 165-166
identification of, 10, 50, 176
Reference location, 3, 20-21, 81, 97
in overlay and index methods, 46, 48, 50
used in selected methods, 46-47, 48
Regional Aquifer-System Analysis (RASA) program, 121
Regional assessments, 37, 50, 173
databases, 45, 114
and process-based models, 53, 59-60
scales, 23
and statistical methods, 61
testing of, 7-8, 78, 80-84
Regional Climate Centers (RCCs), 125
Regression analyses, 60, 61, 62
Regulation, 34, 172-173. *See also* Screening of sites; Zoning activity
California, 152-155
Cape Cod, 139, 141-144
Florida, 146-147, 148-151

overlay and index methods use, 5, 45
statistical methods use, 5, 45
and uncertainty analysis, 75-77
Relative humidity, 123, 124
Remote sensing, 112, 132
Resolution, 3, 23, 24, 36
and zoning activity, 34
Resource allocation, 4, 27, 31, 32-33, 40
and map displays, 36
programmatic, 39
Results. *See* Output
Retardation Factor (RF), 68, 73-75, 176
Risk, definition of, 17
Rivers, 13
Root holes, 21, 94
Runoff, 109
Rural areas
and climate, 123, 124
drinking water, 13, 14
pesticide residues in wells, 14
RUSTIC, 90

S

Safe Drinking Water Act, 35
Salt water intrusion, 18, 145, 156
Samples and sampling
compliance monitoring, 34
equipment, 39
errors in, 65, 84-86
limitations of, 84-86
soils, 10, 113, 115, 120
from wells, 81, 84-86, 97
San Joaquin Valley, California, 9-10, 151-155, 166
Saturated zone
hydraulic conductivity, 10, 175
Scales and scaling, 3, 20, 23-25, 28-29, 173, 174. *See also* Resolution; Time scales
digital terrain data, 110, 112
hydrogeologic maps, 121-123
land use and cover maps, 127
merging of, 11, 177-178

and overlay and index methods, 46, 48
and process-based models, 6, 47, 48, 58, 59-60, 105
of sample measurements, 10, 176
soil surveys, 112-114, 121
and statistical methods, 47, 60
variability in, 65
Screening of sites, 33-34
and process-based models, 56
Screens, monitoring, 85-86
Seasonal variation, 65
and overlay and index methods, 5-6, 48, 50
Second Law of Ground Water Vulnerability, 3, 20, 30, 170-171
Sedimentary basin brines, 2, 19
Selection of methods
and data quality, 37-38
institutional considerations, 5, 27, 39-40
technical considerations, 5, 27, 36-38
and uncertainty, 7, 38
Sensitivity, definition of, 17, 18
Septic tanks, 14, 18
Cape Cod, 139-140
Florida, 145
Shallow aquifers, 21, 22
Simulation. *See* Process-based simulation models
Site selection, 31, 33-34, 56, 67-68
Site-specific databases
soil, 119-120
Site-specific simulation models
data requirements, 37
Size of assessment area, 37
SNOTEL, 125
Snowpack, 124, 125
Soil Classification File (SC), 119
Soil Conservation Service (SCS), 34, 123
Climatic Data Access Facility, 125-126
databases, 90, 120, 125-126, 128, 130-131

maps and mapping standards, 10, 51, 112, 121, 177
models, 91, 92-93
National Resource Inventory, 115, 128, 129, 162-163
Soil Interpretation Record (SIR), 117-118, 120
Soil loss, 92-93
Soil maps, 51, 112-121
standards for, 10, 112, 177
Soil-Pesticide Interaction Screening Procedure (SPISP), 162
SOILPROP, 90, 91
Soil properties
combination with geologic information, 10, 176
databases, 2, 9, 90-91, 112-121, 177, 184
filtration, 13, 48
in overlay and index methods, 48, 49, 51
and process-based models, 37
San Joaquin Valley, 152, 155
in situ measurement, 10, 175, 177
in vulnerability definitions, 17
see also Soil maps
Soil Survey Geographic Database (SSURGO), 112-115, 120-121
Solar radiation, 123, 124
Sole source aquifer, 35, 139
Solution channels, 3, 21, 94-95
Sorption, 2, 19, 42-43, 48, 59, 176
Sources of pollution, 13-14. *See also* Nonpoint sources; Point sources
Spatial Data Transfer Standard, 106, 107, 174
Spatial databases, 8, 9, 20, 96. *See also* Geographic information systems
Spatial scales. *See* Resolution; Scales and scaling
Specific vulnerability, 3, 21, 171
and assessment method design, 46-47, 48
in overlay and index methods, 52
Specificity of contaminants, 3, 20, 21
Spills, 21
containment, 34

Staffing, 39, 40
Standards
for geographic data, 9, 106-108, 174
for soil mapping, 10, 112, 177
State Geographic Systems Activities Compendium, 109
State government
data management, 9, 105, 108-109
GIS use, 87, 92
land use management, 33, 127
monitoring activities, 28
overlay and index methods use, 5, 45, 52
and President's Water Quality Initiative, 15
vulnerability assessments, 16
water-level information, 48
weather data, 123
State-level assessments, 37
databases, 114, 120
scales, 23
use of overlay methods, 51-52
State Management Plans (SMPs), 16
State Soil Geographic Database (STATSGO), 112-113, 114, 115, 120
Statistical methods, 2, 6, 19, 45, 47, 48, 60-63, 173
data quality and availability, 6, 38, 45, 60, 63
parameters in, 60, 62
and uncertainty, 38, 60, 68, 95
Stochastic models, 9, 57, 68, 77
Streams, 13, 21
Surface impoundments, 13
Florida, 145
Surface water and discharge areas, 13, 21

T

Targeting of resources. *See* Resource allocation
Technical assistance, 34-35
Temperature, 2, 43, 91, 123, 124, 125, 126

Tennessee Valley Authority, 127
Terrain. *See* Topography
Testing and evaluation, 4, 7-8, 20, 26, 27, 42, 77-78, 80, 96, 97, 173-174
  equipment, 39
  field assessments, 7, 8, 78-79
  of overlay and index methods, 52
  regional assessments, 7-8, 78, 80-84
  use of statistical tools, 45, 68
Third Law of Ground Water Vulnerability, 8, 96
Time scales, 3, 5, 20, 39, 65, 170. *See also* Seasonal variation
  merging of, 11, 177-178
  and water travel, 10, 19, 39, 81, 137, 176
Time series methods, 60, 61, 65
Topography
  databases, 9, 109-112, 184
  maps, 51, 110
Trace elements, 18
Transport of contaminants. *See* Depth to water table; Flow paths; Leaching of contaminants; Process-based simulation models
Travel time to water table, 10, 19, 39, 81, 137, 176
  Iowa assessment, 137
Trichloropropane, 161
Tritium, 84
Truncated data, 60

U

Uncertainty and error, 3, 7, 20, 26-27, 30, 38, 41, 42, 96-97, 170-171, 173
  analysis of, 5, 7, 11, 67-77
  in data, 3, 7, 20, 38, 63-66
  display of, 9, 11, 20, 37, 92, 96, 174-175, 178
  in method application, 3, 20, 63, 77
  in method execution, 3, 7, 20, 63-64, 66-67
  in process-based models, 57-58

  in soil mapping, 10, 177
  and statistical methods, 38, 60, 68, 95
Underground Injection Control Program, 51
Underground storage tanks, 13, 16
Universal Soil Loss Equation (USLE), 92-93
Universities, 48, 123
Unsaturated (vadose) zone, 2, 19, 42-43
  characterization of, 10, 123, 176-177
  hydraulic conductivity, 10, 175
  in overlay and index methods, 48, 49, 50-51
  solution channels in, 21
  transport through, 2, 6, 43, 45
Urban areas, 124
U.S. Army Corps of Engineers
  GRASS Waterworks, 90, 91
U.S. Department of Agriculture (USDA)
  databases, 128, 130
  hybrid method use, 10, 28, 165, 167
  President's Water Quality Initiative, 15, 162, 164
  vulnerability index (GWVIP), 15, 52, 162-165, 167
  see also Soil Conservation Service
U.S. Environmental Protection Agency. *See* Environmental Protection Agency
U.S. Geological Survey
  National Water Quality Assessment Program, 164
  RASA program, 121
U.S. Geological Survey (USGS)
  maps, 51, 110, 121, 122, 127, 128
  and President's Water Quality Initiative, 15
Uses of assessments, 4, 26, 27, 30-31, 40-41
  constraints on, 4-5, 31, 35, 38, 40-41
  institutional considerations, 39-40
  technical considerations, 36-39
  and uncertainty, 39
  see also Educational outreach; Land use management; Policy analysis and development; Program management

V

Vadose zone. *See* Unsaturated zone
Validation. *See* Testing and evaluation
Variation and variability. *See* Differential geographic assessment;
Differential management;
Geographic variation; Seasonal
variation
Verification. *See* Testing and evaluation
Voluntary activities, 4, 31, 35
Iowa, 28, 35
Vulnerability index, 77-78, 162. *See also* Ground Water Vulnerability
Index for Pesticides

W

Water content, 2, 43, 90
Watershed assessments, 37

Watershed modeling, 59, 91
Water table. *See also* Depth to water
table
as reference location, 3, 20-21
sampling near, 85-86
Weather, databases, 9, 91, 123-126, 182
Weights, 5-6, 45, 52, 95, 173
Wells, 3, 10, 14, 18, 21, 22, 35, 81, 84, 97
Cape Cod, 139, 140
in Florida assessment, 145, 148
in Iowa assessment, 9, 135-136
logs, 48, 122-123
Wind, 123, 124
Wisconsin, 52, 122
Worm holes, 21, 94

Z

Zoning activity, 33-34